NEW FORMATIONS

New Formations is published
three times a year by
Lawrence & Wishart
99a Wallis Road, London E9 5LN
Tel: 020-8533 2506
Fax: 020-8533 7369
Website:www.l-w-bks.co.uk/
formation.html

ADVERTISEMENTS:
For enquiries/bookings contact Vanna Derosas,
Lawrence & Wishart

SUBSCRIPTIONS:
UK: Institutions £120, Individuals £40.
Rest of world: Institutions £120; Individuals £40.
Single copies: £14.99 plus £1 post and packing
Back issues: £14.99 plus £1 post and packing for
individuals; £34.99 plus £1 post and packing for
institutions

CONTRIBUTIONS AND CORRESPONDENCE:
Send to: The Editor, *new formations*
European Studies Research Institute
University of Salford, Salford M5 4WT
s.mccracken@salford.ac.uk

BOOKS FOR REVIEW:
Send to: Timothy Bewes
Reviews Editor, *new formations*
12 Weymouth Street, London WIW 5BY
timothy.bewes@btinternet.com

new formations publishes themed issues, themed sections
and discrete articles. Contributors are encouraged to
contact the editor to discuss their ideas and to obtain a
copy of our style sheet, which can also be obtained on
our website at http://www.l-w-bks.co.uk/style.html

Manuscripts should be sent in triplicate; experts in the
relevant field will referee them anonymously. The
manuscripts will not be returned unless a stamped, self-
addressed envelope is enclosed. Contributors should
note that the editorial board cannot take responsibility
for any manuscript submitted to *new formations*.

ISSN   0 950 237 8
ISBN   0 85315 9440

Text design and setting by Art S
Printed in Great Britain at the I
Cambridge.

D0813202

NOTES ON CONTRIBUTORS

Steven Connor is Professor of Modern Literature and Theory at Birkbeck College. He has published books on Dickens, Beckett, postmodernism, cultural theory and contemporary fiction. His most recent publication is *Dumbstruck: a cultural history of ventriloquism* (2000).

Elizabeth Cowie teaches Film Studies at the University of Kent at Canterbury. She is the author of *Representing the Woman:Cinema and Psychoanalysis* (1997). Her recent work on cinema and psychoanalysis has focused on documentary film, trauma and the spectator in 'The Spectacle of Actuality', in *Collecting Visible Evidence*, Jane Gaines and Michael Renov (eds) (1999); and on *Hiroshima mon amour* in 'Traumatic Memories of Remembering and Forgetting', in *Between the Psyche and the Polis: Refiguring history in literature and theory*, Michael Rossington and Anne Whitehead (eds), (2000).

Jeremy Gilbert teaches Cultural Studies and Media Studies at the University of East London, and sits on the editorial board of *new formations*. He is the co-author of *Discographies: Dance Music, Culture and the Politics of Sound* (Routledge, 1999), and co-editor of *Cultural Capitalism: Politics After New Labour* (Lawrence and Wishart, 2001).

Nick Hubble has recently submitted his doctoral thesis, *George Orwell and Mass-Observation: Mapping the Politics of Everyday Life in England 1937-1941*, at the University of Sussex, where he has also been teaching for the English department.

Margaretta Jolly lectures in Twentieth Century Literature and Culture at the University of Exeter. She is the editor of *Dear Laughing Motorbyke: Letters from Women Welders in the Second World War* and *The Encyclopedia of Life Writing* (forthcoming).

Jeremy MacClancy is a lecturer in Anthropology at Oxford Brookes University. He specialises in Navarre and the Basque Country, and more generally the anthropologies of art, food and Europe. His recent publications include *The Decline of Carlism* (University of Nevada Press, 2000) and, as an editor, *Contesting Art* (Oxford, Berg, 1997) and *Exotics No More: Anthropology of the Front Lines* (University of Chicago Press, 2002).

Laura Marcus is Reader in English at the University of Sussex. Her publications include *Auto/biographical Discourses: Theory, Criticism, Practice* (1994); *Virginia Woolf* (1997) and, as editor, *Close Up: Cinema and Modernism* (1998) and *The Interpretation of Dreams: New Interdisciplinary Essays* (1999). She is currently writing a book on cinema and modernism, and co-editing *The Cambridge History of Twentieth-Century English Literature*.

Rod Mengham lectures in the Faculty of English at Cambridge, where he is also Director of Studies in English at Jesus College. He has written *The Idiom of the Time: the Writings of Henry Green* (1983), *'Wuthering Heights': a Critical Study* (1988), *The Descent of Language: Writing in Praise of Babel* (1993) and *Charles Dickens* (Writers and their Work, forthcoming 2001). He has also edited the short stories of E.M. Forster and *An Introduction to Contemporary Fiction* (Polity, 1999) and has co-edited with Jana Howlett *The Violent Muse: Violence and the Artistic Imagination in Europe 1910-1939* (1994) and with Neil Reeve *Fiction of the 1940s: Stories of Survival* (2001). He is currently working on *Upward Spiral: Edward Upward and the Politics of Writing* for OUP. He is the editor of the Equipage series of poetry pamphlets and co-organizer of the Cambridge Conference of Contemporary Poetry; his own poems have been published under the title *Unsung: New and Selected Poems* (Folio/Salt, 1996; 2nd edition 2001).

Tyrus Miller is Associate Professor of Literature at University of California at Santa Cruz and is currently Director of the University of California Study Center in Budapest, Hungary. He is author of *Late Modernism: Politics, Fiction, and the Arts Between the World Wars* (University of California Press, 1999) and of a manuscript in preparation entitled *Resonances of the Readymade: Finding and Delay in Avant-Garde Art and Aesthetics*.

Drew Milne is the Judith E. Wilson Lecturer in Drama and Poetry, Faculty of English, University of Cambridge. His most recent books of poetry include: *Pianola* and *The Gates of Gaza*. He edits the journal *Parataxis: modernism and modern writing*. For further information see: http://drewmilne.tripod.com

Herman Rapaport is Professor of English at the University of Southampton and teaches courses in critical theory and aesthetics. His most recent books include *Between the Sign and the Gaze* (Cornell University Press, 1994), *Is There Art?* (Cornell University Press, 1996) and *The Theory Mess* (Columbia University Press, 2001).

Adam Roberts is Reader in Nineteenth-Century Literature at Royal Holloway, University of London. He is the author of *Frederic Jameson* (Routledge, 2000) and *Science Fiction* (Routledge, 1999) amongst other things. He teaches Popular Culture on the Royal Holloway MA in Postmodernism.

Dorothy Sheridan is Head of Special Collections at the University of Sussex Library. She has been the Mass-Observation Archivist since 1974 and is currently Co-Director of the Centre for Life History Research. Publications include *Writing Ourselves: Mass-Observation and Literacy Practices* (with Brian Street and David Bloome), (Hampton Press, 2000).

Lois Wheller is a literature DPhil student at the University of Sussex. Her research areas include comedy, ethics, postcolonial theory and contemporary fiction.

CONTENTS
NUMBER 44 AUTUMN 2001

Mass Observation

Introduction:
The Project of Mass-Observation

Laura Marcus

This special issue of *new formations* has a dual focus. Firstly, it explores the history and the cultural politics of Mass-Observation, the movement, founded in 1937, which brought ethnographic fieldwork and observation to bear on everyday life in Britain. Secondly, it brings to centre stage the work and writing of Charles Madge, who founded Mass-Observation with the ethnographer Tom Harrisson and the poet, painter and film-maker Humphrey Jennings. Madge has to date been less prominent in the research and writing on Mass-Observation than Tom Harrisson, as Dorothy Sheridan, Head of Special Collections and Mass-Observation archivist at the University of Sussex, notes in her contribution to this issue. In exploring Charles Madge's writings we intend both to open up the work of an important twentieth-century poet, and to assess the broader significance of poetry and poetics for the Mass-Observation movement. One of the most fascinating aspects of Mass-Observation is the ways in which it negotiated and sought to reshape disciplinary boundaries, and to bring together, as a founding letter-manifesto declares, the artist, the scientist and the mass. Yet the place of 'poetry' in the Mass-Observation project was also a contested issue, as a number of our contributors show. The significance of Mass-Observation as a project and experiment of modernity was not that it reconciled the 'two cultures' - art and science - but that it put into play the possibility and the difficulty of their interrelationship, and, in so doing, raised conceptual questions that continue to resonate today.

By 1937, Charles Madge was a published poet. His work was supported by T.S. Eliot - Faber brought out his collection *The Disappearing Castle* in 1937, followed by *The Father Found* in 1941 - and he was increasingly seen as part of the group of new 1930s writers that included W.H. Auden, Louis MacNeice and Cecil Day-Lewis. He had briefly studied Natural Sciences at Cambridge, but had then switched to the Moral Sciences, with I.A. Richards as one of his tutors. Papers and manuscripts from his schooldays at Winchester reveal him reading widely in psychology and philosophy, as well as science and literature, and writing ambitious essays intended to bring together science and art, or to transcend the opposition between 'mechanism and vitalism'. The work of I.A. Richards and of William Empson was of central importance to him, particularly its attempts to classify and to find 'basic underlying metaphors and structures of comparison' in literary works.[1] Madge joined the Communist Party in 1932, leaving it in 1938. In

1. Charles Madge, *Autobiography*, (*The Madge Papers*, SxMs 71, *Autobiographical Papers* c.), p28.

1933, he abandoned his studies at Cambridge before completing his degree, having fallen in love with the poet Kathleen Raine, then married to Hugh Sykes-Davies.

In 1935, Madge and Raine moved to Blackheath (where they stayed for the duration of their short-lived marriage) in part to be near to their close friend Humphrey Jennings, a contemporary at Cambridge, and by all accounts an extraordinary intellect and character, whose multifarious talents included painting and poetry, and the film-making by which he is now best known. At this time, Jennings was working for the GPO film unit, at the start of his documentary film career.[2] T.S. Eliot found work for Madge on the *Daily Mirror*, and he was employed as a journalist on the paper for two years. In his autobiography, Madge recalls working primarily on human interest stories, and being asked to observe public responses to such major events as the death of George V, and the news of Edward VIII's relationship with the American divorcee Mrs Simpson, followed by the Abdication on 10 December 1936. Madge writes:

> Humphrey Jennings and I had been noticing the way in which the items on a newspaper page, especially the front page, added up to make a kind of 'poem' - or so we interpreted it. There was an affinity between the items at a symbolic level, which must have been due partly to the news editor's assessment of what made front-page news on that particular day, partly to the layout men, partly to the current and shifting concerns of the popular readership, partly no doubt to chance or what is called coincidence. Neither Humphrey nor I were inclined toward Jungian ideas of a collective unconscious, but we had read Freud's essay on the coincidence, which had led to an interest among certain French surrealists, especially Andre Breton, in coincidental happenings of various kinds. [Humphrey Jennings had been involved in organising the International Surrealist Exhibition at the New Burlington Galleries in June 1936.] So when the papers were full of Edward and Mrs Simpson we saw them as in part an expression of mass wishes and fantasies, and were on the look out for other symbolic news-material that might be related to them. At the end of November the Crystal Palace was burned down, and the flames were visible from 6 Grotes Buildings [Blackheath] as a distant glow in the sky: the shock that this seemed to evoke at a symbolic level was perhaps akin to the shock that the abdication crisis brought to our stable monarchy.[3]

Prompted by a letter from Geoffrey Pyke to the *New Statesman*, putting forward the need for an anthropological understanding of the abdication - which Pyke calls a 'sexual situation' - and mass reaction to it, a group met in Blackheath to discuss this possibility - it included Madge, Raine, Jennings, and David Gascoyne, a young poet who had been living in Paris, and whose *A Short Survey of Surrealism* was published in 1935. They drafted a

2. Jennings' films included *Spare Time* (1939), made for the GPO but in fact a Mass-Observation film about leisure time in Industrial Britain. The GPO came under the auspices of the Ministry of Information (later the Crown Film Unit) during WWII; Jennings' films in this context included *Listen to Britain* (1942), *Fires Were Started* (1943) and *A Diary for Timothy* (1945).

3. Madge, *Autobiography*, op. cit., p63.

questionnaire which asked:

> What are your superstitions, in order of importance?
> Do you pay attention to coincidences?
> Do you or did you hate your father, and if so why?
> Do you hate your boss: do you hate your job?
> What is your greatest ambition?
> Did you want the King to marry Mrs Simpson and if so why?
> Were you glad or sorry when the Crystal Palace was burnt down and if
> so why?
> Can you believe you are going to die? Do you want to die?
> What are you most frightened of?
> What do you mean by freedom?

As Ben Highmore has argued, the questions are intended to encourage free-associative responses, and the version of psychoanalysis that underlies them is intended to connect a private and collective 'unconscious', moving from the Oedipal at the private to the public level, and making an implicit connection between fathers, bosses, and Kings.[4] Some twenty people were sent this first directive, and instructed to ask questions of as many people as possible. The directive stated that 'answers should be obtained from the person questioned at a speed which will prevent him [sic] from taking refuge in a merely conventional and socially correct response'.

Geoffrey Pyke's letter also prompted Madge to write to the *New Statesman*. Madge's letter was headed 'Anthropology at Home', and advertises the foundation of a group using 'the accepted principles of anthropology ... of psychoanalysis, and the sciences dealing with the behaviour of man ... to the Crystal Palace-Abdication symbolic situation'. The letter closes with the assertion that:

> The real observers in this case were the millions of people who were, for once, irretrievably involved in the public events. Only mass observations can create mass science. The group for whom I write is engaged in establishing observation points on as widely extended a front as can at present be organised. We invite the co-operation of voluntary observers, and will provide detailed information to anyone who wants to take part.[5]

Madge's letter was published on the page opposite a poem by Tom Harrisson - 'Coconut Moon' - the first and last poem Harrisson ever sent to press. Madge calls it a 'poetic spin-off' from *Savage Civilisation*, the book Harrisson had written about his recent experiences with the cannibal mountain tribes of Maleluka in the New Hebrides, which the socialist publisher Victor Gollancz brought out in 1937. Harrisson, who had dropped out of university in order to pursue his ornithological and anthropological passions, was at this point

4. Ben Highmore, *Everyday Life and Cultural Theory*, PhD thesis, University of London, 1999, p125. A revised version of Highmore's excellent thesis, which contains an invaluable discussion of Mass-Observation, is forthcoming from Routledge, 2001, as *Everyday Life and Cultural Theory: an introduction*.

5. *New Statesman and Nation*, 2 January 1937.

in Bolton, where he had taken a job as a mill-hand as 'an exercise in participant observation'. On reading the *New Statesman* letter, Harrison wrote to Madge suggesting a meeting, which duly took place, and which David Gascoyne, who was also present, subsequently described as a 'talking-match' between Harrisson and Jennings.

The second letter to the *New Statesman* was signed by Madge, Harrisson and Jennings.[6] 'Mass Observation develops out of anthropology, psychology, and the sciences which study man - but it plans to work with a mass of observers', the letter proclaimed, continuing:

6. *New Statesman and Nation*, 30 January 1937.

> Already we have fifty observers at work on two sample problems. We are further working out a complete plan of campaign, which will be possible when we have not fifty but 5,000 observers. The following are a few examples of problems that will arise:
>
> Behaviour of people at war memorials.
> Shouts and gestures of motorists.
> The aspidistra cult.
> Anthropology of football pools.
> Bathroom behaviour.
> Beards, armpits, eyebrows.
> Anti-semitism.
> Distribution, diffusion and significance of the dirty joke.
> Funerals and undertakers.
> Female taboos about eating.
> The private lives of midwives.
>
> In these examples the anthropological focus is obvious, and the description is primarily that of physical behaviour. Other inquiries involve mental phenomena which are unconscious or repressed, so that they can be traced through mass-fantasy and symbolism as developed and exploited, for example, in the daily press. The outbreak of parturition-images in the press last October may have been seasonal, or may have been caused by some public stimulus: continuous watch on the shifting popular images can only be kept by a multitude of watchers. The observers will also provide the points from which can be plotted weather-maps of public feeling in a crisis.
>
> The subject demands the minimum of prejudice, bias and assumption; the maximum of objectivity. It does not presuppose that there are any inexplicable things. Since it aims at collecting data before interpreting them, it must be allowed to doubt and re-examine the completeness of every existing idea about 'humanity', while it cannot afford to neglect any of them.
>
> Equally, all human types can and must assist in this work. The artist and the scientist, each compelled by historical necessity out of their

artificial exclusiveness, are at last joining forces and turning back towards the mass from which they had detached themselves.

The letter focuses a number of important themes. Firstly, we can see how the ways in which the culture of everyday life, and its focus on the random particularities of cultural phenomena, produces an interface between documentary realism and surrealism, the latter most evident in the absurdist juxtapositions in the list of possible topics or 'problems'. Other elements include a possible tension between a reflexive concept of studying ourselves and our own society, and a model of anthropological distance. The emphasis on the objective camera-eye of the trained observer needs to be set alongside Tom Harrisson's reference elsewhere to the necessarily subjective camera-eye of the amateur observer. The distinction may seem to produce a traditional distinction between professional and amateur, but the absoluteness of the divide - like that between objective and subjective - breaks down, producing more complex conceptual figurations.

Other early Mass-Observation publications expand on these themes: thus the pamphlet of 1937, written by Madge and Harrison, refers to the 'new method' with which Mass-Observation will work: 'It intends to make use not only of the trained scientific observer, but of the untrained observer, the man in the street. Ideally, it is the observation by everyone of everyone, including themselves'.[7] In an article for *New Verse* (February-March 1937), titled 'Poetic Description and Mass Observation', Madge and Jennings wrote that 'The process of observing raises him [the 'untrained observer'] from subjectivity to objectivity. What has become unnoticed through familiarity is raised into consciousness again'.[8] As David Chaney and Michael Pickering note, Madge and Jennings 'believed that the seemingly simple project of observing everyday life transforms the literary activity of the observer from that of privileged individualism to that of co-author ... tap[ping] a level of social reality that is best described as implicit in everyday consciousness'.[9]

Although one might imagine that Humphrey Jennings was behind the surrealist delight in incongruity evident in the list of topics to be explored in the second letter to the *New Statesman*, Harrisson, writing in 1940, suggested that Jennings had not approved the factual approach outlined, and Jennings' involvement with Mass-Observation was indeed short-lived. Madge and Harrisson were primarily responsible for taking the project forward. Madge stayed in London, working with a group of volunteers, many of whom had responded to the *New Statesmen* letters and to subsequent newspaper articles on the organisation. (Commentators on Mass-Observation have situated the majority of these volunteers as 'lower middle-class'.) Mass-Observers wrote reports on a range of topics in response to specific Directives - for example, on advertising, clothes, dreams, and smoking. In the first year they were also asked to record their everyday lives, initially in the form of detailed accounts of each 12th of the month. These day-surveys culminated in the observations on May 12 1937, the Coronation day of George VI. The Mass-Observation

7. Charles Madge and Tom Harrisson, *Mass-Observation*, London, Frederick Muller, 1937, p10.

8. Charles Madge and Humphrey Jennings, 'Poetic Description and Mass Observation', *New Verse* 24, February-March 1937, p3.

9. David Chaney and Michael Pickering, 'Authorship in Documentary: Sociology as an Art form in Mass Observation', in John Corner (ed), *Documentary and the Mass Media*, London, Arnold, 1986, p40.

pamphlet referred to the February 12 1937 survey as observation of 'a normal day on which nothing of importance took place', while the 12 May survey will record, it states, 'an abnormal day in social life and consciousness'. Together, these surveys 'give an extraordinary picture of England - extraordinary, though the material they report is completely ordinary'.[10]

10. *Mass-Observation*, p31.

The May 12 survey was published as *Mass-Observation Day-Survey*, edited by Humphrey Jennings and Charles Madge. As the editors write:

> In making a survey of May 12, Coronation Day, various kinds of phenomena had to be observed. There was the life of the streets, existing for that day only, called into being by an exceptional occasion. There was life at home, and in routine environments, disturbed and modified by the demands of the day. More difficult to grasp and define, there was the mass reaction to the events, the floating opinions and counter-opinions which they provoked, and the interactions of individuals and among groups. Such was the varied field to be explored, and in order to make as round a picture as the forces of Mass-Observation would allow, three distinct lines of attack were adopted.[11]

11. Humphrey Jennings and Charles Madge (eds), *May the Twelfth: Mass-Observation Day-Surveys 1937*, London, Faber, 1937, reprinted 1987, p89.

Firstly, the Observers, who had made surveys on earlier 12ths of the month in the year, sent in lengthy reports; 43 of these were received. Secondly, thousands of leaflets were distributed, with questions including: 'What did you do on May 12? Give a *short* hour by hour description of your day'. 77 of these were returned. Thirdly, in the editors' words: 'a mobile Squad of 12 Observers was set to work to confer happenings in the streets of London from midnight on May 11 till after midnight on May 12. They worked in shifts, and kept in touch with the Mass-Observation headquarters by telephone, like reporters and a newspaper office. During the time they were working they took notes almost continuously, and from their notes wrote up lengthy reports'. The editors continue:

> By these three methods, three kinds of focus were obtained, not to mention the individual differences of focus between each of the Observers. Close-up and long shot, detail and ensemble, were all provided. Some recorded just what reaches the threshold of a normal consciousness, others by concentrated effort saw and heard far more than they were normally accustomed to. On the whole, the excitement of the day seems to have stimulated most people's powers of observation to an unusual degree (pp90-1).

The cinematic analogy is central to the *May 12 Survey* in its edited and published form. It uses the techniques of montage and collage to create effects of juxtaposition, fragmentation and diversity, while also assessing the significance of a common perspective. At no point does it attempt to give a single clear image of the actual Coronation ceremonies, staying instead with the partial perspectives of its observers. Thus one of the mobile squad of Observers records:

> An old lady on the shoulders of a respectable citizen: 'I can see the top of them. Dark blue uniforms - rifles - now I see a band - jolly officer with beret, not cap. A magnificent line of bayonets all down Oxford Street. I can see without a periscope. Am I not a strain on you? It's a band. Awfully pleased, that's all. That's why they're making a noise. Now they're Scotties - marching - they always adore Scotties. Now I can only see tops' (p139).

The reports given at this point are those of three Observers, 'who, independently of each other, have arrived in the same crowd at the same time. It is therefore interesting to see how far their accounts correspond. Not only do they agree with each other, but they show the same stimuli affecting different parts of the crowd, and the same impulses travelling through it. Such simultaneous but independent accounts fix the events described with added force – and this force is a direct result of the Mass-Observation method' (p138). The form of the text enacts a vision of mass consciousness as diverse and incapable of resolution into a single narrative whole, but as nonetheless linked in complex underlying ways through collective images, 'mass wishes' and mass fears. The editors comment on the 'surprising or disturbing' element in reports, including a number of recorded dreams: 'They represent in fact that residuum of the day which at present defeats precise analysis or explanation, but which is important as giving it its dominant tone or character, a character which is made up of the totality of the fantasy and image-making of all the individuals' (p328). The importance of the 'dominant tone', or 'dominant image', for Mass-Observation emerges strongly in this passage, as does the concern to link an individual and a social or group unconscious.

***

While Charles Madge was in charge of the volunteer observers or Panel, and operating from London, Tom Harrisson had rented a house in Bolton, and had recruited a number of full-time observers, including the working-class writer John Sommerfield. From Bolton, which they called Worktown in their publications, Harrisson and his team recorded, in the photographer Humphrey Spender's words:

> Information about people's behaviour in all sorts of situations - bus queues, football crowds, people in restaurants, people in pubs, people in church, people walking about the streets, people talking to each other, people not talking to each other, what they were wearing, whether they wore hats, what they wore on their feet – the list was endless, and a great mixture.[12]

12. Humphrey Spender, *Worktown People: Photographs from Northern England 1937-8*, Jeremy Mulford (ed), Bristol, Falling Wall Press, 1982, p15.

Humphrey Spender - Stephen Spender's brother - was recruited to take photographs of working-class life. Harrisson also took with him to Bolton the artists William Coldstream and Julian Trevelyan, who produced his Bolton collages, applying techniques learnt from the Surrealists in Paris to the thing seen, and tearing up pictures of the Coronation crowds to make the cobblestones of Bolton. Trevelyan gives a vivid account of life in Bolton and of Harrisson's extraordinary energies:

> He complained to me at this time that he could not really sleep unless he could feel through the wall the people next door going to sleep; could not work unless the radio was on full blast. Tom went out for his material to the pubs, to the dogs, to the dance halls. He sent a band of willing workers flying round making reports on anything, from the contents of a chemist's shop window to an account of a service in a spiritualist church. 'Bring back a list of the hymns and any other dope you can get hold of, and try and pinch a copy of the sermon', he would say as he sent us out on our mission.[13]

13. Julian Trevelyan, *Indigo Days*, London, MacGibbon and Kee, pp82-3.

One of the first missions of this kind seems to have involved William Empson, who was sent out to make a report on the contents of a sweet-shop window, and returned, Trevelyan writes, with a 'rich Freudian trophy ... a silver cardboard ladder leading up to a golden key from which hung a ring'.

The Bolton (Worktown) side of the operation, which was extended to Blackpool (Holidaytown), included up to sixty investigators at particular times, gathering evidence on such topics as local politics, household budgets, entertainment, including film-going, and religion. They produced an enormous amount of material - some 40,000 pages of notes - testimony to the passion for 'facts' both of Tom Harrisson and of the culture of the 1930s in general. The project was in part funded by Victor Gollancz, who intended to bring out books based on Mass-Observation reporting in the Left Book Club series, though only one of the four volumes planned, *The Pub and the People*, predominantly the work of John Sommerfield, appeared under this imprint. (Gollancz had also commissioned George Orwell's *The Road to Wigan Pier*, his study of life in a Northern mining-community.) Other supporters of Mass-Observation in its early stages included Julian Huxley, who wrote the foreword to the pamphlet of 1937, in which he compared the activities of Mass-Observation to 'bird-watching and natural history observation', and the anthropologist Bronislaw Malinowski, who wrote a lengthy afterword to *First Year's Work*, published in 1938.

Malinowski's essay is entitled 'A Nation-Wide Intelligence Service', and gives a strong sense of the publicity afforded to Mass-Observation in the late 1930s. 'The birth of Mass-Observation', Malinowski writes, 'was in many ways a sensational event', though it is precisely the Press's sensationalizing of it that had aroused the scientific suspicion which Malinowski seeks to allay.[14] Malinowski's is not an uncritical account of Mass-Observation, but it does take it seriously as a contribution to social scientific observation and knowledge. He focuses particularly on the question of the scientificity of mass-observation and on the interrelationship between the 'subjective' and the 'objective' in its methods, arguing that 'the objective treatment of subjectively determined data must start at the very outset'. For Malinowski, writing at a time of intense debate about the relationship of observer to observed, the role of the anthropologist (and he situates Mass-Observation within these terms) is not to submerge himself in the culture he studies in order to become one with it, but to learn how to translate the physiological manifestations of the subjective states of those he observes; the observer and observed, he asserts, cannot be the same person: 'I also understand from my native informants, male and female, that when a white man "makes love" to a native woman, his is not an ethnographic experience. The white man cannot transform himself into a Melanesian. There are either no physiological differences in some of the bodily functions, in which case there is no need to duplicate them, or, if there are racial differences, the white man, as an observer, has to draw the line' (pp99-100).

The context for Malinowski's discussion here is 'Anthropology at Home', the term with which Mass-Observation began and of which Malinowski states: 'From the start of my own field-work, it has been my deepest and strongest conviction that we must finish by studying ourselves through the same methods and with the same mental attitude with which we approach exotic tribes'. While Harrisson was deeply influenced by Malinowski's theories, a number of his writings take a distance from the assumptions of difference and superiority entailed in what James Clifford has termed 'ethnographic authority'.[15] Harrisson was not, moreover, much given to 'draw[ing] the line'.

'Mass-Observation was conceived under conditions of national stress', Malinowski wrote, referring to the Abdication crisis: 'What Mass-Observation could still achieve is a fuller elucidation of what the attitude towards war is among the masses'. The first half of *Britain by Mass-Observation*, published in 1939, analysed Britain at the time of the Munich crisis, with a particular emphasis on press coverage of the events, and the Press's misrepresentations of 'public opinion'. This part of the text is indeed a study of the ways in which 'opinion' is made, with a strongly anthropological understanding of the social unconscious: 'The combination of [Chamberlain's] age and his sky-journey [to see Hitler] made him a father-deity. But his self-sacrificial abasement in going to Hitler made him like the son-deity who descends among the wicked to save them. The piled-up suspense and anxiety could only be dispelled by a gesture of this super-human kind, by a piece of myth-making'.[16]

Tom Harrisson wrote later that 'The war, which started out slowly in 1939, brought M-0 into its own sort of own. Although other

14. Charles Madge and Tom Harrisson (eds), *First Year's Work*, London, Lindsay Drummond, 1938, p83.

15. See James Clifford, 'On Ethnographic Authority', in *The Predicament of Culture: Twentieth-Century Ethnography, Literature and Art*, Cambridge, Massachusetts, Harvard University Press, 1988, pp21-54.

16. Charles Madge and Tom Harrisson, *Britain by Mass-Observation*, Harmondsworth, Middlesex, Penguin, 1937, pp63-4.

organisations had by now sprung up to study public opinion, we could offer a then unique service for the study of private opinion and the interpretation of broad trends; those amorphous marshlands of the mind which in war-time are dubbed "morale". Morale was meat, drink and regular salaries for all in M-O'.[17] Just before the war broke out, Harrisson had offered the 'Panel' of voluntary contributors a choice between continuing to answer Directives (on specific topics) or writing day-to-day diaries covering all aspects of their war-time lives: about 500 wrote a diary, while over 2000 answered at least one Directive - some did both. A Mass-Observation book published in early 1940, *War Begins at Home*, studied the first four months of the war, looking at such questions as the impact of the black out, air raid anxiety, and the Ministry of Information. By the time the book was published, Mass-Observation was in fact working for the Ministry, who commissioned investigations into reactions to the news, expectations and fears relating to the war, and the workings of rumour.

Although *War Begins at Home* might seem to have taken Mass-Observation a considerable way from its early surrealist imaginings, echoes of these do remain. Thus, in one passage, we have the following account, written in the voice of the authors - Madge and Harrisson - of the experience of the black-out, as a preface to the reports from Observers and diarists:

> The first impression of the first night of the black-out was psychological rather than physical. How weird! How rather exciting! How like the unseen forms of indigestion dreams! This groping through familiar streets now unfamiliar, all around you shadows which might turn out to be people or pillar-boxes, while sudden shapes of cars crawl up to you with eyes no more than cats. This contradiction in our civilisation, the unlit city, continues to bewilder for the first thirty seconds every time you go out of doors at night. On dark nights it is really a matter of groping one's way, with nerves as well as hands held out into the future of the next second. In the first weeks of war even small torches were not supposed to be used, though now plenty carry these, and we have the new dream situation, where six or seven strangers walk in a formless crocodile behind the lady with the torch. Torch-batteries remain more valuable than letters from the front? But on moonlight nights, city-dwellers have been forced to discover that not only do they live in a city, they also live under the heavens and patterns of stars. Nothing, no amount of experience, makes you really used to the black-out. And however little it may change your habits, the consciousness of it, waiting for you there, behind the black material of the window, is a threat to any of the pre-war happy-go-lucky. Every evening expedition is now an event, maybe a dangerous adventure. No one in New York or Buenos Aires can successfully imagine what it's like. For when the bright lights of a city are turned off, bright life is turned off too.[18]

17. Tom Harrisson, *World Within*, London, The Cresset Press, 1959, p162-3.

18. Charles Madge and Tom Harrisson, *War Begins at Home*, London, Chatto and Windus, 1940, p187.

While these specific conditions of seeing and not-seeing are particular to the exigencies of war, the description does suggest the ways in which surrealism continued to impact on Mass-Observation: firstly, through the poetic potential of everyday life; secondly, in the importance of coincidence as a way of ordering experience; finally, in the perception of an urban uncanny. The passage on the black-out recalls, indeed, the highly poeticised account of early Mass-Observation given by Kathleen Raine in her autobiography:

> Mass-Observation, concerned with man, was essentially urban. We hoped to discern on the surfaces of dingy walls, on advertisement hoardings, or written upon the worn stones of pavements, or in the play of light and shadow cast by some street-lamp upon puddles at the corner of a shabby street, traces of the beautiful, degraded, dishonoured, suffering, sorrowful, but still the *deus absconditus*. It was a search for the lost lineaments of the most high in the most low; hence the strange sense of dedication, of quest, in which we walked; anywhere, everywhere, we might receive a sign, that hidden and degraded god might sign to us, reproachful, sorrowful, majestic as the face imprinted upon the Holy Shroud.[19]

19. Katherine Raine, *The Land Unknown*, London, Hamish Hamilton, 1975, p84.

The religious vision is Raine's own, and is at one with her habitual and contestable representation of Mass-Observation as a vision of the poets - Madge and Jennings - which was subsequently corrupted by politics and by Harrisson's anthropological focus. Nonetheless, her representation of a surreal, urban ethnography points up elements of Mass-Observation - as a reading of city inscriptions, of the uncanny in the city, of walking rather than writing - which interact in fascinating ways with the documentary aspects of Mass-Observation, and its turning of experience into paper and yet more paper.

Social historians have found in the Mass-Observation records an extraordinary 'history from below' and record of everyday life: excellent work has been done, for example, on the experience of women in wartime. Yet in some ways the mass of material remains opaque and resistant to use. This is particularly true, perhaps, in the case of the dream reports, kept between 1937-48, and discussed by Tyrus Miller in his article in this issue, though I would like to find a way of memorialising the dream of Grace Hickling on the night of 18-19 March 1937: 'Stephen Spender has in some way become inextricably involved in the pattern of a rug I am making'.[20] The recurrence of dreams as a topic and Directive does indicate their importance for Mass-Observation as a project, though this of course took on a particular significance in wartime, when the question of anxiety-dreams became particularly charged, and some of the dream reports were submitted to a Ministry of Information psychologist, who commented on the role of dreams and

20. Mass-Observation archive, *Dreams 1937-8*, TC 28, 28/1/B: 'Dreams and Dominant Images Reports 1937: Women'.

dream anxiety in relation to rumour and national morale.

We can also see in the linking of dreams and 'dominant images' in the Directives something of Madge's fascination with the image more generally. When describing what Mass-Observation had been looking for, Madge wrote: 'the changing colours in the street, the changing shapes of tombstones, these visual elements caught the eye of the observers for whom such observation was not just an amusing exercise in triviality. Some sort of net had been spread to catch that fleeting, glinting apparition, the essence of the time'.[21] The words recall the project of May 12th and the day-surveys more generally, in which the coming together of different elements and optics would ideally constitute the meaning of the whole.

21. Postscript to Tom Harrisson, *Britain Revisited*, London, Gollancz, 1961, pp279-80.

James Clifford, in a footnote to his essay 'On Ethnographic Surrealism', refers to Mass-Observation as a possible example of 'surrealist ethnography', linking it to the French Collège de Sociologie (whose members included George Bataille, Roger Caillois and Michel Leiris), also founded in 1937 and dedicated to exploring the irruptions of the sacred and of ritual moments in everyday life.[22] The question of the surrealist influence on Mass-Observation is a complex one: it would seem that both Madge and Jennings were critical of the aesthetic tendencies in Surrealism and its take up in Britain in particular, which failed to recognise its broad disciplinary base as, in Madge's words, 'a laboratory of studies, of experimentation'. For Jennings, reviewing Herbert Read's *Surrealism*: '"Coincidences" have the infinite freedom of appearing anywhere, anytime, to anyone: in broad daylight to those whom we most despise in places we have most loathed: not even to *us* at all: probably least to petty seekers after mystery and poetry on deserted sea-shores and in misty junk-shops'.[23] Mass-Observation's 'radical positivism', as Ben Highmore has described it, differed from Surrealism in that it insisted on attending to the everyday as a mass project of collecting 'facts', not so much commenting on the everyday as becoming coterminous with it,[24] though its status as 'surrealist ethnography' could be said to emerge in its project of exploring familiar aspects of everyday life as if they were part of an unfamiliar culture, and as a way of revealing cultural meanings.

22. Clifford, *The Predicament of Culture*, 1988, op. cit., p143.

23. Humphrey Jennings, 'Surrealism', originally published *Contemporary Poetry and Prose* 8, December 1936. Reprinted in Kevin Jackson (ed), *The Humphrey Jennings Film Reader*, Manchester, Carcanet, 1993, p220.

24. Highmore, op. cit., p116.

***

The original project of Mass-Observation did not survive the war years. Charles Madge appears to have become increasingly unhappy with Mass-Observation's role in relation to the Ministry of Information, and the dangers of becoming an intelligence organisation, and left Mass-Observation in June 1940, to work, with the support of the economist Maynard Keynes, on a research project on wartime economics and in particular saving and spending behaviour for the Institute of Economic Research. In 1950 he became Professor of Sociology at Birmingham University, a post he occupied until his retirement. Tom Harrisson joined the army in 1942, leaving Mass-Observation in the charge of Bob Willcock, a full-time Observer, and in 1947 accepted a post as Government Ethnologist for Sarawak. After the war Mass-Observation continued to operate as a cross between a government social survey unit and a market research analyst. In 1949 Harrisson passed his rights over to Mass-Observation (UK) Ltd, an independent market research organisation, retaining the rights to the pre-1949 material which was deposited at the University of Sussex in 1970.

Julian Symons, in his account of Mass-Observation in *The Thirties*, focuses on the irony that the techniques developed by Mass-Observation for the scientific examination of human behaviour became a tool of consumer research: 'It was not the masses who had fun with a new science, but science that had its own sort of fun with the masses ... There is nothing more comic than the gullibility of the past'.[25] In returning to Mass-Observation, we are seeking to look beyond this model of comic failure to understand the cultural and political complexities of Mass-Observation.

25. Julian Symons, *The Thirties: A Dream Revolved*, London, Faber, 1975, p103.

Mass-Observation was both of its time - writers on the 1930s have looked to it as a defining cultural and historical phenomenon - and in advance of its moment. Its founders played and fought with the counters of 'poetry' and 'science' in their imaginings of and ambitions for Mass-Observation. It was at one and the same time empirical - called upon to provide 'evidence' of what people thought and felt and dreamed - and utopian. It is a project both contained within its archive and, in conceptual terms, exceeding it.

The essays in this special issue address these and other of the complex and contradictory dimensions of Mass-Observation. Dorothy Sheridan's 'personal note' provides a history of the Mass-Observation archive and its founders. It also reminds us of two important aspects of the archive: firstly, the central role played by women Mass-Observers and secondly, that Mass-Observation is a 'living archive', not only preserving past material but managing the ongoing project, begun in 1981, of recording the present, in the shape of the autobiographical responses of a panel of volunteers. Rod Mengham's essay discusses the work of Charles Madge and Humphrey Jennings in relation to French surrealism, and takes up the question of the Mass-Observer's 'quality of looking', that 'of the figure in the crowd, whose view is frequently obscured, by other passers-by and by traffic; which is shifting, transitory, partial'. Mengham also provides a reading of Madge's prose poem of 1936, 'Bourgeois News', which makes concrete the profound imbrications of surrealism and documentary.

Tyrus Miller explores in detail one particular element of the Mass-Observation archive: the material on dreams, which was gathered from members of the voluntary Panel between 1937-48. Miller uses the dream material to open up the significance of the 'dominant image', for Madge and Jennings in particular, and to discuss the ways in which the dream project, at one level so central to Mass-Observation's attempt to find a bridge between individual consciousness and the social imaginary, was at another a 'relative failure'. Investigating the terms of this failure, Miller opens up the nature of the desire fuelling the dream-diarists' endeavours to record their dreams - and at times their resistance to their dreams and their recording - linking this to broader questions of psychic and political life in war-time and raising fundamental questions about the use of dreams as historical evidence.

The question of perspective raised in Rod Mengham's essay is pursued by Steven Connor, whose contribution examines the representation, in Charles Madge's poetry and *May the Twelfth: Mass-Observation Day Surveys 1937*, of two contrasting forces: transcendence and relapse (the latter connected, perhaps, to the image of 'Abdication' which Mengham discusses both as a political event and a poetic trope), elevation and drowning. These pairings are manifested in *May the Twelfth* in the 'dominant images' of the periscope (the instrument and optic through which the May 12th crowd sought to see the spectacle of the Coronation and which becomes an image of Mass-Observation itself) and the sea of paper under the feet of the crowd, itself linked to Mass-Observation's archival excesses. Connor explores these images in conjunction with the temporal, evolutionary preoccupations of Madge's verse, and the ways in which it plays out the relationship between natural and human time. Drew Milne's essay also addresses Madge's poetry, taking up the question of 'the relation between poetry and social science in his political imagination', and exploring more generally the role played by poetry and the idea of poetry in English socialism. 'New kinds of socialist aesthetics', Milne argues, 'are needed to read Madge's work, along with new kinds of historically nuanced and formally reflexive criticism'. He raises key questions about the relationship between Madge's poetry and his politics, the place of poetry and poetics in the Mass-Observation project, and the 'uncertain social function of poetry' in the present day.

Nick Hubble pursues the question of the politics of Mass-Observation, and, like Milne, explores the connection between Madge's early and later works. He discusses Madge's collaborations with Keynes and Beveridge, and the 'centrality of Madge's own role within the rational-technical social eidos of the post-war British state that he wanted to criticise'. Working through Madge's early writings, and the first years of Mass-Observation, Hubble opens up the implications of Madge's own perception that empirical investigation into opinion formation had been unproductive because Mass-Observation had not worked out how broad social influences - press, radio, friends - actually interacted with individual consciousness to produce opinion. This raises questions about the class politics of Mass-Observation, its perceptions of the passive citizen-consumer, and about attitudes towards the need for active leadership and social planning which bear in crucial ways on the social and political formations of the post-war period. Jeremy MacClancy addresses the attitudes of social anthropologists towards Mass-

Observation, including those of Malinowski and Raymond Firth, and discusses the reasons for the neglect of the innovatory work of Mass-Observation in historical studies of twentieth-century anthropology. He points to the fact that 'the broader consequences of M-O were implicitly subversive of university-based anthropologists' attempts to establish the professional nature of their endeavours', and the ways in which the democratising impulses of Mass-Observation threatened the privileged intellectual status of academic anthropologists. In this, and in its surrealist origins and imaginings, MacClancy suggests, Mass-Observation anticipated the programmes of postmodernism.

Elizabeth Cowie's essay takes up the question of the documentary film and the documentary project, looking at the roles of observation and testimony in films of the 1930s, including those of a 'lost' film-maker - Ruby Grierson, whose brother, John Grierson, was the most influential figure in British documentary film-making of the period. 'Giving voice and image to the ordinary - the anthropology of our own culture', Cowie writes, 'is clearly not straightforward, but both Mass-Observation and film-makers like Ruby Grierson were concerned to authorise the ordinary'. Margaretta Jolly's article takes up the question of observation and testimony in relation to the diaries kept by volunteer Observers, and looks at the ways in which these unpaid volunteers (to be contrasted with Harrisson's team of radical amateur anthropologists) rose to the challenge of providing an 'anthropology of ourselves'. Focusing on three diarists in particular - Nella Last, Edward Stebbing and Naomi Mitchison - Jolly opens up the function of diary-writing, both for the project of Mass-Observation and for the diarists themselves. She explores the thesis that 'a cultural sociology of writing is part of the logic of M-O itself', and discusses the current work of the Mass-Observation Archive in this light.

This special issue also includes an account of mass observation in a different context. Karen Fang's essay, 'Arresting Cinema: Surveillance and the City-State in the Representation of Hong-Kong' argues that surveillance is the distinctive characteristic of the city state. In an illuminating account of Hong Kong cinema before and after re-unification, Fang describes the inter-relationships between new technologies of surveillance, law-enforcement and the media, and concludes that Hong Kong is 'the product of a police-entertainment industrial complex'.

Most of the articles in this special issue are based on the conference Mass Observation as Poetry and Science: Charles Madge and his Contexts, *held at the University of Sussex on 12 May 2000. We would like to thank all those who contributed to the conference and its success, including Andrew Crozier, David Mellor, Stuart Hall, Peter Jay and Millie Oliver, and, for their expert help in organisation, Margaret Reynolds, Joy Eldridge, Anna Green, Bet Inglis and Anna Nomikou. Dorothy Sheridan was, as always, a source of great knowledge and energy. We would also like to express our special thanks to Dr Victoria Randall,*

Charles Madge's daughter, whose donation of her father's papers to the University of Sussex library was the original inspiration for the conference and hence for the new work we present here.

Those interested in further information on Mass-Observation can consult the web-site at <http://www.sussex.ac.uk/library/massobs/>

The catalogue for Charles Madge's papers can be found at <http://www.sussex.ac.uk/library/manuscript/lists/madgelist.shtml> *Charles Madge's selected poems were published by Anvil Press in 1994 as* Of Love, Time and Places.

CHARLES MADGE AND THE MASS-OBSERVATION ARCHIVE: A PERSONAL NOTE

Dorothy Sheridan

In the thirty years between his leaving the organisation in 1940 and the establishment of the Archive at the University of Sussex, Charles Madge seems to have kept particularly silent about his involvement with Mass-Observation. Perhaps he might have remained silent if the Archive, under the ebullient stewardship of Tom Harrisson, had not begun to attract the attention of the media and, more gradually, of the academic community during the early 1970s. To tell the story of Charles Madge's involvement, however, I should first describe the inauguration of the Mass-Observation papers as a public archive.[1]

The papers came to the University of Sussex in 1970 as a result of negotiations between the then vice-chancellor of Sussex, Asa Briggs, and Len England, at that time Director of Mass-Observation UK Ltd. The deal was effectively a rescue operation. By the late 1960s, Mass-Observation had evolved into a small but fully fledged market research company (M-O UK Ltd), working mainly for commercial clients. Its original commitment to the study of social questions and the production of books and articles with popular appeal had long been abandoned together with its recourse to qualitative and ethnographic methods of research. It is not surprising, then, that the staff of M-O UK Ltd were anxious to find a new home for the dusty trussed up old files of papers which were taking up expensive storage space in their London offices. Had Briggs not acted when he did, the papers might easily have been destroyed. Already some of the printed material and copies of survey reports from the collection had been hived off to the Imperial War Museum and integrated into other collections relating to World War Two. At the time there was almost no recognition of the research potential of the collection. Only two scholars had managed to track down the collection before its transfer to Sussex - Angus Calder for his monumental work, *The People's War*, and Paul Addison for his study of wartime politics, *The Road to 1945*.[2]

When Harrisson first employed me at the Archive in 1974, it was his name which eclipsed all others whenever Mass-Observation was mentioned. It was Harrisson whom Asa Briggs had invited to the University to set up the Archive and Harrisson who had retained strong links with the people working in the organisation during its transition into a market research company. Even though Harrisson had spent the 1950s and 1960s far away from Britain, either in Southeast Asia or in the USA, his continued enthusiasm for the research activities and for the early papers (over which

1. For a history of Mass-Observation, see Tom Jeffery, 'Mass-Observation: a short history', Brighton, University of Sussex, Mass-Observation Archive Occasional Paper no. 10, 2000. For information about the holdings of the Archive and access to it, see www.sussex.ac.uk/massobs

2. Angus Calder, *The People's War*, London, Jonathan Cape, 1969 and Paul Addison, *The Road to 1945*, London, Jonathan Cape, 1975.

he made a probably uncontested claim of ownership) made him a natural champion of the newly opened Archive. Indeed, for many years after his quite unexpected death in an accident in January 1976, the Archive was called 'The Tom Harrisson Mass-Observation Archive' in his honour. This title acknowledged both Harrisson's substantial role in Mass-Observation especially during the early years of the Second World War as well as his efforts in establishing the Archive. However, despite my own considerable personal debt to Harrisson, I always had reservations about the title. It unfairly obscured the contributions of a whole team of other Mass-Observers, many of them women, who did a good deal of hard graft under Harrisson's direction. Above all, it relegated Harrisson's fellow-founders of the organisation, Humphrey Jennings and Charles Madge, to second place. Jennings had died many years before the establishment of the Archive, but Charles Madge was very much alive and well, having retired from his professorial post at the University of Birmingham to live in the South of France.

To give him credit, it is clear that Harrisson was keen to re-involve Madge in Mass-Observation. He had successfully recruited other former Mass-Observers (for example, Humphrey Spender, Bob Willcock and Celia Fremlin) back into Mass-Observation-related projects. Several original members of the team offered help with his last book, *Living Through the Blitz*, which was published posthumously by Collins.[3] Not only was Harrisson keen to demonstrate the value of the wartime papers as resources for new books, he also still nurtured ambitions to re-launch Mass-Observation as an active research organisation. Looking back through Harrisson's correspondence for the early 1970s, I found a copy of a letter to Charles Madge, dated 20 May 1971, in which he said that he was 'taking a unit to the Bromsgrove by-election' and 'it would be very nice indeed if you would consider re-associating yourself with the project'.[4]

It appears that Madge was not to be wooed. Nor did he attend the Archive's formal opening party organised in 1975 by Asa Briggs at Sussex. At the time, I was puzzled by Madge's reluctance not to share in some of the limelight, but the reasons for his reserve became clearer once he began to express some of his ambivalence about his time with Mass-Observation. Significantly, it was only after Harrisson's death that Charles Madge chose to emerge as a commentator on Mass-Observation. He wrote a long review of *Living through the Blitz* for the *Times Literary Supplement* in which he described in some detail his own personal situation in 1937 and the gestation and birth of what became known as 'Mass-Observation'.[5] It was, he said, the culmination of his own developing belief in the possibility that 'history and social self-knowledge could be served by organised collective observation'. The review goes on to describe his relationships with Harrisson and Humphrey Jennings, the evolution of the research, and his own eventual departure to join the newly founded National Institute of Economic and Social Research in 1940.

3. Tom Harrisson, *Living Through the Blitz*, London, Collins, 1976.

4. Mass-Observation Archive (M-OA): Tom Harrisson (TH) correspondence boxes, 1971.

5. Charles Madge, 'The Birth of Mass-Observation', *Times Literary Supplement*, 5 November 1976, p1395.

Much has been made of Madge's principled objections to undertaking research for the government. Harrisson had negotiated with his friend Mary Adams at the Ministry of Information to supply Home Intelligence with regular reports on the morale of the civilian population based on Mass-Observation's observations and surveys.[6] Madge described this work as 'home front espionage' but I have never been convinced that it was the government work alone which was responsible for alienating Madge from Mass-Observation. In the same review, he goes on to say that despite its lack of rigour and the many problems which were to dog its footsteps, Mass-Observation was 'a trail blazer and trend setter' and it was 'ingenious and enlightening also'. His verdict on Harrisson's book is, in the end, remarkably generous. This, despite the fact that for most of their collaboration between 1937 and 1940 (as can be observed from their vituperative correspondence) they were at loggerheads - two very different kinds of men whose passions creatively and complicatedly overlapped, but only for a while.[7] What is surprising about their differences at the time is that it was Madge rather than Harrisson who was concerned about social scientific rigour. Madge saw Harrisson's approach as much more romantic than his own and this also led to a rift. However, the difficulty which Madge was experiencing in his personal life was at least as important a factor as his conflicts with Harrisson. His marriage to Kathleen Raine ended in the early months of the war, and as a way of coping, Madge escaped from London by taking Harrisson's place leading the 'Worktown Study' in Bolton while Harrisson returned to lead the London end of Mass-Observation. In Bolton, Madge undertook his last work for Mass-Observation, a study of saving and spending habits.[8]

After Harrisson's death in 1976, and the Archive established at Sussex,[9] Madge began to be approached for interviews about his experiences. In conversation with Nick Stanley in March 1978, he said:

I find it difficult to be fully truthful about [Mass-Observation and his own role], looking inside myself to know what I did, what my philosophy was at that time, because afterwards in looking back inevitably one tries to improve on the truth – to make it more convincing, more self-critical than it was in fact.[10]

Contact with academics and research students opened up a new relationship with the Archive for Madge but it was not until 1983 that I first met him. I attended a lecture he gave on Mass-Observation at the City University in London on 11 March which was probably his first public lecture on Mass-Observation. After that we engaged in an occasional but warm exchange of letters. He wrote kindly of the first Mass-Observation anthology which Angus Calder and I edited in 1984 commenting that he had never found the re-presentation of Mass-Observation material an easy task but he had enjoyed our efforts.[11]

6. The reports on morale are part of a sequence of 3,000 File Reports (see website for list and index of titles). They have been published on microfilm by Primary Source Media.

7. M-OA: History of Mass-Observation box 1: correspondence between TH and Charles Madge (CM) 1938-40.

8. For further discussion of Madge's role, see Liz Stanley, *The Archaeology of a Mass-Observation Project*, University of Manchester, Department of Sociology Occasional Paper, 1990.

9. Among the people who spoke to him during the 1980s were Angus Calder, Nick Stanley and Liz Stanley.

10. M-O A: Former Mass-Observers boxes: Madge File: interview of CM by Nick Stanley who published his PhD thesis on early M-O: N.S. Stanley, *The Extra Dimension: a study and assessment of the methods employed by Mass-Observation in its first period 1937 - 40*, CNAA.

11. Angus Calder and Dorothy Sheridan, *Speak for Yourself*, London, Jonathan Cape, 1984. A number of other books drawing on the collection have also been produced since the Archive was established including three edited diaries. See the website for details.

12. Ian Potts directed *Stranger than Fiction* for Channel Four, broadcast in 1987 and available for hire from the British Film Institute.

13. The full on-line catalogue to the Charles Madge Papers, prepared by Elizabeth Inglis, is available at http:\\www.sussex.ac.uk\speccoll

14. From a BBC Radio script, *They speak for themselves*, broadcast on 1 June 1939; also M-OA File Report A26.

15. The Mass-Observation Project was launched from the Archive at Sussex in 1981 and continues to the present-day under the direction of the present author. In terms of numbers of writers and duration it has long outstripped the original panel of diary-writers and others who answered the M-O 'directives'. An account of this phase of Mass-Observation can be found in Dorothy Sheridan, Brian Street & David Bloome, *Writing Ourselves: Mass-Observation and Literacy Practices*, Cresskill (NJ), Hampton Press, 2000.

16. From the BBC script, p3, as note 14.

The opportunity arose in the mid 1980s for him to re-locate himself within Mass-Observation. Ian Potts, a film director who had previously been at the BBC, decided to make a feature length film about Mass-Observation using a mix of contemporary newsreel, still photography, interviews with the few surviving former Mass-Observers and reconstructions of Mass-Observation activities using actors. Madge was invited to be the narrator of the history. He agreed and, although the 'take' on Mass-Observation is decidedly Potts' own, Madge's authorial voice gently and unassumingly pervades the film.[12] The film represents the re-integration of Charles Madge, and to some extent of his friend Humphrey Jennings too, into the complex story of Mass-Observation.

Charles Madge's part in *Stranger than Fiction* was filmed in the Archive at Sussex. This was his one and only reunion with the papers he had so conscientiously collected (and struggled with) in the late 1930s. It was gratifying, then, after his death in 1996 at the age of eighty-three, that the process of reconciliation could be continued. His younger daughter, Dr Victoria Randall, agreed, on behalf of his family, to donate his papers to the University of Sussex. Because they consist largely of his literary work and include many volumes of his poetry note books, the collection was not incorporated into the Mass-Observation Archive but established as a collection in its own right as one of the University's literary manuscripts collections.[13] The collection also includes his unpublished autobiography, many family photographs, a remarkable collection of over 2,000 letters written to his mother, Barbara, during his school years, and later correspondence with his first wife, the poet Kathleen Raine and with his second wife, Inez Spender (née Pearn), whom he married in 1942. One unexpected gem which we found when a second batch of papers arrived at Sussex was his correspondence with J.M. Keynes between 1939 and 1944, which began during the time he was withdrawing from Mass-Observation.

I am not now sure how Charles Madge would feel to be remembered most decisively for his three turbulent years as a founding Mass-Observer. I hope it would please him to know that his idea of a national panel of 'ordinary hard-working people'[14] recording their everyday life has been an inspiration for a re-launch of an autobiographical project which still calls itself Mass-Observation.[15] Mass-Observation, he suggested in 1939:

… immediately puts us in touch with a section of people in the population who were at one and the same time ordinary hardworking folk and also intelligent and interesting enough to want to help us. We did not regard these people as being themselves scientists studying the mass, nor did we consider them as being a random sample of public opinion. Their position was something different. They were observers, untrained but shrewd, placed at vantage points for seeing and describing in their own simple language what life looks like in the various environments which go to make up England.[16]

It is easy now to criticise Madge and his friends for their naivety, and to cringe at the casual use of the words 'folk' and 'simple', but for me as archivist, having spent more than half my life surrounded by the results of their imaginations and energies, I feel grateful for their chutzpah, not only Tom Harrisson's (who was always larger than life), but also Charles Madge's who in his quieter way ensured that Mass-Observation was intriguingly, outrageously and abidingly original.

BOURGEOIS NEWS: HUMPHREY JENNINGS AND CHARLES MADGE

Rod Mengham

This essay explores first how the experimental methods employed by Charles Madge and Humphrey Jennings in their poetic writings may be related to the example of French surrealism; then it considers how this relationship may bear on the subsequent development of both Mass-Observation and a certain style of documentary film-making.

The main trends and groupings within English surrealism of the 1930s reflected the structural changes that had previously affected French surrealism, changes identified in, and conveniently marked out by, André Breton's first and second manifestos, published in 1924 and 1930, respectively. The first manifesto had emphasised the liberation of the individual unconscious mind, laying heavy stress on the importance of dreams and on the exploitation of automatic writing methods. The kind of writing produced during this phase of French surrealism was likely to consist of highly subjective examples of what Breton referred to as 'pure psychic automatism'. The second manifesto showed much more interest in the surrealism of everyday life, in the attempt to discover where 'surreality resides in reality itself' - in material reality and in a public, social world. The writing of this phase showed less concern with a crisis of the subject and more concern with what Breton referred to as a 'fundamental crisis of the object'.

The second phase of French surrealism was associated, unsurprisingly, with a more self-conscious and more overt commitment to a left-wing politics, indicated most simply in the change of title of the main journal concerned, from *La Revolution Surrealiste* to *Le Surrealisme au service de la revolution*. Looking back on the change of direction, in a lecture entitled 'What is Surrealism', given in Brussels in 1934, Breton divides the history of the movement into two epochs: in the first or 'intuitive' epoch, 'thought is supreme over matter', while in the second or 'reasoning' epoch, the reverse is the case; thought's supremacy over matter is replaced by the 'supremacy of matter over mind'.[1] Breton dates the second epoch as beginning after the outbreak of the Moroccan War in 1925, an event which politicised a number of the movement's associates.

This basic distinction between different ways of working along surrealist lines was fully grasped by English practitioners. David Gascoyne, in his brief but crucial book, *A Short Survey of Surrealism*, published in 1935, specifies how things changed from what he refers to as a 'more or less passive attitude prior to the *Second Manifesto*' to a 'new, active attitude'

1. André Breton, 'What is Surrealism', in Franklin Rosemont (ed), *What is Surrealism: Selected Writings*, London, 1978, p116.

during the 1930s, when 'super-reality' is conceived of as 'existing in the material world, objectively, as well as subjectively, in the automatic thought of the unconscious'.

Clearly, not all the English writers and artists connected with Surrealism during the 1930s can be lined up neatly behind either one or the other of these tendencies. However, I think it is the case that a number of those who subsequently turned out to be among the more interesting and significant figures did tend to concentrate their efforts on developing one of these areas rather than the other. Gascoyne, for example, despite his grasp of surrealist doctrine, in most of his 1930s work, represents a continuity with the earlier, individualist mode, inclining towards automatic writing. Whereas, it is in the work of writers initially associated with Cambridge projects and publications that one sees a more comprehensive attempt to explore the implications of the second mode. The absolutely key journal in this respect was *Experiment*, a magazine started by undergraduates in 1928, where the early works of William Empson, Jennings and Hugh Sykes Davies appeared.

The real interest of this early work does not necessarily have to do with its intrinsic qualities, so much as with the implications it carries for interpreting the course of British cultural history during the 1930s and 1940s. Jennings's concern (shared later by Madge) for the cultural object, in existing texts, and in social reality, makes their work at once both intensely English - because it is an English social reality that they are closing with - and more closely connected with a modernist poetics than the majority of their surrealist colleagues. And it is because of their involvement in Mass-Observation, and because of Jennings's pioneering work in documentary film, that one can begin to think about a very paradoxical line of development in English culture in which Surrealism is the formative influence upon both the origins of sociology in Britain and on a war-time and post-war new realism concerned with the portrayal of working-class culture.

There are obvious ways in which the beginnings of Mass-Observation look surrealistic that have to do with a surface manner. What was effectively the original manifesto for the Mass-Observation group, the letter published in the *New Statesman and Nation* on January 30, 1937, under the title 'Anthropology at Home' and signed by Madge, Jennings and Tom Harrisson, includes a bizarre 'plan of campaign' listing an assortment of topics for observation on a nation-wide basis. It is worth recalling the sheer daftness attached to the beginnings of what was to develop into such an intensely serious enterprise, treated with respect, eventually, even at government level:

We are [...] working out a complete plan of campaign, which will be possible when we have not fifty but 5,000 observers. The following are a few examples of problems that will arise:

Behaviour of people at war memorials.

Shouts and gestures of motorists.

The aspidistra cult.

Anthropology of football pools.

Bathroom behaviour.

Beards, armpits, eyebrows.

Anti-semitism.

Distribution, diffusion and significance of the dirty joke.

Funerals and undertakers.

Female taboos about eating.

The private lives of midwives.

The playfulness of this list, its deliberate silliness at times, is in perfect accord with the more facile subversions of surrealist humour. Beyond that, the implicit research interest in the links between bodily functions and dispositions and unconscious social behaviour would be just as much the natural concern of an exclusively surrealist enterprise as of an anthropological enquiry. According to David Gascoyne, who was present when the famous letter was drawn up, the relationship between the surrealistic and anthropological elements of the experiment was an antagonistic one from the start; he remembers the occasion in terms of the physical attitudes of Jennings and Harrisson, perched at either end of a mantelpiece, and was struck by the likelihood that the movement then just beginning would end up going 'in either this direction or in that'.[2]

Jennings's methods as a documentary film-maker betray a superficial allegiance to surrealist techniques by incorporating the accidental into a film-text that also has a layer of repetitive, obsessional imagery - a repertoire of images recurrently dominated, according to the film historians Hodgkinson and Sheratsky, by evocations of horses, both zoological and mechanical, groups singing, smoking chimneys and catastrophic fires.[3] The horse and the iron horse crop up again and again in Jennings's work in all media: poetry, painting, photography, film. They have been given an individualising, biographical origin, in the unpublished account of his childhood, 'Beyond the Life of Man',[4] a manuscript in which Jennings records his memories of horses passing in front of the family house while trains ran along the back; but they also conjoin in the first two commissioned films Jennings ever directed: *Post Haste* and *Locomotives* (both 1934); and they persist all through his work as a pair of motifs, constantly provoking questions about the role of art, and of the artist, in an age of mechanical reproduction.

However, a much more thoroughgoing and systematic means of establishing uniformity in his principles of composition throughout the oeuvre is achieved by Jennings's employment of a modernist poetics of superimposition. In his very earliest critical writings, published in *Experiment*, Jennings very clearly perceives and values the kind of artistic practice in

2. Personal communication.

3. Anthony W. Hodgkinson and Rodney E. Sheratsky, *Humphrey Jennings: More than a Maker of Films*, Hanover and London, 1982, pxxiii.

4. Quoted in Mary-Lou Jennings (ed) *Humphrey Jennings: Film-Maker, Painter, Poet*, London, 1982, p6.

which collective experience is reflected and preserved; it is an adaptation of an Eliotic notion of tradition and the individual talent which is open to, and accepts, more popular forms than the high modernist example normally allows. In *Experiment* (Spring 1931) he celebrates the kind of African rock paintings in which

> a single work may have been painted at different times by different men with no apparent consciousness of the consequences of superimposition. Figures overlay, definite planes are abandoned, rhythms intersect and above all, scale is widely varied.
> Space in these paintings is not bounded; they have no planes, but this does in no way exclude depth.[5]

5. *Experiment*, 7 (Spring 1931), 37.

For Jennings, the modern artist occupies the position of the observer, effectively the Mass-Observer, who grasps the relation between any given historical moment and the series of superimposed paintings, drawings, or texts, that comprise the work of art. There is a constantly shifting temporal point, which means that the observation of the spatial arrangements has to be constantly revised.

The role of the artist-observer (analogous to Madge's notion of the 'poet-reporter') is an extremely active one. Two years before the rock-painting piece, Jennings recommends, in the second (February 1929) issue of *Experiment*, that the visitor to the Fitzwilliam Museum in Cambridge should ignore the curated order of the paintings in order to discover a personal sense of the relationship between different paintings. He is effectively recommending that one should operate a proto-Situationist *derive* among the monuments of official culture. In his subsequent career, Jennings established for himself the vocation of *bricoleur* of English culture. His works draw on, are frequently straightforwardly composed of, the elements of English culture, of both high and popular varieties.

This sense of participation in a collective enterprise is absolutely fundamental to Madge's work in his first volume of poetry, *The Disappearing Castle* (1937). All of the poems in that volume pre-date, but also in some sense anticipate, the formation of Mass-Observation. According to Malinowski, in his 1938 essay 'A Nation-wide Intelligence Service', 'Mass-Observation was conceived of under conditions of national stress, of dramatic circumstances which compelled every man and woman to think and feel, to react towards a definite issue - that of the Abdication'.[6] This perception has a particular bearing on Madge's work, because there is a sense in which the subject matter of the early poems has to do with abdication, with the fear of renunciation, of abandonment by default, with the sense of cutting oneself off from, or of being cut off from, a collective identity, a sense of belonging. Questions of belonging haunt the early works. When the Abdication occurred, in December 1936, it was only the most spectacular expression of a set of

6. Malinowski, 'A Nation-Wide Intelligence Service', in Charles Madge and Tom Harrisson (eds), *First Year's Work 1937-8 by Mass-Observation*, London, 1938, p108.

issues that Madge had already been contemplating for several years. And of course the first major project undertaken by Mass-Observation, *May 12*, concerned the coronation of George VI, which functioned as an act of national restitution, a restoration of collective identity, as Malinowski was quick to recognise, seeing it in economic terms as a regaining by Britain of the requisite amount of cultural 'credit'. If anthropology needs to begin at home, that is partly because 'Home is gone' as Madge's poem 'In Sua Voluntade' puts it in 1933.[7] So many of these texts centre on the experience of feeling strange, of being a stranger, in one's own land. In the very earliest works, humankind is most often figured as species, positioned within geological epochs and in elemental settings, rather than as a congeries of social beings within a recognisably human history. When the social dimension is featured, it is more often than not fraught with obstruction and impasse, as in 'The Hours of the Planets'(1934). A marginal note - 'The rise of the bourgeoisie' - is offered in apparent explanation of a process of socialisation which involves 'All equal all in inequality / Looking not one to one but each from each / Different in self-indifference',[8] where the very concept of social relations is founded on antithesis. The structures of these early poems are frequently abdicative, obliging the reader to progress through a dereliction of meanings and occasionally of syntax in a way that corresponds to, without exactly matching, the procedures devised by Jennings during the same period.

Almost exactly contemporary with Madge's 'Bourgeois News', which I shall discuss later, is Jennings's 'The Boyhood of Byron', first published in the December 1936 issue of *Contemporary Poetry and Prose*, edited by Roger Roughton. One of the reasons that Jennings chooses to write about Byron is because Byron represents for him the paradox of a poet of rational control in a Romantic age. And it is significant that in the same issue of *Contemporary Poetry and Prose* containing 'The Boyhood of Byron', Jennings also publishes a review of *Surrealism*, the volume edited and introduced by Herbert Read and including articles by Breton, Hugh Sykes Davies, Georges Hugnet and Paul Eluard. Jennings uses most of the space available to him to resist Read's idea that Surrealism should be founded on 'the universal truths of Romanticism', advocating in place of this a re-use, or a new use, of classicism, which in his view is currently being misused by a 'classical-military-capitalist-ecclesiastical racket' (by which he can only mean T. S. Eliot).[9]

What interests Jennings in Byron is Byron's very conscious regulation of the formal aspects of his work, and this is reflected in the organisation of 'The Boyhood of Byron'. The text is comprised of extracts from a variety of sources, and these extracts are juxtaposed sometimes quite violently, so that as a series of paragraphs, the text can be extremely elliptical. And yet within the bounds of each paragraph, the writing is extremely cogent, even sometimes quite strictly disciplined:

7. Charles Madge, *Of Love, Time and Places: Selected Poems*, London, Anvil, 1994, p17.

8. Ibid., p26.

9. 'Surrealism' in Roger Roughton (ed), *Contemporary Poetry and Prose*, (December 1936), 167-8.

From Livadia the travellers proceeded to Delphi. The huge locomotive, the more gigantic for being under cover, was already quivering with that artificial life which rendered it so useful and so powerful a servant. Its brasses shone with golden lustre, its iron cranks and pistons glittered with a silvery sheen, while the oblong pit over which it stood glowed with the light of its intense furnace.[10]

It is very odd, but a matter of record, that some of the most grammatically decorous and self-consciously polished writing of the period comes from the Surrealists Humphrey Jennings and Hugh Sykes Davies. It is a paradox which is caught nicely by the references to Greece in the text: these include a reference to Delphi, one of the original sources for oracular speech, for the texts of 'psychic automatism', and yet the reference is enclosed within a paragraph of very carefully poised and regulated writing, using proper sentence structure.

Jennings's use of existing materials in his poetry - which is reflected in the way he painted as well, working the subjects of his canvases up from originals in photographs, postcards and prints - when put alongside his recommendation of classicism, does give his work a modernist dimension. Unlike perhaps the majority of Surrealists, he was concerned to preserve the culture of the past, not jettison it; indeed, his work insists on a continuity with it. Where both Jennings and Madge diverge most obviously from the priorities of high modernism is in their attitude towards popular culture. Jennings actually planned to call a volume of his poems of the 1930s that never came out, *Popular Narratives*, and in any case he habitually ascribed his prose poems of the 1930s to the genre of 'reports'. The notion of the poem as 'report' and of the poet as 'reporter' is one of the things that links Madge's and Jennings's procedures as Surrealist writers with their activities as Mass-Observers.

The point of view of the Mass-Observer is absolutely crucial here, because it contrasts dramatically with other points of view that are given a high profile during the 1930s. The poetry of the period is frequently associated with the hawk's eye view; this is by no means as uniformly present in those poems of Auden where it has often been identified by critics, but it does appear with sufficient frequency in his work and in that of his epigones for it to have become a standard topos in terms of the reception of the work. The poetry of the Auden gang and the films of Jennings share a rhetoric of apostrophe, in which the reader or spectator is enjoined to 'observe', 'inspect', or 'look at' the data of English social reality: 'Look, stranger, at this island now' begins one of Auden's most famous poems. The difference between Auden and Jennings contrasts the point of view of the hawk or the helmeted airman, a position of supreme advantage, from which to dominate imaginatively a given landscape and reduce it to order, with the point of view of the Mass-Observer, which is that of the figure in the crowd, whose view is frequently obscured, by other passers-by and by traffic; which is

10. 'The Boyhood of Byron' in Roger Roughton (ed), *Contemporary Poetry and Prose*, (December 1936), 146-7.

shifting, transitory, partial. The 'stranger' in early to mid-Auden, and in the readings of that material, is a completely different figure from the 'stranger' in Jennings and Madge. And the quality of observation employed can be different as well: the 'look' of Auden's stranger is associated with spying and surveillance, with an exclusive, Masonic knowledge; the 'look' of the Mass-Observer turns that process of introversion inside out, to display, and share with others, the knowledge of a public reality - the observing is part of a process of accessing information rather than of encrypting it.

Jennings's last textual project, actually left unfinished at his death, was *Pandaemonium*, that collection of extracts from the eighteenth and nineteenth centuries bearing witness to the coming of the machine and its impact upon the texture of everyday life. What Jennings was doing, effectively, with this project was awarding Mass-Observation, retrospectively, to the eighteenth and nineteenth centuries - treating the authors whose words he borrowed as if they were members of one of the survey teams. In the Introduction to this volume, put together by Madge out of notes left by Jennings, there's an account of the motivation for this project that makes it sound like an attempt to repair a breach that has opened up in the cultural fabric as a result of something that resembles very closely Eliot's notion of the 'dissociation of sensibility'. Jennings/Madge argue that there has been an increasing specialisation of discourse coincident with the progress of the Industrial Revolution, which necessitates the presentation of a multiplicity of viewpoints in a quasi-simultaneous fashion, using the methods of poetry. The trouble with poetry, they say, over the last two hundred years is that it has been expropriated by poets.

The question of points of view, single or multiple, is far more than a merely technical problem in Madge's 'Bourgeois News'; his extraordinary prose poem of 1936. 'Bourgeois News' takes the form of a news report about a culture dominated by bourgeois values, and by implication it issues a warning about what is likely to happen to that kind of culture. It incorporates numerous effects of a surrealistic whimsy, but its closest connections to surrealism are to the concerns of the second stage of surrealism, as revealed in its editing together of separate, apparently pre-existing documents; so that it is documentary in the literal sense. The news report focuses on a catastrophe, on a seemingly natural disaster of apocalyptic proportions: a universal flood, hitting a culture in which universal floods are normally inflicted as penalties for universal transgression. The culture this flood obliquely overwhelms is represented by several things: by a description of working conditions in a small business; by a communiqué about government and the conduct of government-appointed bodies; and by an anthropologist's interpretation of a distant, alien, tribal culture. It is in effect a report on the British, who have been made the object of the kind of scrutiny which an anthropologist would bring to bear on the so-called primitive rituals of an exotic tribal culture. In this it pre-dates but anticipates how anthropology will 'begin at home'.

And it also parallels or shadows Malinowski's project, as stated retrospectively in 1938: 'From the start of my own field-work, it has been my deepest and strongest conviction that we must finish by studying ourselves through the same methods and with the same mental attitude with which we approach exotic tribes.' Interestingly, given the role of surrealistic humour in Madge's prose poems, Malinowski also emphasises the importance of humour as a means of achieving what he calls the 'home-coming' of anthropology, in order to 'gain a new sense of proportion with regard to our own institutions, beliefs, and customs'.[11]

11. Op. cit., p104.

What binds together the separate documents, the sometimes very disparate elements of the text, is ultimately the movement of the prose. Semantically, 'Bourgeois News' is full of inconsequentiality. Syntactically, and rhythmically, the sentences, the paragraphs, and finally the whole text, are bound together into some sort of unity. Most of Madge's jokes work because he manages to achieve a certain unity of tone which gives the impression of a scientific attitude. It is what the prose *sounds* like when you read it aloud (or in your head) that binds it together: the music of a certain kind of speech, and that perhaps is reminiscent of something that Jennings once said in connection with his own methods of composition in creating documentary films: 'any two shots can be cut together - the soundtrack will connect them'.[12] (A good example of that would be *Listen to Britain* (1942) with its 'anticipatory soundtrack', where you get the sounds of one sequence - of the next sequence - coming in and overlapping with the last few images of the previous sequence, so that there is a constant syncopation of sound and image.) But the soundtrack of 'Bourgeois News' holds all the dangers of a voice-over enforcing connections; it does not allow the reader to assume the responsibility for editing together, collating, the disparate materials of which it is composed. Malinowski was aware of the necessity for the editors of Mass-Observation not to abdicate from the responsibility of providing an objective interpretation of subjective data, and yet he referred to the editorial team as the 'General Staff', a phrase which is immediately suggestive of the facility with which that interpretation might become subjective, a form of spokesmanship, a method of speaking *for* subordinates, rather than letting equals speak for themselves. The model of spokesmanship, of public speaking, of political oratory, is endemic to the literature of 1936; it is most spectacularly evident in Auden's 'Spain', and it is most destructively gaining ground in Edward Upward's prose. Malinowski claimed that Mass-Observation would never be allowed in a totalitarian state; in 'Bourgeois News' it may be that autocratic and democratic perspectives are still being held in tension. 'Bourgeois News' is one of those texts in which history is Janus-faced; a movement which could go in either this direction or in that.

12. Quoted in Hodgkinson and Sheratsky, op. cit., p25.

In The Blitz Of Dreams: Mass-Observation And The Historical Uses Of Dream Reports

Tyrus Miller

The Means of Vision - matter (sense impressions) transformed and reborn by Imagination: *turned into an image.*
The Means of Production - matter is transformed and reborn by *Labour.*
Humphrey Jennings, Introduction to *Pandaemonium*[1]

In the imaginary dimension proper, existence *is* signification.
Cornelius Castoriadis, 'The Imaginary'[2]

1. Humphrey Jennings, *Pandaemonium: The Coming of the Machine as Seen by Contemporary Observers, 1660-1886*, M-L. Jennings and C. Madge (eds), New York, Free Press, 1985, pxxxviii.

2. Cornelius Castoriadis, 'The Imaginary: Creation in the Social-Historical Domain', in Castoriadis, *World in Fragments: Writings on Politics, Society, Psychoanalysis, and the Imagination*, David Ames Curtis (ed and trans), Palo Alto, Stanford University Press, 1997, p11.

3. Charles Madge and Tom Harrisson, *Mass-Observation*, London, Frederick Muller, 1937, p38.

4. Charles Madge, 'A Note on Images', in Mary-Lou Jennings (ed), *Humphrey Jennings: Film-Maker, Painter, Poet*, London, British Film Institute, 1982, p47.

An assumption held in common by the three founders of Mass-Observation, Charles Madge, Humphrey Jennings, and Tom Harrisson, was that the predominant social anxieties and wishes of the age express themselves most readily in the idiom of 'images'. The image, as they defined it, has a peculiar two-faced character, in which ideas are sensualised and sensations given ideational content. The image is 'more vivid than an abstract idea', Madge and Harrisson wrote in the 1937 pamphlet *Mass-Observation*; yet 'it is more intangible than a concrete sensation'.[3] Humphrey Jennings, as a painter and filmmaker, gave the term a particular psychological and aesthetic spin, as Charles Madge noted retrospectively. In a text for a pamphlet produced by the Institute of Contemporary Arts shortly after Jennings's death in 1950, Madge wrote that Jennings conferred on the term 'image' - 'a meaning personal to himself and bound up with his early researches into poetry and painting. His use of "image" is not far off from the way it is used in psychology, in literary criticism and in surrealist theory, but it is not quite identical with any of these. It has resemblances to the psychological concept of the *gestalt*'.[4] Implicit in a later consideration of the 'image' by Madge, again in relation to Jennings, is a more complex notion of a sort of intersemiotic translation, from one medium such as a text to visible or imaginatively visualisable form. Thus, in his editorial preface to Jennings's collection of textual quotations about the rise of the machine in the modern age, quotations called 'Images' by Jennings, Madge writes:

> In his notes for an introduction, Humphrey calls his extracts 'images', a term which, in the way he uses it, can cover a wide range of meanings. He chose the extracts because, for him, they had an imaginative impact ... What gives this its force as an 'image' is its place in Humphrey's 'unrolling film' ... Humphrey undoubtedly had an eye for such passages,

a painter's eye, and a film-maker's, for whom the visual complement of the written word was never far away.[5]

5. Charles Madge, 'Editorial Tasks and Methods', in Jennings, op. cit., pxviii.

Madge thus sees two main features compounded in Jennings's 'image': it translates a sign-system that is not necessarily pictorially evocative into a visually striking image, and it allows a dispersed or hidden pattern to be discerned and rendered explicit as a visible whole, a *gestalt*. While in this second passage, Madge has in mind the narrow context of Jennings's 'text-images' in *Pandaemonium*, it is easy enough to see this as a special case of a more general application of the image to a wide range of media, from arrangements of objects, to built spaces, to rituals and everyday practices, to explicitly symbolic artifacts. The image is a general interpretative tool for rendering conscious and presentable previously hidden constellations of social meanings.

In the domains of everyday life, from personal grooming to popular superstition to home decoration to movie-going, practices and beliefs in which the ideational and ideological contents remain largely a matter of implicit knowledge, the M-O directors believed that 'dominant images' would emerge that could be detected and possibly rectified by the activist sociologist. In this regard, the Mass-Observation project was guided by assumptions that would become increasingly articulate in the interpretative sociology, ethnography and cultural studies of the last three decades. Practices, it suggested, are not merely functional and instrumental. They are also meaningful, and the meanings they bear need be neither evident nor derivable from the manifest 'rational' intention of the practice. In at least some cases, one could legitimately speak of a 'repressed' meaning and hence a distortion of social knowledge that keeps important aspects of the practice's effective nature hidden from those most directly involved in it. In other words, while avoiding the more metaphysical and archaic-mythic aspects of Jungian symbol theory one could conceive of a certain 'collective unconscious' residing in the material textures of modern social life.

In this respect, Mass-Observation showed a remarkable prescience, anticipating in a genuine way what would become a paradigmatic conceptual orientation of contemporary cultural theory. Especially as it has become possible to reconceive 'psychic' agencies as embedded in linguistic, semiotic, informational, and ecological systems, this 'deallegorisation' of collective representations in contemporary theory has advanced rapidly. Without conjuring up mythic psychic entities like 'racial memories' or the 'national mind' or the like, it has nonetheless become possible to talk coherently about transindividual agencies for preserving and transforming meanings such as 'culture', 'collective memory', and 'archives'.

If the concept of the image, as formulated by the M-O directors, offered an epistemological entry into the social investigation of collectively produced meanings, it is in turn evident why the everyday (or everynight) process of dreaming would have attracted their interest. Dreams seem more than just entities to be interpreted as 'images'; they already *are* images. To M-O, they seemed to offer a readymade object and model for the work of the sociological collector and interpreter of images. Moreover, the foundational status of dream interpretation in the development of psychoanalytic theory meant that the M-O directors could count on a fairly authoritative body of theory about dreams that might be extended into the broader reaches of social images they wished to investigate. While the dream project ultimately represented only one among many areas of Mass-Observation's interest - and could hardly be said to be their most important work - from a *theoretical* point of view, it was critical.

II

> The sociologist ... is ill-equipped for anything more than examining dreams as they appear on the surface. His job is not to dig deep into the unconscious lives of a few individuals, but rather to explore wider fields, at a more superficial level. His interest is not so much in individuals and depth, as in masses and extent.
>
> Mass-Observation, 'A Report on Dreams', March 1949 [6]

6. Mass-Observation File Report 3096, March 1949, Mass-Observation Archive, University of Sussex.

Despite its apparent promise, however, Mass-Observation's project of collecting dreams from its participant observers resulted in something less than a definitive new knowledge of the collective psychic life of the British populace. The project, as I have indicated, began in the late 1930s as an outgrowth of the broad and brash programmatic ideas that situated the dream research among a number of areas of 'mass-observation', data collection, and interpretation in the pursuit of collectively shared images. Although throughout the war, Tom Harrisson, the prime mover of the M-O dream project, encouraged his correspondents with promises of valuable comparative results from the collection efforts, he seems to have realised fairly early that the submitted dreams were not really backing up the theories motivating the collection.[7] By the last major document of the project, the 'Report on Dreams' prepared in March 1949, the note of abortiveness is palpable. This project, maintained at least nominally for a full decade, did not, in the end, pan out.

7. Harrisson personally corresponded with the dream reporters, gently chiding them when they were lax about sending in reports and offering encouraging words about the usefulness of their efforts. By the outbreak of the war, he seems to have taken exclusive charge of this project, even advising in a letter to the Mass-Observers dated 21 September 1939, 'for this dream material, though not for anything else, please send in to me personally at the above W.II address'. M-O Directive Replies 1939 (microfilm), Roll 8, July-Sept 1939 (Dreams), in M-O Archive, University of Sussex.

For the scholar engaged in research using the M-O papers (or analogous collections of documents), the relative failure of the dream project poses some key methodological questions about the significance of dreams as social, cultural, and historical evidence. First there are issues related to the project itself. The documentation is rather scant at the directorial end. There are a few directives, a few hesitant attempts to evaluate the evidence, and little else in the way of theoretical or interpretative reflection related to the project. One has to assemble scattered statements in the early M-O writings and ponder the practical shape of the documentary evidence itself to be able to come to a clearer sense of what Harrisson and company were up to with the dream project.

But an even stickier set of problems relates to the material side of the project as it was realised. The infrequency and intermittence of the dream directives only allow a few of the individual observers, those especially eager and hence perhaps unrepresentative dream reporters, to emerge as particular personalities among the mass of scattered dreams sent in by other reporters. Yet on the other hand, the relatively small number of reporters and hence the relatively small sample of dreams does not amount to data for significant statistical analysis. A point of comparison will help bring in focus the betwixt-and-between character of the M-O dream evidence. In September 1940, the directive sent to the observers included questions about dreams among other questions about the air war and its role in bringing about changes in daily habits, mental attitude, reading, and radio listening. Tom Harrisson's report written on the basis of the responses, dated 14 November 1940, quantifies the results. He notes that 123 men and 77 women answered the questions. Of these, only 102 men and 58 women provided any reference to dreaming. The large majority (83 per cent of men, 70 per cent of women) reported no change in their dreams, and a look at the responses themselves will show that in most cases, these respondents gave no more information than to note this fact. Only 16 per cent of men and 30 per cent of women reported dreams in which there were references to the war, one of the topics that Harrisson was particularly hoping to find reflected in dream-life. Roughly estimating, this means that only about 20 women and 20 men reported war dreams.[8] By comparison, an American study of dreams carried out in the late 1940s and early 1950s collected over 10,000 dreams for statistical analysis. A single subgrouping, eighteen- to twenty-eight-year-olds, provided a sample of 1819 dreams to the investigator.[9] This comparison is not meant to ridicule the numerically dwarfed M-O efforts, but it does highlight the relative backwardness of quantitative method and the very limited resources available to Harrisson to conduct this kind of study of dream.

Aside from these methodological weaknesses in the way the project was conducted, there are serious issues related to the intrinsic character of the dream reports as historical evidence. Evidence of what, socially significant patterns or idiosyncratically personal preoccupations? - a sceptic might justifiably ask. Many of the dreams reported, clearly, have a purely private significance, the background of which can no longer be reconstructed, even were it of interest to do so. And even if the dreams collected by M-O might be in some 'collective' way significant - for example, as a window on an intimately experienced, but widely shared emotional life - serious problems persist in assessing and interpreting such documents. The partialness of the sample, the unsystematic nature of the collection effort, the absence (in most cases) of the dreamer's associations with the dream images, the possible influence of the survey itself on what was dreamed or recorded, and the 'irrational' figural form of the dreams themselves would together

8. Mass-Observation File Report 492, 14 Nov 1940, M-O Archive, University of Sussex.

9. Calvin S. Hall, 'What People Dream About', *Scientific American*, 184, 5 (May 1951), 60-63.

appear to render them intractable to the historian's methods.

As a biographical aside, I will note that my interest in the M-O dream reports involved the frustration of my own theories about their historical significance. I initially approached them with the hope of shedding light on the putative 'surrealist' influence on M-O's formation. Beyond reconfirming the obvious loose ties with the aesthetic and psychological interests of the founding directors, however, the dream project does not really confirm a subterranean surrealism in M-O. There is very little in the way of elaborated interpretation or engaging textual montage of dream materials on the part of M-O. On the contrary, despite the weaknesses of their methods, the directors collected dreams in the genuine hope of using them as sociological data, for the diagnosis and solution of social problems. Now, as a reader in the archive, one is struck above all by the sheer facticity of the dream reports rather than the imaginative, aesthetic interest of their imagery: the enigmatic presence that preservation itself has lent these sometimes boring, sometimes fascinating little narratives dutifully written down and sent in by people from all over Great Britain. Flying in the face of my own suspicions of futility - for what was I really going to do with all those pencilled notes and photocopies of dreams dreamed six decades ago? - over three or four successive visits from the United States to the University of Sussex, I worked my way slowly through the archived papers.

Two things continued to hold my attention, and it is these, I would argue, that offer me a thread towards a possible reinterpretation of the M-O dream project that does not merely dismiss its documents as residues of an 'ethnographic surrealist' phase, abandoned along the way to a more sound scientific orientation.[10] First, if I may stretch a Freudian distinction beyond any legitimate psychoanalytic construal, I became fascinated by the 'form' of the dreams, their *Darstellungform* as an archival collection, as much as any theme or manifest content that might be represented in any one of them. The mode of the reports and their accumulation seemed to reduce to a common two-dimensional plane the most hilariously silly and terrifyingly vivid dreams, and even within single dreams, to place in a single perspective both thudding banalities and fantastical details. At times, the form of the report itself took on the quality of an oneiric artifact, complete with illegible passages, incongruous interpolations and revelations, and complex layerings. Perhaps my favourite example is in a dream report by a zealous young male observer, in his waking life a newspaper reporter. His M-O reports reveal a method shaped by his occupation. He regularly abbreviates articles, conjunctions, prepositions, and other function-words with letters or symbols. Moreover, he evidently took abbreviated notes of the dream at the moment of waking, which he often quotes into his report, then explains what he 'must have been dreaming'. Sometimes, however, the waking notes are obscure to the observer himself. In one instance, he inscribes an unreadable scrawl into his report, imitating what he wrote to himself, noting 'The remaining note I can't read, so soon after waking

10. For the concept of 'ethnographic surrealism' with reference to the development of French anthropology in the 1930s and 40s, see James Clifford, 'On Ethnographic Surrealism', in *The Predicament of Culture: Twentieth-Century Ethnography, Literature, and Art*, Cambridge, Massachusetts, Harvard University Press, 1988, pp117-151.

11. For example, the cafe proprietress who reports: 'Feeling I was rather letting you down, I rushed round my friends trying to rake up some nice dreams or nightmares for you, and was rather surprised to find that their dream world was much the same

must I have written it. It looks like [scrawl] if that helps you'. This obscurity seems to have genuinely weighed on this young man, however, for in a later report, the 'repressed' returns, this time in a much weirder form. He writes to Tom Harrisson that there was a note that he hastily jotted down 'in a befuddled state' and asks the M-O director to 'have a go at it'. A triangular piece of paper is stuck to the page, a fragment of the real waking note with the scrawl earlier imitated. And then an appended note (I am unpacking the shorthand): 'Not being at the office with a pastepot handy, I'm afraid I've had to stick it to this page with a bit of chewing gum'. I could not believe my eyes when I first read this on microfilm; so as the final act of this perverse drama of unintelligibility, I asked to see the original paper, confirming that he had indeed stuck the scrap of dream-debris to the page with chewing gum!

If the material form of dream reports constituted one pole of fascination for me, the unexpected ways in which the dream reporters fulfilled or failed to fulfil their assignments also gripped me. In some cases, as in the newspaper reporter with his illegible note, or a woman who sent in not only copious dreams but also reports of visions she saw in her fireplace, or the correspondents who eagerly collected additional dreams from family and friends,[11] the dream-directives of Mass-Observation sometimes occasioned an excessive attachment to the project that itself seems socially meaningful. One is led to ask: what sort of desire underlies this kind of hyperfulfilment of the assignment to observe and report on oneself? What sort of pleasure is at stake for the participant? Is there any broader social significance to this 'socialisation' of intimacy made possible by the social science research itself?

The 'biopolitical' significance of statistical study in the human sciences has been made abundantly clear by the work of Michel Foucault, Ian Hacking, Paul Rabinow, Ferenc Fehér and Agnes Heller, and other recent historians of science and philosophers. These scholars have followed Foucault's lead in considering the genesis and implications of a social order in which 'life and its mechanisms' are brought 'into the realm of explicit calculations' and the resulting networks of 'knowledge-power' act as agents of 'transformation of human life'.[12] I would suggest, however, that these questions might also be approached from, as it were, the opposite pole. The dream project, in other words, may provide access to the *affective* and *phantasy* life of biopower, as it was experienced by individuals. If biopolitical theory has primarily asked how the classification, quantification, and processing of data about life and death has led to new structures of knowledge/power that Foucault called 'governmentality', I am asking what affects might be occasioned in individuals living within the emerging biopolitical order. Precisely because of its amateurish, ineffective organisation, the M-O dream project registered, rather than methodically extirpated this unauthorised dimension of its intended study (a dimension indiscernible, for instance, in the relatively 'successful' American dream

as my own. Even a most deadly bore who used to have whole novels to relate about her dreams complains that her dreams have lost form and shape'. (Female correspondent, 1939).

12. Michel Foucault, *The History of Sexuality, Volume I: An Introduction*, Robert Hurley (trans), New York, Vintage Books, 1978, p143. For further discussion of the concept of biopolitics, see Michel Foucault, 'The Birth of Biopolitics', in Foucault, *Ethics: Subjectivity and Truth*, Paul Rabinow (ed), New York, The New Press, 1997, pp73-79; Ian Hacking, 'Biopower and the Avalanche of Numbers', *Humanities and Society*, 5 (1983), 279-295; Ian Hacking, 'How Should We Do the History of Statistics?' in Graham Burchell, Colin Gordon, and Peter Miller (eds), *The Foucault Effect: Studies in Governmentality*, Chicago, University of Chicago Press, 1991, pp181-195; Ian Hacking, *The Social Construction of What?*, Cambridge, Massachusetts, Harvard University Press, 1999; Paul Rabinow, *French Modern: Norms and Forms of the Social Environment*, Cambridge, Massachusetts, The MIT Press, 1989; Ferenc Fehér and Agnes Heller, *Biopolitics*, Brookfield, Vermont, Avebury, 1994.

study mentioned earlier).

If in some cases, the M-O correspondents fulfilled the task of collecting dreams with excessive zeal, in others, their responses register overt or covert resistance to the assignment. Often, however, these apologies and complaints are more revealing than the dreams themselves would have been, for in making excuses for not reporting or not dreaming 'in the right way', observers could be quite unguarded about referring to their daily life, sexual attitudes, family relations, beliefs, and personalities. Some of the responses, for example, are dutifully regretful at not having satisfied the assignment of reporting particular kinds of dreams: 'I feel I've missed your point - I am not getting at the sort of public images you want'. (Male correspondent, 1937); 'Unsatisfactory - I'm sorry. I don't think I could make my images intelligible to anybody else'. (Female correspondent, 1937).[13]

For one female respondent, the failure to fulfil the task of reporting to Mass-Observation became the self-reflexive content of the dream itself: 'There was a further chaotic dream in which the National Registration form and MASS OBSERVATION MSS. were involved. I had apparently given too much or too little information in one or both, anyhow trouble was brewing for me with "the authorities" (Female correspondent, 1939).

Another respondent prefaced her report with an epigraph and ironic heading, revealing her sense of silliness about reporting her dreams:

If there were dreams to sell
What would you buy.
Dreams I wouldn't buy (Female correspondent, 1939).

Others expressed trepidation about the dreams that they were reporting, suspecting that a clever dream interpreter might be able to ferret out embarrassing meanings in them: 'This dream is completely daft, and contains no sense. But I tremble to think what terrible Freudian complex it may show'. (Unidentified correspondent, probably 1940). In contrast, a young female medical student appears to welcome the chance to hint at the racy action going on in her bed, at least in her dreams: 'My dreams have changed enormously. Previously, if I dreamt at all, it was quite innocuous, but since the war began my dreams have become so erotic that it horrifies me sometimes. I dream so much more often than usual and oh boy, do I dream!' (Female correspondent, 1940). A similar tone of winking jocularity is struck by a young male respondent: 'Strictly dirty, with B, reads my note. Freudfulness has nothing to do with horrors of war' (Male correspondent, 1939). Popularised Freudianism is also the occasion of a female correspondent's temporary suspension of her reporting:

Dear Mr Harrisson,
I have neglected to keep a record of further dreams because, it

13. Except where otherwise noted, quotes from the M-O dream reports are from one of two sources: the topic files about 'Dreams', read in paper form from the original letters or typescript copies made by Harrisson (in a few cases); the directive replies from 1939 pertaining to 'Dreams' and from 1940 pertaining to 'Air Raids', read on microfilm. All the primary text materials referred to in this paper are housed at the Mass-Observation Archive at the University of Sussex. I would like to take this opportunity to thank archivist Dorothy Sheridan and all of her staff past and present for their kind hospitality and knowledgeable help as I conducted my research there.

seemed to me, that I am becoming as abnormal as some of Freud's patients and that therefore my dreams were not really typical of the times. (Female correspondent, 1939)

This same correspondent, however, having received an encouraging word from Harrisson, writes back eight days later:

Dear Mr Harrisson,
Your flattery or my natural inclination towards mild exhibitionism urges me to continue the dream-diary. (Female correspondent, 1939)

A young male correspondent to the 1939 directive remarks with amusing irony on the culture of dreams among his family and friends:

I've had to listen to recitals of dreams and dissertations upon their meanings both at home, and, a few times, at work. There is nothing so utterly boring as the recital of someone else's dream, punctuated by incoherent explanations and bursts of incomprehensible laughter. But my own occasionally remembered dreams are very interesting, or so I think, and so occasionally I inflict them on the rest of the family. (Male correspondent, 1939)

Still others reveal irritation with the project, suggesting its tautological influence over the psychic life they are supposed to be observing and reporting: 'I think it's pretty hopeless collecting dreams. Just what do you expect? ... On receiving your letter, I promptly dreamed you a war dream the next night. + look at it. Hopeless cooked. I bet I never dreamed that. Censor sitting waiting and all gone literary long before it got to me'. (Male correspondent, 1941).

In a response that reports an absence of war-dreams (a predominant concern of the M-O dream project during the war), an unidentified correspondent reveals both the memorial texture of his (or her) dreamlife and the uncanny affect connected to it:

I have had hardly any war-dreams, not even when I have lain awake shivering lest a Jerry should drop a bomb on the roof ... I often see my father (who died in 1899); also my brothers, one of whom vanished in 1914, and the other died in 1937. He is the only *recent* inmate of my dreams. I think he must be trying to communicate with me. (Unidentified correspondent, 1942)

Finally, as the last example in this by no means exhaustive sample, the dream response may become the occasion for a revelation that is unrelated to the dream reported but appears even more pressing for the reporter. Appended to a dream dated 29 September 1939 (hence, in the first weeks after the declaration of war with Germany) is the following 'Note':

> From the point of view of research as suggested by T[om] H[arrison]'s letter it is only fair to state that my personal life has been hurricaned in the last month, not by the war particularly, but by having to decide *not* to 'live in sin' after trying it for a few days. The decision was forced by personal fastidiousness and a longing for my Mother, both unexpected factors. (Female correspondent, 1939)

Responses to the M-O directives, in short, become the vehicle for communicating a wide range of attitudes, emotions, and personal information. Far from being noise muddling the 'real' information of the M-O dream archive, they should stand on an equal evidentiary plane as the dreams themselves for the historical interpreter. Precisely in *not* properly fulfilling the task of supplying reliable information into the hidden realms of their psychic life for the social-psychological analysis, they become historically valuable. For such 'aberrant' responses leave traces of another sort: indices of an on-going negotiation between individuals and governmental institutions, in which psychic, epistemic, and political spaces are being interlaced in new configurations.

III

> 1 Sept 1939: Woke from nightmare to realise that at least it hadn't happened yet: so until after breakfast.

> 29 Sept 1939: The nightmare quality grows; one thinks one will wake up.

> 23 May 1940: Nightmares. Almost inevitable.
> Naomi Mitchison, from her wartime diary [14]

14. Naomi Mitchison, *Among You Taking Notes: The Wartime Diary of Naomi Mitchison 1939-1945*, Dorothy Sheridan (ed), London, Phoenix Press, 1985, pp32, 43, 59.

I have up to now emphasised the methodological and interpretative problems that may have contributed to the relative failure of the dream project to identify 'dominant images' with a social generality and efficacy. I have also suggested that the project's documentary leavings may have their greatest historical importance as evidence of something intended neither by the M-O directors nor their respondents: the affective experience of biopolitical governmentality, in which social and psychological scientists play a crucial role as the interface between individuals and institutions. The emotional bond created between the observers and the investigation and negotiated in concrete ways by a variety of agents is, I am arguing, readable in the interstices of the dream project. I do not, however, mean to imply that the dream materials are without meaning or value within their intended framework. As statistical material, admittedly, they probably are unusable; but at the more intimate level of individuals, as 'anecdotes' occupying the shifting borderline between the personal and the historical, there is much of interest in them.[15]

Part of their interest is negative: they provide an important index that Hitler's campaign of terror from the air did not succeed in radically disrupting the domestic life of the British dreaming psyche, the largely private inner life that one might expect to find in a modern, liberal, individualist society. In his book *Living Through the Blitz*, Tom Harrisson notes that despite predictions based on psychoanalytic and psychiatric theory, the air raids of 1940 did not really occasion major increases in traumatic psychic states among the populace. Indeed, if anything, the statistics show a decreased incidence of nervous episodes, if the reports of medical professionals reliably reflect the state of affairs at the time:

> Dr (now Professor) P.E. Vernon recorded under 1.5 per cent out of more than a thousand London shelter hospital patients with any sign of nervous trouble. At a specialist London hospital up to 2.5 per cent of the intake suffered from a malady which could be in some way related psychologically to air-raids. Overall, however, nervous admissions dropped with the end of peaceful nights and then went down further in 1941 - as did female suicides during the blitz years.[16]

The dream research of this period supports this picture. In the September 1940 survey already quoted above, the overwhelming majority of respondents reported no change in their dreams since the air-war began and only a small number of people reported vivid war dreams or significant increases in the number of dreams recalled. Many individual responses, by both male and female observers, sound a similar note of relative indifference:

Male respondent:
Frequency of dreams about war, air raids, etc. is not noticeably increased. If anything, I'd say it was less. I expected to have a nightmare the night after the lethal raid, not having previously seen corpses, but I slept like a log, probably because I was tired out. I don't think I dream differently, but my father tells me that for the first time in my life I talk and even succeed in whistling in my sleep.

Female correspondent:
I have fewer 'next war' dreams now than I had a year ago. I know of at least one other woman of whom this is true. Actuality destroys fantasy. I usually dream quite a lot but since the war, I've been ambulance driving each night and therefore have had to make up sleep at odd times such as lunch hour etc. which doesn't seem to induce dreaming. I get into bed feeling 'Oh well thank goodness I can't fuss any more about this

15. For discussion of the concept of 'anecdote', see Joel Fineman, 'The History of the Anecdote: Fiction and Fiction', in H. Aram Veeser, *The New Historicism,* New York, Routledge, 1989, pp49-76.

16. Tom Harrisson, *Living Through the Blitz*, London, Collins, 1976, pp308-309.

until the morning' and sleep without dreaming. I crossed the Channel during the first night of this war, and knew that if I stayed up I should worry about the possibility of torpedoes and raids, so I went below and slept until we landed.

Had Harrisson's respondents reported war dreams in large number and in preponderance over other dreams, we might be able to take this evidence of Hitler's effectiveness in using the blitz as a 'propaganda of the deed'. But as it happened, the inner psyche may have played its most effective historical role by maintaining its interior distance from the history that was happening all around. Dreams resisted being 'addressed' politically or militarily, and the relative imperviousness of the British dreaming psyche to terror may have helped keep the fabric of everyday life intact - a blessing for the war effort, if a frustration for the sociologically-minded dream researchers.

While it is important to emphasise this 'negative' background - that much of the war-time dream life seemed to have preserved its solipsistic detachment from history - dreams in which the terror and fear of the historical circumstances find entry into the intimate psychic world are certainly not absent in the M-O reports. Indeed, one might say that the minority of reported war-nightmares offers an important index of what the majority managed to ward off and allows us to imagine what a more psychically effective terror might occasion in a populace. In some cases, for instance, the internalisation of war terror in bad dreams could injure people from within by robbing them of the ability to refresh themselves through sleep: [17]

17. This exacerbated sleep-loss can be seen as a genuine extension of war by other means. In a poll conducted in early October 1940 in London about how much sleep people had had the night before, 31 per cent reported that they had had none, 32 per cent less than 4 hours, 22 per cent 4-6 hours, and only 15 per cent more than 6 hours. Cited in Leonard Mosley, *London Under Fire, 1939-1945*, London, Pan Books, 1971, p202.

In order to get a little peaceful sleep last night had to take sleeping tablets - just a stupor - no dreams. (Female correspondent, 1939)

The bad dreams during the infrequent sleeps - mostly so lousy that they've been censored even in sleep. Begin to dread sleeping, as well as need it. (Unidentified correspondent, 1940)

I used to look forward to my dreams, often continuing them from night to night and pondering them during the day: but I am beginning to dread them and put off going to sleep: which will be useless, really. (Female correspondent, 1940)

War dreams and especially war nightmares, moreover, do seem to exhibit something about the 'dominant images' of the immediate pre-war period and the first years of the war. In my archival research, I found myself almost naturally copying out a number of dreams grouped around common topoi, even if the tone and specific narrative articulation of the dreams varied widely. These topoi included air raid dreams, invasion dreams, spy ring dreams, dreams in which the dreamer kills or is killed, and dreams in which

Hitler appears. Rather than illustrate these various topoi separately, I have chosen to provide a series of examples of one sort, the Hitler dreams, to exhibit the range of affect experienced by British dreamers in their dream-encounters with this arch-enemy:[18]

> He said he dreamt he was at our new library and art gallery which had just been opened. After the ceremony they were looking round the Art gallery, when Hitler marched in, and said in a loud voice, 'This is mine'. So we all had to clear out, he said. (Man of about 26, recounted by male correspondent, 1939)

> I dreamt I saw Herr Hitler standing (at attention) in a Court of Law (the court was quite empty but for him) he was delivering a *silent* speech (speaking without voicing) (do you understand?) perfect silence. He was dressed, square cut, half-way coat and convict's hat. (Female correspondent, 1939)

> I was arguing with Hitler, but I don't know what about. (Female correspondent, 1939)

> Dreamed of trying to tidy up a room, floor littered by sheets of paper, chiefly brown wrapping paper because I felt Hitler was possibly coming. I awoke before he appeared. (Female correspondent, 1939)

> I dreamt that Hitler was going to be hung, and that I was in charge of the proceedings. There was a carriage and a troop of soldiers waiting for me but I was worried as to whether I should wear a lounge suit or evening dress. I asked someone who said, 'Evening dress certainly'. (Man of 60, recounted by female correspondent, 1939)

> Had argument with Hitler in German (I can speak it quite well, but not altogether so fluidly as I did in the dream), ending with a long harangue on my part as to the rights and wrongs of the present war. He was fairly humble, but obviously unconvinced. (Male correspondent, 1939)

> I dreamt that Hitler was kissing me. I had a feeling of disgust as I saw his beady eyes and his small moustache coming towards me, but my disgust didn't last. Later in the dream I thought he was making a fuss of my son who seemed like a little boy again of ten years old. He began to cry and I remembered that I had heard that Hitler had a reputation for liking boys, and I was going to kill him. I then saw him as one of a crowd in a big railway station. I was grateful to find that it said in a dream book that all would be well if you dreamt an enemy was kissing you. (Female correspondent, 1939)

18. In *Living Through the Blitz*, Harrisson singles out this type of dream, which in his view exhibits 'love-hate ambivalence (the affectionate enemy)' towards the Germans. Yet dreams in which Hitler (or other Nazis) appears as benign or reasonable stand alongside dreams in which Hitler is terrifying; Harrisson cites the former selectively to support the thesis of ambivalence.

I saw that a German threw something on to the path by me and I knew as though I were reading it in a paper that this was a scorpion and that they were throwing scorpions among us. I seemed to be pretty annoyed at this and dashed back up the path again towards them and shouted at Hitler who was standing on the path 'You swine!' He was quite insulted at this and shouted back 'I'll have you reported for that', and began to advance, getting out a revolver. I had no ammunition myself and hurried back again. (Male correspondent, 1939)

I find myself in a desert followed by Hitler and a dog, and go to an earlier school. Here I capture Hitler, and he is arrested by R.A.F. men, and taken to the hall of this school, where the headmaster enters. By this time the Fuehrer has changed into a dish of steak and bacon, in which form he is given to the headmaster, whereat I awake. (Male correspondent, 1939)

I dreamt a man got into the house and it was 'Hitler'. (Boy of 11, recounted by female correspondent, 1940)

A night or so ago I dreamed, in perfectly real and serious terms, of overhearing the conversation at the Brenner between Hitler and Mussolini … The tenor of the conversation between the two Dictators was, in my dream, alarmed and defeatist. On waking and thinking this over, I suddenly remembered hearing, whilst fully intent on something else, a 'rag' version of this interview in 'Cockledoodle-doo!' on the wireless. Here there were also two guards, but the words of the guards and the Dictators, in the sketch, were completely absurd. In the dream, there was a terrible brooding sense of fatefulness about the whole scene. (Male correspondent, 1940)

I have just dreamt of Hitler looking aged, with grey hair, humpbacked and round shoulders, dressed in British khaki, and looking cowed and ashamed. (Female correspondent, 1940)

I seemed to be interviewing Hitler. There were some books of which he asked for some, designating one or two. I refused to hand over the books asked for but gave instead, 'Christ and the New Age'. (Male correspondent, 1942)

The other night I had a dream in which Hitler came here to tea. He spoke, as far as I remember, English. I wondered if he would understand what I meant if I asked for an autograph. (Male correspondent, 1942)

A final example, fascinating for its length, imagistic vividness, and gamut of emotional tones, was submitted in April 1941 by a female correspondent.

I will quote it in full as an epitome of the psychic struggle that could be provoked by the enemy's penetration deep into the home front, behind the line of dreams:

I dreamed I went to bed as usual and woke up with a cold resolve - like when the boys were small and tried my patience until I gave way and resulted in a good slapping. I felt THIS HAS GOT TO *STOP* and I got up and dressed myself and also Clifford who was a small sleepy little boy. He said, 'Where are we going?' - and I said, 'I'll go and see Hitler myself!' We seemingly 'flew through the air with the greatest of ease!' - for next thing we were before a big iron door which had a little opening 'grill'. I was so interested in it for I'd not seen one like it before. And I must have rung or knocked and a tall fair man came out dressed in a black uniform. I heard my voice say curtly, Mrs L ... to see Mr Hitler - at ONCE please! He bowed and escorted me into a room where a man was writing at a desk and went out and closed the door. The man looked up and said 'Ah Mrs L ... , so glad you got here before sundown and we can have a look around. We went out - it was Hitler himself - and strolled along a road which suddenly started to 'slope' steeply and soon we were going up a mountain road.
In the far distance were high snow clad mountains but the slopes near at hand were wooded. I walked on the left of Hitler and on my left the sheer drop of the mountain fell and the sound of running splashing water came from the depths. Cliff ran busily on in front - so interested - and Hitler said 'you are not afraid then he will fall?' I said 'Oh yes, but I've told him to have a care and he must learn to stand alone and choose for himself - I cannot always guard him'. The air was sweet and lovely and then I heard singing and round the bend came a group of young men with curiously bulging thighs. I felt so concerned but Hitler said 'oh it's with them always walking on a slope and their muscles swell'. They were carrying huge branches of lovely berried holly - the brightest and largest berries I had ever seen and I cried how lovely, 'do let me have a little piece - I would like to try and 'strike' it in my garden'. Hitler said - 'I'll send you some with blood red berries for Christmas. I'll not forget'. I said 'I'd love a little tree too if the woodmen can spare it'. And I knew by his frown I had spoken unwisely somehow. He said 'They are MY trees. ALL AND EVERYTHING is MINE' and I felt sorry I had asked for one. The next thing we got to a highly placed house where there was quite a crowd of people - all men. Up to now a curious feeling of static well being had wrapped me but now I held Cliff's hand tightly and said 'stay close by me darling'. His bright eyes twinkled up at me and his wide mouth opened in a flashing smile and he said 'only for a little while Dearie'. I felt wildly frightened and suddenly I felt danger all around and knew it came from Hitler. I stood so alone with my loved little boy and then I saw a way out and still holding his little

hot hand I sauntered carelessly to the open window hearing a queer noise behind of hurry and banging like bombs in the distance. Standing on the edge of the open window - such lovely wide 'french windows' that was a living picture of mountain scenery - I stepped calmly and fearlessly out with the feeling I'd chosen my own way. I fell or rather floated downward on gracefully on a parachutist but I lost my little boy and woke with a start *and feeling* of desolation. That was all. (Female correspondent, 1941)

IV

The history of dreams remains to be written, and offering insight into it means to break by means of historical elucidation the superstitious bias towards nature. Dreams participate in history. Beyond the charms of the anecdotal landscape, dream statistics would advance into the wasteland of the battlefield.

Walter Benjamin, 'Dream Kitsch'[19]

I have never had a dream 'come true'. (Female M-O Correspondent, 1939)

The history of dreams, seventy years after Walter Benjamin's resonant call for their incorporation into historical writing, remains to be written after all. I will conclude with a brief discussion of two contemporary historians who have taken up the challenge of dreams, offering methodological reflections on how they might be used in historical writing.

In an essay published in *Annales* in 1973, Peter Burke re-posed the argument that Benjamin had proposed almost fifty years earlier: that 'dreams have a history' and that it should be possible 'to write a social history of dreams'.[20] Burke argues that the dream can provide the social historian with data at two distinct levels. First, in a thesis akin to that of Mass-Observation's notion of the 'dominant image', Burke suggests that attention to the manifest contents of dreams in a particular epoch can help reveal the changes in the 'psychologically efficacious or pertinent' images and myths of the society. Second, he argues that dreams represent a form of indirect communication of that which is forbidden or repressed in a society, and hence can serve as testimony to forces and factors that might otherwise remain hidden in more official forms of discourse and documentation. On the basis of a comparison of dreams recorded by clergymen in the seventeenth century and the same American study of dreams from the 1950s I cited earlier, Burke goes on to suggest that different epochs may exhibit different degrees of unity and transindividual coding of dream contents. The specific documentary basis for Burke's comparison seems to me dubious. The fact that within a professional caste like the seventeenth-century clergy one might find a certain shared dream-imagery does not let us conclude that this dream-imagery is characteristic of the

19. Walter Benjamin, 'Traumkitsch', in Rolf Tiedemann and Hermann Schweppenhauser (eds), *Gesammelte Schriften*, 2/2, Frankfurt a/M, Suhrkamp Verlag, 1977, p620, my translation. For further discussion of Benjamin's dream historiography see Susan Buck-Morss, *The Dialectics of Seeing: Walter Benjamin and the Arcades Project*, Cambridge, Massachusetts, The MIT Press, 1989, esp. pp253-286; and Tyrus Miller, 'From City-Dreams to the Dreaming Collective: Walter Benjamin's Political Dream Interpretation', *Philosophy and Social Criticism* 22, 6 (1996), 87-111.

20. Peter Burke, 'L'histoire sociale des rêves', *Annales: Économies, Sociétés, Civilisations* 28, 2 (1973), 329.

period; we do not know whether a corpus of dreams from twentieth-century Episcopalian priests would not show a similar cohesiveness of imagery.

Nevertheless, the underlying theoretical point seems to me potentially valid. If modernity entails the historical emergence of an unprecedented social mobility, instability of class and caste codes, new forms of intimacy, increasingly nuclear family structures, and so on, then it would be surprising if this development of the modern subject did not leave some traces in the dream-process. For instance, might we not expect a greater privatisation and individual articulation of dream-content in a modern democracy than in an authoritarian, socially rigid, patriarchal society? Moreover, if this hypothesis turned out, upon further study, *not* to be the case for dream life, this in itself would be a significant fact about the historical character of subjectivity.

I have already made a somewhat covert allusion to Burke's argument in my suggestion that the M-O dream project, in its failure to identify clear-cut 'dominant images', may be offering historical testimony to the psychic differentiation fostered by modern liberal societies. An interesting contrast may be offered by Charlotte Beradt's celebrated study of dream life in the first years of the Nazi dictatorship, based on dream reports from 1933 to 1939, *The Third Reich of Dreams*.[21] Beradt sees the dream texts she assembled as parodic distortions of reality which, paradoxically, exhibit a peculiar realism in representing the real distortions that Nazism itself imposed on everyday life. 'Set against a background of disintegrating values and an environment whose very fabric was becoming warped', she writes:

> these dreams are permeated by a reality whose quality is unreal - a combination of thought and conjecture in which rational details are brought into fantastic juxtapositions and thereby made more rather than less, coherent; where ambiguities appear in a context that nonetheless remains explicable, and latent as well as unknown and menacing forces are all made a part of everyday life.[22]

Beradt's book provided the occasion for a far-reaching meditation on dreams and historiography by the German historian of political and historical thought Reinhart Koselleck, his essay 'Terror and Dream: Methodological Remarks on the Experience of Time During the Third Reich'.[23] Koselleck's reflections take off from an 'eighteenth-century experiential shift, in which history was formulated in terms of a new reflexive concept', making 'the line dividing the camps of historians and creative writers … osmotically porous'.[24] This shift is the 'discovery' of the placement of the historian *within* 'historical time', now conceived as a kind of flowing medium in which the events that constitute the basis of any historical writing have occurred and will continue to occur. This new conception of historical time entails, however, that the historian-in-time necessarily writes from a perspectival point requiring him not merely to

21. Charlotte Beradt, *The Third Reich of Dreams*, Adriane Gottwald (trans), Chicago, Quadrangle Books, 1968 [German original, 1966].

22. Ibid., p17.

23. Reinhart Koselleck, 'Terror and Dream: Methodological Remarks on the Experience of Time During the Third Reich', in Keith Tribe (trans), *Futures Past: On the Semantics of Historical Time*, Cambridge, Massachusetts, The MIT Press, 1985, pp213-230.

24. Ibid., p214.

set down history, but to 'compose' it:

> It was this knowledge of historical perspective which forced historians to become aware of the devices of fiction ... if they wished to pass on meaningful histories. The historian was confronted with the demand, both in terms of techniques of representation and epistemologically, that he offer not a past reality, but the fiction of its facticity.[25]

25. Ibid., p215.

Koselleck goes on to argue that given this distinctively 'modern' framework for thinking and writing historically, dreams must not only be considered legitimate historical sources, but they also may serve to underscore essential presuppositions of historical evidence as a generic concept. 'Dreams do occupy a place at the extremity of a conceivable scale of susceptibility to historical rationalisation', he writes. 'Considered rigorously, however, dreams testify to an irresistible facticity of the fictive'.[26] In other words, Koselleck's argument about dreams as sources is analogous to what I asserted earlier about dreams as, in a sense, both 'images' and 'meta-images', models for M-O's larger concerns. Dreams for Koselleck are one among many forms of modern historical sources, but they also lay bare the very logic of sources as the elements of those factual fictions called 'histories'.

26. Ibid., p218.

Koselleck goes on to discuss Beradt's collection of dreams of terror during the early Nazi period, comparing them to other dreams recorded by concentration camp inmates. His conclusions offer a striking contrast to the picture I have sketched out of the M-O dream project. The terror dreams collected by Beradt, Koselleck argues, have an essentially *political* function; they are, as it were, political shock troops carrying Nazi power deep into the psychic haven of sleep. The accumulated dreams of embarrassment, fear, shame, betrayal, self-exposure, and cravenness documented in *The Third Reich of Dreams* are not merely narratives in which terror is represented. They *are* terror, the affective vehicles of terror itself. 'They are physical manifestations of terror but without the witnesses having fallen victim to physical violence. In other words, it is precisely as fiction that they are elements of historical reality', Koselleck writes: 'Even as apparitions, the dreams are instrumentalisations of terror itself'.[27]

27. Ibid., p220.

Concentration camp dreams, in contrast, are radically different. If terror dreams are all too comprehensible in their immediate reference to historical circumstances, concentration camp dreams slip free of the index of reality almost completely. Koselleck notes that utopian camp dreams, which projected a lost past into a hoped-for future, most commonly portended death. In the unreal, yet brutally factual world of the camp, hope for survival lay in a kind of depersonalisation, an acceptance of a post-temporal existence in which a few were able to endure the unendurable and survive. Koselleck sees this dissociation of the self as a final form of resistance, in which the inmate saves a margin of himself by no longer offering a self to the operations of power. Yet this also makes concentration camp dreams, in his view, essentially illegible in historical terms. They exist in a realm ontologically outside of the temporal, social, and political dimensions that give definite shape to the 'historical':

> the inferential path from individual salvational dreams to general behaviour specific to one social stratum is blocked, for they contain no signals of reality that are politically or socially legible. If you like, the whole point of such dreams is to be apolitical. One could even go so far as to see in them covert enactments of a disposition to resistance. But even this anthropological finding can no longer be socially generalised.[28]

28. Ibid., p224.

Koselleck's provocative essay allows me to venture one final remark about the constraints on the use of dreams as historical evidence: their 'availability' for historical writing may be itself socially, politically, and historically circumscribed, which in turn allows them to be used self-reflexively, as positive and negative indices of these conditioning factors. The dreams reported by the M-O observers proved, in many cases, deficient in their social referentiality, in their systematic 'mass' registration of historical circumstances. I suggested that this might, indeed, give evidence of the strong underlying continuity of domestic privacy, individualism, and liberalism of British society at mid-century, even in the midst of air-raids and wartime hardships. So too, for opposed reasons, the concentration camp dreams that Koselleck discusses are deficient in historical referentiality - not because individual, inner selves remained too durable in the face of historical circumstances, but because these contracted to an almost indiscernible point of posthumous and posthistorical survival. It may only be in the range in between these antipodes, frighteningly narrow after all, that the dream may turn its face frontally towards the historian's profane illumination.

'A DOOR HALF OPEN TO SURPRISE': CHARLES MADGE'S IMMINENCES

Steven Connor

The sense of imminent cataclysm, of tremendous things trembling on the brink of happening, is recurrent in Charles Madge's poetry of the 1930s and early 1940s. Often, he writes out of a sense of anticipatory pause or lull, tense with waiting, as

> time prepares for us his tidal wave
> To sweep our harbour clear, and wash the shore
> And we surrender to the final pain [1]

1. Charles Madge, 'The Lull', *Of Love, Time and Places: Selected Poems*, London, Anvil Press, 1994, p135. References hereafter to *OLTP*.

The early poems in his first collection, *The Disappearing Castle*, enact this sense of urgent desire through the use of incipient and unfinished sentences, which strain for completion, like the uncompleted conditionals of 'On One Condition', which wind down into a crushed pluperfect without, as it were, ever having been present:

> If there were an open way...
> A door half open to surprise...
> If the writing in the road
> Had led a stranger's foot nearer that door and in...
> If it had been [2]

2. Ibid., p15.

The transfiguring change that is awaited, imagined and wooed in these poems is seen against the background of a vision of a sterile England, huddled in conformity, sexual repression and shrivelled purpose: in a version of the modernist anti-modernism of Lawrence, Eliot and Auden. Sometimes, Madge imagines the excited liquefaction of this locked and narrow world, for example in the 'Man Maniform' section of his mock-alchemical 'Hours of the Planets', in which an evolutionary tide of near-human exile-creatures floods across the Thames:

> Life, more persistent than thought, continues to flow
> Out of Europe grown gaunt and old
> Multiple genera untabulated
> Carrying pouches, tufted behind ears,
> Splay-footed, hammer-fingered, hooked, humped [3]

3. Ibid., p29.

Nevertheless, the poem still yearns for some further, more definitive catastrophe:

> O reich of riches, urbs of all superb
> When will you break your banks [4]

4. Ibid.

The fourth section of his 'Instructions' suggests that, as well as bearing witness to it, poetry might itself inaugurate and conjoin with the racing spate of the new:

> This poem will be you if you will. So let it.
> I do not want you to stand still to get it.
> You will have it if you go high-speed [5]

5. Ibid., p127.

Madge wrote in the early 1930s of his desire to be caught up in the irresistible current of the new, which he saw both in the dynamism of America and the even more irresistible dynamism of Russia, which, he wrote in 1936, America shadowed. He represented American writers as 'straws, caught up in an overwhelming current, even if individually they may not amount to much. Existence in America, and its reflection in print and photography, is a terrific force. The addition of a signature to such material does not add anything but simply takes away the anonymity which is its virtue'.[6] In a fragment of the 1930s, he wrote excitedly 'we hear cries and noise of steel/ And run to join the turning of time's heroic wheel'.[7]

Modernist experiment is part of the liquefying surprise of the new, of the 'all that is solid [that] melts into air' that Madge was fond of quoting in his political writing. Like the Auden whom he admired, and like so many young writers in the 1930s who imitated him, Madge had an ambivalent relation to modernism. He entertained a public suspicion of modernist experiment and private obscurity and proclaimed the historical necessity of socialist realism. Indeed, at times he saw Mass-Observation as the self-authorship of the mass in the production of socialist realism. He also shared Auden's desire for lightness and directness - though not always Auden's ability to mine the mechanisms of light verse with surprise. And yet he was also capable of conceiving a modernism joined to mass expression, or, as in this rather interestingly idiosyncratic account of Joyce's late writing, presumably in *Finnegans Wake*, retreating so far into the self as to escape from it back into the world:

6. Review of *American Writers' Congress*, Hart (ed), *Left Review*, 2 (1936), 405.

7. *OLTP,* p62.

> A careful study of Joyce reveals that his progress has always been further and further into the recesses of the self, until at last by a process of exhaustion he arrives back at the real and external world. His latest works are not about the self but about the world; however, the language he uses is that of the self, which, smashed into a thousand atoms, begins to recompose itself, in a picture of the world.[8]

8. Review of Gorki et al, *Problems of Soviet Literature*, *Left Review*, 2 (1936), 230.

This suggests that Madge's version of socialist realism (which, he says, might well take a hundred different forms) could be achievable by a passage through modernist intractability and obscurity. His own mildly, jocosely Joycean experiments in 'The Hours of the Planets' perhaps support this idea.

Only occasionally does Madge allow himself to characterise in any detail what the poem 'Instructions' calls 'The new world lying in ambush round the corner of time'.[9] But in this somewhat incautiously specific poem, Madge does evoke the new dispensation, with uncharacteristically raking Whitmanesque fervour:

9. *OLTP*, p128.

> we hear on all lips a new song in the street all day,
> Spreading from house to house without wires. This new song has come
> to stay.
> We shall be differently aware, we shall see all things new
> Not as a craze or a surprise, but hard, naked, true.[10]

10. Ibid.

The Madge of poems like this, who looks, not to the inflammation of emergency, but to the emergence of undeluded lucidity and definitive truth, is paralleled by the sometimes rather grimly exhilarated assertions of belief in historical necessity that appear in his prose writing of the 1930s, in which Madge argues that the turmoil and obscurity of a modernism already withering are just the necessary preliminary to a mass consciousness, and the socialist realism that would express it: 'Socialist realism, like the socialist revolution, not only *is* being invented, but it must inevitably be invented. It is the beginning, and only the beginning, of this long-drawn-out historical process that we see in England to-day'.[11] The sequence of 'Landscape' prose-poems in *The Disappearing Castle* sometimes seem like enactments - if overlaid with the queerly outer-space atmosphere to be found in Humphrey Jennings's prose poems - of the anonymous, solar precision of the promised new way of seeing. These poems attempt to go beyond the effervescence of mere surprise or rejuvenating alienation, and also beyond the factitious obscurities and disorientations of modernism, which can be seen as part of the structure of neurotic fixation rather than the means of its cure. The 'Delusions' sequence in particular repeatedly voices the suspicion of surprise, whether in the false transcendence of 'the blissful moment of surprise/When the dull bourgeois can become divine' of 'Delusions I', or the traveller who returns home 'without surprise' in 'Delusions VI'.

11. Review of Gorki, op. cit., p230.

However, the poems in *The Disappearing Castle* often join Prufrockian indecision to revolutionary apprehension. Rather than the imminent insurgence of new life from the collapse of the old, the poems elaborately recreate the sense of stubbornly plugged impediment:

12. 'In Sua Voluntade', *OLTP*, p17.

> I cannot have the round world in my hands.
> I cannot join with the ascending light.
> ...England is fallen. Home is gone. Time stands.[12]

Madge's poetry travels between the two perspectives signified in his 'Philosophic Poem', of 'workaday things and a white rising planet': the world of historical, human time, in which the pain of choice and change is pressing, and a natural or elemental time in which change is so generalised as to be numbly self-annulling. In his poetry, Madge attempts to make out apertures of possibility; but he does so against the sense, which is usually more oppressive than it is consoling, of the indifferent unchangingness of nature.

Time, in Madge's poetry, is always liable to freeze or be compressed into space; into inhuman landscapes, blankly convulsive oceans, moon-irradiated deserts, in which the possibility of change is whispered, cryptic, figural, as in the anonymous dust of the thousands who live 'in ignorance and pain' in 'Delusions IV', covering everything except 'the uncanny sphinx, their hieroglyph',[13] which is both formed from dust and the form of it.

13. *OLTP*, p51.

If the self could be swept up in the dynamic emergency of historical time, it could also be drawn into the reverie of recurrence, or elemental time, imaged in this fragment, as so often in Madge's writing, in terms of the sea:

Our wills are dissolved as we
Contemplate in reverie the beautiful motion of tunicates
And remember our origin in the ambiguous sea [14]

14. Ibid., p64.

This fragment parallels and answers another one from the same period, which marks out an emblematic contrast between unselfconscious, submerged existence and the historical being of creatures who have evolved into uprightness, civilisation and a higher form of collective life:

While in the deep cold sea
Simple sponges and gregarious fish
Exert brief lives without a wish.
To be a vertebrate is to be a street.[15]

15. Ibid., p63.

This busy timelessness is enacted in 'Saeclum', a poem which uses the coming and going of waves to express the flowing together of before and after, the urgent gatherings and buildings of present time and the unchangingness of past or recollected time, imaged in sun and moon:

Solemn, contrite fusion
Of the centurion tides
Conveying the moons after
The moons of gone tides
Shadows that with water mix
And daily races of the sun
Over the perennial treetops [16]

16. Ibid., p33.

The poem swirls together three meanings of 'race': a Marvellian notion of a race against time figured in the 'races of the sun', the historical 'race' which is beyond racing and impulsion, both swirled together in the idea of the tide-race:

> The villagers repeat
> The proverbs of a former race,
> And the ungathered sun and corn
> And water belong to the race [17]

17. Ibid.

Natural and human time are mediated by the figure of Darwin. Madge takes Darwin as the forerunner of both Marx and Freud, and often returns to the idea of evolution to underpin his faith in the historical development of collective self-consciousness. However, in Madge's poetry, the figure of Darwin is as often used to ask a question of natural existence: to wonder whether natural history can be said to have an itinerary rather than a simple commotion, the 'commotion born of love' that humans are said to be in 'Solar Creation'.[18] The 1937 poem 'Rebirth' troublingly reverses the sense of the necessary evolutionary push of time. The poem begins with the question 'Where are our sons?' but then represents the apprehension of the necessary emergence of the next generation as a kind of haunting by the future:

18. Ibid., p23.

> Where are our sons? Their tow-coloured hair
> Forces its way through the stones and the pavements.
> The fibrils of their being are everywhere.
> It is useless to avoid them, stepping to one side
> From the small shadow and the puddle in the rain:
> Once found they will not lose you again.[19]

19. Ibid., p83.

The poem which bears the name of Darwin, written at the end of the War, is much less confident that natural impulses have fitted us out for necessary self-transcendence, and ends carefully stymied between vectorial possibility and the more elementary itches and twitches of impulse:

> Have pity on people: within them dwells
> Propulsion to an end.
> There is a reason for all that running to and fro.[20]

20. Ibid., p147.

THE PAPER AND THE PERISCOPE

The Darwinist and biologistic cast of so many of Madge's poems of the 1930s, at a time when so much of his other life was bound up with the exploration of social life, as journalist and then as social investigator, is curious. I want to see it as a contrast between different ways of apprehending time: of the somnolent time of purely material existence, and the emergent historical time of mass society; the time of mere commotion and the time of life-story. Madge wrote in 1937 that his fourteen months as a reporter on the *Daily Mirror* 'taught me to understand the queer poetry of the newspaper and the advertisement hoarding, and not to dismiss it simply because it is sensational and vulgar'.[21] Mass-Observation stood half way between Madge's different lives as newspaperman and poet. Both Madge's poetry and his work for Mass-Observation allow an enquiry into the part that poetry might have in the temporality of mass self-consciousness - or the movement of temporality into consciousness.

21. 'The Press and Social Consciousness', *Left Review*, 3 (1937), 285.

Madge valued the newspaper and the hoarding because they were 'vehicles for the expression of the unconscious fears and wishes of the mass'.[22] In his work with Mass-Observation, Madge sought, or said that he sought, to bring these mass fears and wishes to consciousness. The use he makes of Freud's later writings can suggest the necessity of a form of understanding which will dissolve the fixative force of neurotic wishes by giving them expression. His essay 'Magic and Materialism', which we may read as a personal manifesto for Mass-Observation, proclaims as roundly as anyone might wish that 'Our common front is the application of materialism to superstition'.[23] It is not entirely clear whether the bringing to light of the 'mass wish' or the 'mass fear' is intended to make them visible and substantial, or to abolish them, as a preparation for the emergence of some less encumbered and distorted form of consciousness. Perhaps a combination of the two: perhaps it is expected that mass feelings, once given form or visibility, will lose their neurotic character, though without disappearing or being superseded altogether.

22. Ibid.

23. 'Magic and Materialism', *Left Review*, 3 (1937), 34.

One can see the signs of this uneasiness in the treatment of some of the material gathered together in the *May The Twelfth* Mass-Observation anthology. For the most part, the editors, Madge and Humphrey Jennings, attempt simply to let observers and their observations speak for themselves. But the most telling parts of the anthology are the footnotes and editorial comments which the editors occasionally permit themselves, such as the anthropological gloss on the contribution from the sceptical Platonist observer in which he describes the application of restorative hair-oil to himself, in what we are told is an identificatory self-anointing.[24] At other times, the editors point to odd conjunctures and congruities emerging from the material. Perhaps the most arresting of these concerns paper. They first point to the multitude of forms and uses which were found for paper during the Coronation day:

24. Humphrey Jennings and Charles Madge (eds), *May The Twelfth: Mass-Observation Day-Surveys 1937 By Over Two Hundred Observers*, London, Faber and Faber, 1987, p317.

> Out of many possible studies of the Coronation crowds, it seems worth while attempting to list the uses to which they put paper. Paper was used in newspapers, notices, tickets, maps, programmes, radio-lists,

plates, drinking-cups, for wrapping cigarettes, knives, forks and food, as bunting, flags, house decorations, hats and suits of red, white and blue, for rosettes and streamers, in fireworks, in cardboard periscopes, for sitting on, for sleeping on, to shelter people from the rain, and when thoroughly wet the stuff was thrown about as a kind of bomb.[25]

25. Ibid., p145.

As so often, one wonders quite what the practical point might be of compiling such a list, while marvelling at its weirdly purposive poetry. Perhaps one point about paper is just that it is the visible and tangible form of a nothing, of the very ephemerality and arbitrariness not only of the day but of the exercise of recording it. After all, Mass-Observation itself was a machine or organism for turning events or experiences into piles (*piles* and piles) of paper.

The long footnote moves from paper as polymorphous stuff to paper as the carrier of news, with an admiring account of the organisation of runners to carry photographic plates to motor launches on the Thames, which enabled special editions of the evening papers, with pictures of the procession which had arrived at the Abbey at 11.00, to be on sale on the Buckingham Palace Road an hour and twenty minutes later. But this movement, which turns paper into meaning, has already been countermanded by the observation (we are still in Madge and Jennings's long footnote), that this 'triumph of organisation which brought out early editions of evening papers was not well rewarded in London itself'. This seems not just to have been because the crowds were getting their news from the radio loudspeakers all along the route, but also, Madge and Jennings suggest, because of a sense of nauseated surfeit at the sheer mass of paper: 'The stands and pavements were positively drowned in paper ... People came to feel that there was so much paper about that you did not want any more'.[26] So the footnote, which begins with paper as polymorphous substance, and ends with the triumph of paper as expressive medium, actually points to an inverse movement, in which paper begins as expressive and meaningful, and ends up as pure waste, an exhausted, scribbled-over, screwed-up swamping of signal by noise.

26. Ibid.

This connects with one newspaper-vendor's interesting pitch, which reads like a bit of Leopold Bloom: '"Coronation Number - Keep from going mad, doing nothing: Read while you wait"'.[27] Another, slightly flummoxed footnote refers to Q.D. Leavis on the use of newspapers to stave off boredom, and concludes sniffily that the use of reading as a sedative 'gives a striking view of our universal education and neurosis'.[28] Madness is held at bay by the newspaper, but because the newspaper is only just this side of the nausea of the discarded, the used up, the already read, it participates in this threat of madness too.

27. Ibid., p109.

28. Ibid.

This footnote might have been suggested by the observations recorded in Humphrey Jennings's own report in particular, rendered as 'CM.1'. CM.1

was one of the 'Mobile Squad of 12 Observers' who acted as a kind of shadow press, keeping in touch with the Mass-Observation headquarters by phone, taking notes continuously and writing up their accounts in the form of lengthy reports.[29] CM.1 records this arresting image from 11.25 am in St James's Park:

29. Ibid., p90.

> In the Park behind the stands there is an area of black mud strewn with pieces of torn newspaper. A woman sits alone in the mud surrounded by the paper, her head in her hands.[30]

30. Ibid., p124.

The same observer records a version of the battle between the radio and the newspaper, or significance and insignificance, in terms of what can be made out by the ear and eye, and what is in contrast ground underfoot:

> A girl lying on the grass pulls back her hand from under the Guardsmen's feet just in time. At this moment from the loudspeakers in the Mall the Abbey music begins. Fanfare. Prelude. The choir. Reproduction of music excellent. Drowning the sound of rustling paper under people's feet. Drowned in turn by the crunch of the Guards' feet as they return. Waterloo steps are covered with torn newspapers and broken bottles.[31]

31. Ibid.

In fact, another diagonal reading that one might imagine of the *May the Twelfth* survey would focus, as Madge's own poetry does so often, on height and uprightness, on the endlessly renewed struggle for elevation and the distinct perspective that it gives. New information keeps the possibility of distinctness and uprightness alive; but it is liable at any moment to collapse or reverse to the ground, as in this sequence recorded by CM.2:

> Girl sitting on soiled newspaper is reading Daily Mirror. The caption reads 'Three women wait 25 hours; lead line up for the big parade.' A man's folding stool collapses; girls giggle, rather hysterically.[32]

32. Ibid., p109.

The crowds swarming and struggling to obtain the best vantage points are encouraged by the sale of periscopes all along the route. One of the first mentions is at 6.30 in the morning:

> A middle-aged woman, a tripper, says 'We shall have to get one of these 'ere glasses' - she holds up her fingers to indicate periscope - 'It's the only way now.'
> A police wireless van takes up position, guarded by 7 policemen - a curious crowd swarms round and submerges it - youths climb on back to get a better view of route - police do not prevent them - hawker cries 'Genuine periscopes, the only periscope you can see through - see over the top of your car - see your next door neighbour whenever you like.' A girl in the crowd who has purchased one says 'The

33. Ibid.

periscopes are quite good, but (with grim humour) there's a long time to wait yet'.[33]

In a series of fascinating non-sequiturs, the last one stands out. What has elevated vision to do with time? It is as though time had congealed into a soupy substance, the substance of the mass, which only the eminence of the periscope could lift you clear of.

So many of Madge's own poems of the 1930s image the aspirations to transcendence of man in terms of the painful attainment or maintenance of the vertical ('To be a vertebrate is to be a street'), against the temptation of relapse, the gravitational pull of the ground or of the sea. 'Man Under Taurus' begins with 'The strain of being upright in the flat world' endured by 'Man more than man mechanical skyward genius'.[34] Periscopes join also with the binocular or stereoscopic vision that is so recurrent a preoccupation of Madge's poetry.

34. *OLTP*, p19.

I have been unable to substantiate in Madge's own poetry my intuition that here paper becomes the mediating image of mass existence - though I will just mention the final night which falls at the end of 'Drinking in Bolton', like a 'pack of cards'.[35] But the thematic of elevation and drowning is particularly marked in some of Madge's poetry, especially 'Through the Periscope', which imagines a drowned, undersea urban landscape. It is as if the periscope becomes an image for Mass-Observation itself, enabling one to look out over the mass and see the stammering King who is perhaps nothing more than the reflection of the crowd's own previously unremarked being; or the mass itself, achieving a kind of tautological perspective on itself, but in splinters and fragments. (Some members of the crowd brought along shaving mirrors and other improvised reflective devices to make their observations.)

35. Ibid., p108.

What is the perspective offered by Mass-Observation: gawping observation of the mass, eyes out on stalks (as object), or the mass engaged in the act of stalking itself? The periscope, which is as apt to let you see your neighbour's secrets, or somebody fainting in the crowd a hundred yards away, as the Royal Family passing in state, is a perfect symbol of this flickering between immanence and eminent self-transcendence. The events of 12 May 1937 provide a coincidental mapping of the two temporal axes of Madge's world: the time of insensate substance, and the time of sensate beings. On the one hand there is the periscope, associated with prospects and perspectives, and with time lengthened out into desire and anticipation; on the other hand, or, rather, underfoot, there is the churning, formless condition of paper, or mire. The commutability of the two dimensions is neatly emblematised by the fact that so many of the periscopes used and discarded on the day were in fact made of cardboard.

But there is another kind of perspective which is increasingly in evidence in Madge's poetry through the 1930s, which is somewhat at odds with the confident assumptions regarding the necessary emergence of a lucid, mass self-knowledge. For Madge is also increasingly interested in minority, in incipience: the diminutive stirrings and twitchings of awareness and forms of life at the lowest level. Thus, for example, the last section of 'Visions of Camden Town', a poem which reflects on the material destruction of the War and the prospects of urban reconstruction, celebrates the emergence, not of a naked, necessary lucidity, in which everything will coincide with itself, and nothing any more be hidden, but of a more fugitive set of 'awkward and gentle shapes', which 'emerge, tentatively free', like the fragile, disregarded, formless appearances of nature to be found in the city.[36] The Hardyesque poem 'Inscription' of 1946 ends its meditation on some lines carved in memorial stone with a registration of the humble forms of minor life that they enable: they are 'Good grooves for lichen spores and chance connections'.[37] Madge, who had been at the beginning the most insistent in his promises that Mass-Observation would be the agency of a new and definitive form of mass consciousness, soon found an opportunity of mitigating his claims. Where, in the inaugural pamphlet for Mass-Observation, Tom Harrisson was urging that the movement might itself constitute 'a new synthesis' of social thought, Madge characterised his position in the following, much more modest ways:

36. Ibid., p145.

37. Ibid., 148.

> In the other author's opinion, Mass-Observation is an instrument for collecting facts, not a means for producing a synthetic philosophy, a super-science, or super-politics. The availability of the facts will liberate certain tendencies in science, art, and politics, because it will add to the social consciousness of the time. *Mass-Observation* is not a party, a religion, or a philosophy, but an elementary piece of human organisation and adaptation. It is one part of a general deflection of emphasis from individual to collective effort. It is not enough in itself to ensure mass regeneration, and has no pretence to being the salvation of anybody, either spiritually or politically. It is each man's job to find his salvation as best he can.[38]

In this passage, the deflection from the individual to the collective has no sooner been stated than it is itself deflected back into a disconsolate individualism. Increasingly, Madge's poetry will be characterised by its attention to the minor, the peripheral, the surprise of the disaggregated, the repeated imminence of small ways of making a living amid the general life. Tellingly perhaps, one image of this distinctly entomological perspective is almost entirely silent. In 'Countries of the Dead II', the only thing that seems to allow for the continued possibility of new life or connections, in a Gothic habitat of decay and decrepitude, is the meandering inscription of the worm traced by the ellipses in each line, the feeble, but insatiable appetite that, living indifferently both on

38. Charles Madge and Tom Harrisson, *Mass-Observation*, London, Frederick Muller Ltd, 1937, pp47-8.

human bodies and on the paper to which they entrust their lives, marks out the minor surprise of persistence rather than the definitive, irreversible, for-good-and-all of transfiguration:

39. *OLTP*, p61.

```
        an inscription                difficult
   no scholar can decipher           forces        unknown
        or negatively                groping
   on to the end                                of tactile sensation
           restoring          a dead man
           life           in that
        underworld               overgrown
      a little crevice          centipedes find
   a way through                          solitude.[39]
```

Charles Madge: Political Perception And The Persistence Of Poetry

Drew Milne

The second last poem included in Charles Madge's collection of poetry *Of Love, Time and Places* is a brief poem entitled 'Somewhere'. The poem concludes:

> Myth, history, panic fear
> Sweeping dilated horizons,
>
> Red flag in tatters, a flashing knife,
> Clouds that hold dark promise of the breast.[1]

This poem is one of three poems dated in the selection as being written in April 1971. Read in relation to the title of the collection, the indeterminacy of place evoked in this poem suggests a reflection on the uncertain horizons, both historical and geographical, of international socialism. The political significance of these lines is difficult to read, partly because supporting evidence from other poems is fragile, and partly because the lyric register is impersonal. An early poem such as 'Solar Creation' (1934) rather too grandly opens with the claim that 'The sun, of whose terrain we creatures are, / Is the director of all human love ...'[2] Cosmological reflections are evident in many of Madge's poems, perhaps most notably 'The Hours of the Planets' (1934), which mixes astrological and astronomical figures, while juxtaposing figures of modernity with more primordial terms. Read forwards into a much later poem such as 'Somewhere', then, it is of some consequence whether what is offered indicates personal despair or something approaching historical or more universal judgement. This essay explores ways in which the persistence of Madge's commitment to poetry suggests a revision of some canonical conceptions of the politics of modernist poetry and the continuing relevance of poetry for radical social formations.

In what sense could Madge's poem 'Somewhere' be read without some related conception of the historical role of poetry in the articulation of political perception? The level of 'difficulty' is not hermetic or notably obscure, but reading comes under pressure here to assess the limits of 'close' reading, especially the protocols of practical criticism associated with the culture of 1930s criticism familiar to Charles Madge from his teacher I.A. Richards. In question are the commitments and intentions of Madge's life and work, not least the conflict between socialist ideals and the idea of poetry, a conflict which can only with some awkwardness be read as a

1. Charles Madge, *Of Love, Time and Places: selected poems*, London, Anvil, 1994, p207.

2. Ibid., p23.

'materialist' problem. Madge's commitment to poetry might be read as supervening over his political perception of socialism's conditions of possibility, acting as some kind of aesthetic solace amid political ruins. More challengingly, his commitment to poetry suggests affinities between the political perceptions of socialism and poetic imagination.

Different traditions of historical memory converge on the colour symbolism of the red flag figured in tatters in 'Somewhere'. Predominant among these traditions is commemoration of the blood shed by the communards in the brutal suppression of the 1871 Paris Commune, during which some seventeen thousand people, including women and children, were massacred. Although the First International played a limited role in the 1871 Commune, the hopes of the communards resonate in the memory of socialist struggles, not least because the Commune put the question of communism at the heart of Europe. Madge's poem 'Somewhere' could be read, then, as marking a hundred years of socialist struggle, struggles with new global dimensions in the late 1960s and early 1970s and associated in the political imagination with Paris, Prague and Vietnam. Poetry might attempt to articulate the place - 'somewhere' - from which the perceptions of international struggle can continue to be imagined, and yet it would be hard to say whether the authority of poetry or of this poem is more tattered than that of socialism. An earlier poem entitled 'Apparition' asks 'Who is it stands, is stained with red / At the tragic portal?' and this tends to suggest a generic theatre or, as the poem puts it, a 'dark proscenium'.[3] Such images represent poetic perspectives capable of a more Olympian purview than anything grounded in individual experience. Indeed many poems sing across time and place in ways that suggest classical topoi of divine vantage. The following poem exemplifies some of the imbrication of classical, solar and uncertainly modern resources of figuration:

Mars

Low and with contracted Power
Lies the centre of the eye,
Issuing forth its fantasy
With the sound of midnight rage.

From the broken window frame
The squares of darkness
In perspective
Are the faces
Of the dead chieftain
Returning in his blindness
To storm above the field
Where the noise of harps might be
Mistaken for the rustling of grass. (1935)[4]

3. Ibid., p151.

4. Ibid., p38.

Madge was born in Johannesburg in 1912, and his father, Lieut. Colonel C.A. Madge, was Director of the Information Bureau at Defence Headquarters. Such autobiographical locations of 'place' suggest a juxtaposition of classical poetics with what might be read as experiences located in the Africa of British imperialism. Many of Madge's poems attempt to figure intimations of solidarity through the long shadows cast by the British empire. The poem 'Lusty Juventus', for example, offers a more playful version of such motifs:

A giant that threw a stone at Caerodunum
Transforming England into a salty pancake
Lichen-alive governed in gametosporous colonies
Crescented with calciform corollae, a great stone marsh
With the dragons of dead Hercules debating [5]

5. Ibid., p137.

The poem sets up this mix of vocabularies and registers in relation to 'the Young Bolshevik Bolus' such that the poem can be read as an attempt to co-ordinate a left-wing sensibility with the metaphysical conceits of modern scientific language and an idiomatic classicism. The sense that this might owe something to readings of renaissance poetry and drama argued for by T.S. Eliot is supported by recognition that the title 'Lusty Juventus' is shared by an interlude by John King, published circa 1565.[6] It seems likely that Madge too sought to associate otherwise disassociated sensibilities. Madge's early work also suggests comparison with the austere wit and concision of Auden's early poems. Auden's poem 'Who stands, the crux left of the watershed' (*Poems* 1928 & 1930),[7] provides some terms of comparison for Madge's series of poems 'Countries of the Dead'. A poetics of twentieth century waste lands lends itself, accordingly, to socialist interpretation of questions regarding the vantage from which poetry articulates its political perceptions. Returning to the reading of 'Somewhere', the resistance of Madge's poetry to the forces of myth, history, panic and fear, might offer less sweeping horizons of political perception, articulating, albeit in a mode of modernist fragmentation, something of what Madge called the 'society in the mind'.

6. W.W. Greg, *A Bibliography of the English Printed Drama to the Restoration*, vol. 1 Stationers' Records, Plays to 1616, London, The Bibliographical Society, 1970, pp119-21.

7. Edward Mendelson (ed), *The English Auden: Poems, Essays & Dramatic Writings, 1937-1939*, London, Faber & Faber, 1977, p22.

Madge retired as Professor of Social Science at Birmingham University in 1970, so the persistence of poetry in his writing in the early 1970s suggests intriguing questions as to the relation between poetry and social science in his political imagination. As regards publication, it is unclear how far Madge's published work as a poet was halted by changing conditions in poetry publishing after 1945. The papers in the University of Sussex archives suggest that Madge continued to work on collections of poems in the post-war period, despite the many other demands on his intellectual energies, but his earlier, relatively warm relation with Faber & Faber, through T.S. Eliot, appears to have cooled, though this was true of a number of interesting poets who emerged in the 1930s. The archives also provide abundant evidence that Madge wrote poetry persistently from an early age onwards, even if it was not until the Anvil collection published in 1994 that this persistence was more publicly affirmed. Indeed the apparent severity of Madge's selection criteria suggests a determination to indicate quality rather than quantity.

How far, then, did poetry inform Madge's socialism, and how far did socialism inform his poetry? Poetry and the idea of poetry have played a significant role in the life and work of many English socialists, despite the apparent marginality of poetry to the traditions of historical materialism. A life-long commitment to poetry *and* socialism was shared, for example, by E.P. Thompson and continues to figure in the work of John Berger. Understood historically, this connection between poetry, socialism and political perception could be traced back to the politics and poetry of the Chartists, and beyond that to Keats and Shelley,[8] but was probably most evident in the 1930s, the years formative for Madge's poetry and for his intellectual development. Even if Madge's poetic oeuvre is somewhat fragmented and developed at a tangent to more established bourgeois or modernist conceptions of poetry, part of the interest of his poetry is that it is informed by a socialist poetics of perception that implies a revision of the literary historical terms conventionally applied to the poetry of the 1930s and poetry more generally. Madge's work might be compared, for example, with the work of his contemporaries Hugh Sykes or Joseph Macleod, or indeed with the poetry of left-wing 'objectivists' such as Louis Zukofsky or George Oppen. The critical difficulty is to develop appropriate reading protocols against the grain of left-wing critiques of the ideology of poetry and aesthetics dominant in supposedly progressive criticism. New kinds of socialist aesthetics are needed to read Madge's work, along with new kinds of historically nuanced and formally reflexive criticism.

The poetry of Madge suggests, indeed, that the awkwardly incomplete formation of English modernism was not solely the province of the authoritarian politics and aesthetics associated with T.S. Eliot and Ezra Pound, but included attempts to develop a poetics of socialist and Marxist modernism. These attempts have important differences from the politicised aesthetics more familiarly associated with Bertolt Brecht and Walter Benjamin. The poetics of Mass-Observation nevertheless have suggestive affinities with Benjamin's political poetics of Paris, everyday life and historical memory, affinities evident in superficial similarities between Benjamin's *Arcades Project* and Humphrey Jennings' *Pandaemonium*, the latter posthumously edited by Mary-Lou Jennings and Charles Madge.[9] In the essay which Madge wrote to accompany *Pandaemonium*, he writes:

Among the notes for an introduction to *Pandaemonium* is the pencilled sentence: 'The poets are guardians of the Animistic system, the scientists of the Materialist system.' In the conflict between these two basic systems, it is the materialist system which has prevailed and Humphrey

8. See Drew Milne, 'Flaming robes: Keats, Shelley and the metrical clothes of class struggle', *Textual Practice* 15,1 (2001), 101-22.

9. Walter Benjamin, *The Arcades Project*, Howard Eiland and Kevin McLaughlin (trans), Cambridge, Mass. and London, Belknap Press of Harvard University Press, 1999; Humphrey Jennings, *Pandaemonium 1660-1886: The Coming of the Machine as seen by contemporary observers*, M-L Jennings and C. Madge (eds), London, Andre Deutsch, 1985.

[Jennings], for all his essentially poetic vision, accepted that this must be so. But he could see and feel the immense loss which it had brought upon his own and succeeding generations. Perhaps he was not able to surmount this contradiction, but in the latter part of his notes for an introduction, where he sets forth a post-Marxist position in which the means of production are paralleled by equally important means of vision, he is thereby able to escape, if only poetically, the constriction inherent in Marxism.[10]

A mechanist or crudely scientistic conception of Marxism might indeed appear to strangle the poetic imagination. Read critically, however, the more restricted conception of poetic 'vision' is one which is avowedly escapist. As Benjamin's work also dramatises, the role of poetic imagination is difficult to specify politically. The formulation offered by Jennings claims 'that the poet's vision does exist, that the imagination is a part of life, that the exercise of the imagination is an indispensable function of man like work, eating, sleeping, loving'.[11] This suggests some grounds for thinking that the animism of poetic perception is anthropologically or existentially constitutive of human materiality, but it hardly needs stating that there is many a slip twixt poetic 'vision' and actual poems. One man's poetic vision often turns out to be another person's historical nightmare. Madge appears to have shared some of the sensitivities dramatised here, wanting to affirm poetic perception and practice as activities central to his life, while recognising the challenge from more scientific and materialist conceptions of society, not least the possibility that 'poetry' has become a romantic form of anti-capitalist escapism.

Understood in these terms, it becomes possible to see why poetry and the idea of poetry should continue to play a significant role in the mediation of nonconformist and dissident social tendencies within all levels of society, despite the apparent marginality and vulnerability of poetry as a historical medium. Despite or perhaps even because of the often quasi-aristocratic anti-bourgeois class orientation of the history of English poetry, an early interest in poetry has played a significant part in the making of English socialism and what might be called the radical intelligentsia. The persistence of poetry as an interest sustained beyond youthful enthusiasm is perhaps more unusual, but Karl Marx is only one among a range of socialist intellectuals whose imaginative horizons continued to be informed by poetry even after early aspirations to write poetry had modulated into different types of literary activity. Many socialist writers have emerged from a sustained imaginative engagement with poetry. Trevor Griffiths, for example, a socialist playwright not noted for his interest in poetry, referred in 1972 to his own experience of 'the kind of mandatory ten years of poems' he underwent by way of literary training.[12] Despite charges of effete neurasthenia or political irrelevance often directed at poetry, poetry has been a decisive educative influence, in part through the utopian aspirations

10. Madge, 'Editorial Tasks and Methods', ibid., ppxvi-xvii.

11. Ibid., pxxxix.

12. Trevor Griffiths, quoted in 'A Play Postscript: Trevor Griffiths talks to Nigel Andrews', *Plays and Players*, 19, 7, issue 223 (April 1972), 82.

projected onto the idea of poetry and in part through the practices of reading and writing poetry.

The power of poetry to shape the political orientation of significant class fractions is perhaps most evident in the radical agency ascribed to poetry by a number of writers and intellectuals in the 1930s. W.H. Auden remains the most visible protagonist in retrospective accounts of this historical conjunction of poetry and politics. Writing in the *New Statesman* in 1933, for example, Julian Bell observed that: 'As far as an interest in literature continues it has very largely changed its character and become an ally of Communism under the influence of Mr Auden's Oxford group. Indeed, it might, with some plausibility be argued that Communism in England is at present largely a literary phenomenon - an attempt of a second post-war generation to escape from the Waste Land'.[13] This helpful characterisation of the context in which Charles Madge emerged as a poet needs to be amplified with some reference to the Cambridge contexts experienced by Madge, and the ambitious conceptions of poetry developed by I.A. Richards and William Empson, along with poets such as Hugh Sykes and Humphrey Jennings associated with the journal *Experiment*. A broad range of local political commitments and affiliations were prompted and informed by such interests in poetry.

More recently, however, the relation between poetic and political commitments has come under sustained pressure from attempts to subsume questions of poetry within the sociology of culture or cultural materialism. Much energy has been devoted to showing how claims for poetic value reflect ideologies of the aesthetic. The reductive tendency of such criticism becomes evident as the return of the repressed in the use of the term 'poetics' for modes of thinking in which poetry itself is the last form of culture to be deemed worthy of attention. Over-investment in the value of poetry is often significant in the intellectual formation of those most enthusiastic to engage in the radical critique of any claims for the value of poetry. The uncertain social function of poetry, its purposeful lack of purpose, remains the site of conflicts in which the idea of poetry is almost more potent than the continuity of poetry as a practical and aesthetic orientation to social being. In this sense, the interests negotiated through the idea of poetry inform the aesthetic dimensions of culture and politics in ways which are incommensurate with the more modest facticity of particular poems. The idea of poetry continues to generate conflicts of interpretation which exceed the evident limits of poetry as a material form within the prose formations of the capitalist world.

The work of Charles Madge provides an eloquent illustration of this paradox, to the extent that Madge's interest in poetry and poetics informs the project of Mass-Observation beyond the conventional terms of what is meant by poetry. The sociological and anthropological orientation of Mass-Observation appears to involve the scientific suspension of those questions of value, social perspective and aesthetic judgement so central to poetic artifice. It is nevertheless possible to recognise that Mass-Observation was motivated by an understanding of the relation between politics and poetics which involved a radical new conception of the social function of linguistic testimony and poetic perception. But just as the idea of poetry seems to stimulate the radical imagination to exceed the parameters of existing poetic production, so the idea of Mass-Observation is perhaps more stimulating for rethinking the politics of the imagination than anything embodied by the actual results of Mass-Observation as an existing social practice. The extensive archive generated by Mass-Observation practices somehow fails to provide the testimony of imaginative activity and ideological resistance so evident in the historical records of poetry. Very few of Madge's poems suggest themselves as attempts to appropriate insights gathered from Mass-Observation. The most notable exception is 'Drinking in Bolton' (1939), which illustrates the problems involved, by suggesting a lack of solidarity in the vantage from which the 'I' and 'you' of the poem might converge. The search is evident:

> I am drawing
> (Towards imagination) gills of mild,
> The industrial drink, in which my dreams and theirs
> Find common ground.[14]

14. Madge, *Of Love, Time and Places*, op.cit., p108.

But while the poem assembles a number of appropriately 'industrial' images, the tendency is to suggest the impossibility of sharing the imaginative significance sketched:

> So final night
> Falls, like a pack of cards, each one of which
> Is fate, the film-star and the penny pool.
> You sit there waiting for the spell to break.[15]

15. Ibid., p108.

A somewhat later poem 'Visions of Camden Town' (1944) talks of 'mass children', but nevertheless suggests a less alienated experience of urban collectivity: 'Millions like us live in these towns / Whose buildings lie heavily on the soil / And press it down, mile upon mile'.[16] However suggestive it is to read Madge's poems in the light of a poetic derived from Mass-Observation, the poems testify to the pitfalls of co-ordinating the political aspirations embodied in Mass-Observation with specific conditions of individual perception. There is a significant gulf between the ability of any individual to generate their own images and the significance of these images understood as a mode of collective political perception.

16. Ibid., p144.

Mass-Observation's failure to integrate a poetics of radical subjectivity with the objectivity of social anthropology is perhaps comparable, then, to the failure of radical poetics to integrate poetic practice with politics and social criticism. Even if Mass-Observation cannot, in the end, be understood as a new kind of poetics, the idea of Mass-Observation owes something to the persistence of poetry as an aesthetic dimension informing the political imagination. The difficulty for criticism, however, is the gulf that opens between the idea of poetry and the more limited evaluation and critical analysis of particular poems. This gulf is made all the more profound where new conceptions of poetry as a relation to social being involve a critique of the social hierarchies, historical assumptions and formal conventions associated with poetry. Given that much of the recent criticism written about poetry has been more concerned with conceptualising poetry's conditions of possibility than with the consideration of existing poetic practices, it has become increasingly difficult to judge the value of particular poems beyond the most local contexts of their production. The risk, applied to the poetry of Charles Madge, is that consideration of the significance of Madge's poems becomes secondary to an account of the idea of poetry in Madge's work as a whole. The more awkward task is to recognise the dialectical relation between the social projects implicit in different ideas of poetry, and the negotiation of historical and linguistic experience in particular poems.

Madge's poetry has not yet received much critical attention, and it remains unclear how far admirers would wish to claim a more canonical role for his poetry. Any attempt to make Madge's poetry more central to the understanding of modern English poetry would require substantial revision of existing priorities. It seems more likely that what is needed is a nuanced account of the instability of poetic value and poetic tradition in particular poems, in part because Madge's poems have residual affinities with the better known work of T.S. Eliot or the early poems of W.H. Auden, while also implying a rather different socialist idea of the significance of poetry. Indeed, it is at least plausible that one of the radical implications of the poetics of Mass-Observation is the need to displace ideas of poetry which seek to privilege particular, pseudo-individualised 'voices', experiences or expressions of linguistic individuality. This would suggest a socialist conception of poetic impersonality concerned less with the need for greater literary objectivity than with the need to eradicate the commodified or privatised voice-style as the signature possession of an individual, bourgeois writer. The new challenge would be for a socialist poetics of collective inter-personal poetry rather than for an impersonal 'objectivism' that denied the possibility of individual engagements with social experience. But if a socialist poetics necessarily involves a more inclusive sense of the variousness of poetic practices in opposition to the feudal hierarchies and pantheons of canonical poetic traditions, this also threatens to consign the work of individual poets to critical oblivion and social neglect. Without some shared sense of the value of poetic traditions, it is hard to see how poetry can persist as more than an idea.

Some of these questions are highlighted by Peter Jay's 'Publisher's Note' (1990) in the collection *Of Love, Time and Places*. Jay describes how Madge initially 'rejected many poems for a variety of reasons: either because they seem to him now to have been factitiously composed, or to have lacked a hard enough poetic core, or because their interest seemed narrowly historical'.[17] It remains unclear what kind of self-criticism is implicit in the notion of 'factitious' composition or a 'hard' poetic core. Nevertheless, the decisive question is whether Madge's poems are 'narrowly historical', of value merely for reasons of historical interest, or whether there is a qualitative poetic achievement whose value persists beyond the initial contexts of its production. Any such judgement depends on deciding which of Madge's poems are most important. Somewhat contentiously, for example, Jay claims that 'The socialist and surrealist elements in his early work ... are subsumed into a broader vision in his more mature writing.[18] It might be suggested, however, that the tensions between socialism and surrealism generate Madge's most interesting poems, precisely by offering a more radical and suggestive approach to the situation of poetry than available within more conventional modes of poetic form. The idea of 'mature writing' often involves limiting the sense of social potential within writing which might be more historically specific or unfinished while remaining available for as yet unrealised re-appropriations. Against the tendency to value poetry which tries to transcend its historical specificity, it could be argued that it is poetry which is most acutely articulate about its historical specificity which most effectively resists being subsumed within history. In this sense, the persistence of poetry would not be a value appropriately ascribed to poems that seek to transcend history, but a quality of poems whose recognition of historical provisionality allows the radical historicity of poetry to remain open-ended as a potential mode of social being. The poems of Charles Madge are torn in this way between a provisional sense of poetry's historical materiality and desires to reanimate and reaffirm aspects of poetic tradition which are at odds with contemporary historical forces.

If Madge's poems are animated by questions about the persistence of poetry as a meaningful horizon of social being, such questions also emerge in his critical and sociological writings. The relative paucity in *Of Love, Time and Places* of poems written after the early 1950s may reflect a diminished interest in the writing of poetry, or perhaps more external features such as new conditions for publishing poetry. He continued, however, to write poems at least occasionally, and his persistence with the question of poetry is implicit elsewhere in his writing. In 1949, for example, Madge wrote an essay on Ezra Pound's use of the 'ellipse' in the *Pisan Cantos* in which he offers a defence of the persistence of that poetry 'which has lived a long time, and which we therefore call classical', claiming that once stripped of the historical falsifications of their reception 'when anybody is able to win access to them, to break a way through, these classics can still recreate our insight into the present and the future'.[19] Madge comments on the difficulty of composing poems without producing elliptical and ambiguous effects, and offers suggestive

17. Ibid., p5.

18. Ibid.

19. Madge, 'The Ellipse in the Pisan Cantos' (1949), in Peter Russell (ed), *Ezra Pound*, London, Peter Nevill, 1950, p119.

remarks on the visual appearance of poems on a printed page. In some respects the interest in ellipsis could be traced back to Auden's early poetry. Adrian Caesar suggests that in *Poems* (1930): 'Auden's fondness for ellipsis, for abstract nouns, and for definite articles placed against indefinite nouns, ensures a "difficulty", a "mysteriousness" [...]'[20] The permanent or future-oriented value Madge ascribes to the classic does not, however, quite extend to confident claims for the status of Pound's Cantos:

20. Op. cit., p47.

> [...] where Pound has left a yawning gap in argument or syntax, it is difficult to prove that the implied statement, and its aura of feeling, is of a poetic order. The gap might simply mean that Pound did not know what to say, or could not say it, or even that there was nothing to be said. The final decision as to whether the empty space does or does not contain a living spirit is very largely a matter of testimony. I can testify to what I find in the poem, but I cannot be sure that others will find it [...] To me it appears that Pound is bringing to the surface by a process of free association certain elements in the cultural unconscious which are painful and harmful. By so doing, he is enlarging the consciousness of a future age, but he is also provoking mental resistances which are naturally strongest in those who come nearest to his meaning [...] Each Canto is in fact like a psycho-analytical session, probing the cultural unconscious of literature and history. As the analysis proceeds, events are taking place in the outer life of contemporary history and of Pound's personal history [...][21]

21. Madge, 'The Ellipse in the Pisan Cantos', op.cit., p126.

Further lines of investigation are suggested by Michael Roberts' intriguing comment concerning 'the great passages in Whitman, where, Charles Madge has pointed out, the ego passes over all the earth and eventually "dissolves in lacy jags"'.[22] I have, as yet, been unable to trace the source from which Roberts here cites Madge. From amid the Faber and Faber stable of poets who emerged in the 1930s, Madge's willingness to write sympathetically about the value of Pound's work in the late 1940s suggests his continuing affinities with the earlier literary modernism of Eliot and Pound, and it is tempting to explore these remarks as an interpretative template for reading Madge's own poems.

22. 'Introduction', *The Faber Book of Modern Verse*, Michael Roberts (ed), London, Faber & Faber, 1936, p23.

Perhaps more important, however, is Madge's reluctance to claim any more objective value for his own testimony as a reader, and what this suggests about the social indeterminacy of the meaning of elliptical or paratactic form in modernist poetry. References to 'free association' and the 'cultural unconscious' also indicate the persistence of surrealist conceptions of poetic practice rather different from the ideas of poetry more commonly associated with Pound. The persistence of such questions is evident in Madge's 1964 book *Society in the Mind* in which he outlines two post-Enlightenment tendencies:

The first is the tendency towards objectivity and away from ethnocentric bias: this is in keeping with the scientific, rational, critical trend of the period. But the other tendency, already explicit in Vico, is to seek in the archaic and primitive an element of poetry which is felt to be disappearing from the modern world. This tendency is obvious enough among modern artists and poets, but it has, I think, also motivated anthropologists, historians and scholars and has entered into their interpretations, and into the interest of a wide public in their work. Along with the shift to rationality, and partly because of it, there has been a broad nostalgic turning back towards what is, psychologically, the lost world of childhood: what Vico called 'the world's childhood'. It is of course possible for the two tendencies to be united: it is possible to be both nostalgic and objective.[23]

23. Madge, *Society in the Mind: Elements of Social Eidos*, London, Faber & Faber, 1964, p30.

It is also possible to see how the project of Mass-Observation sought to articulate the persistence of poetry with some critical objectivity. It is less evident, however, how these tendencies are to be understood historically. Madge, for example, defines 'eidos' as 'the predominant character of the whole stock of ideas available in a society or group',[24] but appears committed to the possibility that literature and the arts can somehow articulate an 'unsocial eidos'. Thus Madge claims that:

24. Ibid., p13.

> The canons of mature un-social eidos are more personal and more elusive. They have taken shape over the past two hundred years largely through the activities of poets, painters and novelists, whose influence has been felt not only through their artistic works and manifestos but through the example of their own private lives.[25]

25. Ibid., p139.

The lived commitment to artistic practice embodies the idea of poetry or art more generally as a private, almost anti-social resistance to dominant values, a resistance implicated not just through the impersonal testimony of works produced but by the challenge posed by different ways of living. The world of modern art is increasingly irrelevant to the dominant social eidos, but persists as a residual alternative, idiosyncratic and unscientifically personal.

The sense that art's significance is diminishing echoes a broadly Hegelian conception of the withering away of art through the impact of modern scientific rationality and the world of prose. Madge cites Marx and Marcuse to support a radical conception of the aesthetic dimension of the potentials within social being, but this utopian aspiration is tempered by a sense of its diminishing persistence within aesthetic practices. Indeed, Madge poses the problem of art's persistence within a curiously romantic kind of nostalgia:

> Can we ever reinvent a 'vision of the world' which will satisfy us aesthetically, or shall we have to hoard, as long as we can, the aesthetic capital we inherit from classical Athens, Renaissance Italy and other

past 'flowerings'? Are the arts to become a 'dead language', whose meaning can only be relearnt by a reconstruction of the kind of life that was lived in the pre-scientific stages of civilisation?[26]

26. Ibid., p149.

These terms suggest the extent to which Madge shares the conceptualisation of poetic 'vision' ascribed by Madge to Humphrey Jennings in the essay introducing *Pandaemonium*. Jennings, moreover, provides specific examples relevant to Madge's conception of the historical persistence of poetry, such as the following citation from Charles Darwin (1881):

> [...] if I had to live my life again, I would have made it a rule to read some poetry and listen to some music at least once every week; for perhaps the parts of my brain now atrophied would thus have been kept active through use. The loss of these tastes is a loss of happiness, and may possibly be injurious to the intellect, and more probably to the moral character, by enfeebling the emotional part of our nature.[27]

27. H. Jennings, op.cit., p344.

Darwin also appears as something of a pivotal historical figure in Madge's work. The poem 'Darwin' dated November 1944 offers statements on creation from amoeboid pain to ruined cities, almost as if Darwin could be said to have provided an evolutionary account of human anthropology. In an earlier review of Beddoes published in *Criterion* (1936-7), Madge suggests that 'It was left to Charles Darwin, and to his successors in the anthropological and psychological domains, to possibilise human science and human poetry'.[28] Such hints as to the anthropological tendency and scientific interests underlying Madge's poems suggest that the quality of abstraction in many of his poems reflects an attempt to articulate poetry across otherwise disassociated sensibilities. Hints regarding the anthropological concerns of poetry can be compared with the more historical and sociological account expressed by Charles Madge in *Art Students Observed*:

28. Review of *The Works of Beddoes, Criterion*, 16 (1936-7), p149.

> Art is an extreme case of a traditional activity - other examples being those of the army or the clergy - which has been continuously redefined in an attempt to give it new validity in contemporary terms. Perhaps more than those of any other such activity, its values are remote from those which predominate in industrial societies, which are, however, prosperous enough to allocate resources to art on a considerable scale, in total probably greater than at any time in history. On the other hand there is little or no consensus either among artists or among their public about the nature and purpose of artistic activity.[29]

29. Charles Madge and Barbara Weinberger, *Art Students Observed*, London, Faber & Faber, 1973, p15.

This lack of consensus necessarily informs any attempt to develop appropriate reading protocols for Madge's own poetry.

There is more work still to be done to develop an understanding of the critical apparatus implicit in Madge's reviews and unpublished work, as

well as in relation to his friends and collaborators. What seems to emerge from the investigations sketched here, however, is that any sustained reading of Madge's poetry needs to reckon with the tension between Madge's poems and the ideas explored by Madge regarding the crises of modern poetry and poetic cognition. This tension suggests that many of Madge's poems dramatise the limits of poetry's ability to serve or support critical reflection on various metaphysical, historical, sociopolitical, ethical or personal concerns. Madge's reticence regarding the cognitive status or value of poetry, both in his poems and in his prose writings, suggests the need for comparable scepticism in the critical reading of his work. This would help to motivate an understanding of the moments of uncertain quality in Madge's poems, moments in which the urge to transcend particular identities of love, time and place appears blocked or awkward.[30] In some respects the awkwardness is historically and politically motivated. In other respects the most germane questions concern the continuing viability of poetry as a way of understanding or representing contemporary social experience. The pressure of contemporary colloquial idiom, for example, is felt only occasionally in Madge's poems. This is most decisive with regard to the significance of verse conventions used by Madge, conventions appreciable within conventions of close reading, but which appear newly arbitrary and anxious, somehow incomplete. The sense of incompletion or interruption is often a mark of modernist seriousness, a reluctance to over-state convictions of connectedness where imaginative leaps have over-stepped existing grounds or conditions of perception. More often the sense of register and vantage is socialised through the forms of verse tradition, even if the persistence of verse tradition is viewed with some scepticism.

The impact of the poetics of Mass-Observation on Madge's poetry is surprisingly slight. Although Mass-Observation suggests the need for a radical revision of the class divisions of poetic diction, aesthetic experience and political imagination, Madge's poems appear more confident that the materials of verse history can support renewed attention to contemporary society. The risk is that this suggests that the idea of poetry persists in his work merely as a kind of formal literariness which can pose certain kinds of rhetorical problem, but without achieving the reassociation of sensibilities implicit in modernist arguments for poetry's continuing viability. The uncertain grounds from which the seemingly Olympian or cosmological perspectives of imaginative poetry are projected then become vulnerable to scientific scepticism. Madge's poetry is intimate with such difficulties, but the question as to whether such difficulties can be resolved in particular poems suggests the need to read his poems both for the particular insights they offer and through a politicised conception of the ideas and values poetry embodies. The need to renegotiate the tension between particular poems and a historical understanding of poetic traditions suggests that Madge's apparent marginality as a poet should be reconsidered, not least as an argument for the persistence of poetry within the traditions of socialism.

30. Compare Simon Jarvis, 'A Burning Monochrome: Fisher's Block', in John Kerrigan and Peter Robinson (eds), *The Thing About Roy Fisher: Critical Studies*, Liverpool, Liverpool University Press, 2000, pp173-92.

CHARLES MADGE AND MASS-OBSERVATION ARE AT HOME: FROM ANTHROPOLOGY TO WAR, AND AFTER

Nick Hubble

Persons are indoors
Show no divinity to mine, or tread
No more in chorus the inherited space

Charles Madge, 'View from a Window' (February 1951)

One of the few apparent constants of Madge's varied career from 1932, when he first started selling the *Daily Worker* in the backstreets of Cambridge during his time as an undergraduate, through to the late 1970s and his work on inner city poverty with the Institute of Community Studies, was his interest in the environment of the working-class home. Implicit within his concern was a belief in the everyday plenitude of working-class life - that resistive quality that lies at the heart of the English radical tradition as recorded from William Cobbett to E.P. Thompson. This belief is perhaps most clearly stated in his 1964 book *Society in the Mind* - an attempt to map out the social and historical structure of social eidos (the mental framework of society in which we all operate). This, for all Madge's typical diffidence and understatement, is a powerful questioning of the ideology and instrumental reason present in what he describes as our contemporary stage of social eidos, where 'along with a plentiful inheritance of mystery and morality, there is an overriding tendency to look on society as a working system, which can be made to work better and better by rational-technical means. Central to this conception are first, the idea of progress, second, the economics of the market and third, the politics of the ballot box'.[1] Against this, Madge describes the role of inarticulate resistances such as 'the resistance to school' - echoing Cobbett and Orwell - and non-participation in religion and politics.[2] This is what he calls the un-social eidos, which cannot be simply identified with 'laziness, indiscipline or incomplete socialisation'.[3] Arguing that 'the canons of mature un-social eidos ... have taken shape ... largely through the activities of poets, painters and novelists',[4] Madge advocates relaxing the socially coercive bonds of society by redirecting social eidos towards an aesthetic teleology. A project he pursued in his subsequent book, *Art Students Observed*.

What makes this focus on an aesthetic un-social eidos significant is the very centrality of Madge's own role within the rational-technical social eidos of the post-war British state that he wanted to criticise. For he had been a

1. Charles Madge, *Society in the Mind*, London, Faber and Faber, 1964, p55.

2. Ibid., pp123-4.

3. Ibid., p138.

4. Ibid., p139.

close collaborator of Keynes and Beveridge, its two most influential technocrats and leading architects. According to Angus Calder, after research on saving and spending in the run-up to the 1941 Budget, 'Madge had announced that working-class people were far more worried about the immediate physical problems of blitz and food shortage than a few bob a week more or less on taxation, and his findings had convinced the Treasury that Keynes' theories were acceptable in practice'.[5] Consequently, income tax was extended to four million new payers, thus making the deep bite into working-class incomes Keynes deemed necessary to close the 'inflationary gap'. The Chancellor of the Exchequer, Sir Kingsley Wood, quoted directly from Madge's reports during the course of his financial statement presenting the Budget.[6] The purpose of these passages - described by Keynes as 'quite one of the bright moments of the afternoon'[7] - was to allay the fears of the House by demonstrating a working-class willingness to pay.

From September 1942, Madge worked on the staff of Political and Economic Planning (PEP). At the same time he was editing the 'Target for Tomorrow' series, concerned with publicising how the post-war future could be planned, for the Pilot Press under an editorial board led by Beveridge, who wrote forewords to the books. When Michael Young, the secretary of PEP, left in February 1945 to become research secretary to the Labour Party, Madge was offered the vacancy. Instead, he stayed with the Pilot Press, where he was now a salaried partner, and started the quarterly, *Pilot Papers*, which could be claimed as the first cultural studies, theory and politics journal. Here, essays on sociology and economics were placed next to analyses of Butlins' holiday camps and cartoon strips, reports on the Communist squatters' movement and lengthy working-class autobiographies. The journal was a victim of the financial problems of 1946-1947, but Madge was able to take an interest in housing questions, that he had developed in his editorial commentaries, and put it into practice as Social Development Officer of the New Town of Stevenage. Three years later he was appointed to the Chair in Sociology at the University of Birmingham, one of the first of such positions outside London, and part of the post-war foundations of the boom in the subject that was to follow.

It is fair to say that Madge believed in, and was fully committed to, the notion of planned progress which encapsulated the post-war settlement. His advocacy can be seen at its most forthright and (over) optimistic in the 1945 *Pilot Guide to the General Election*. Here, the discussion of non-voters is particularly at odds with the position that Madge was to adopt in 1964: 'Of course, a large number of people are too lazy to go. But we may not be losing much by missing their votes. We ought not to be satisfied with less than a 95 per cent poll at a General Election'.[8]

The temptation at this point is to consider the well known social history of this period - the budgetary problems, the Cold War, the 1951 election, Suez and Hungary - and to see this as the context to which Madge reacted,

5. Angus Calder, *The People's War*, London, Pimlico, 1992, p238.

6. Hansard, 7 April 1941, Columns 1301-2.

7. John Maynard Keynes, Letter to Madge, 7 April 1941, Box 21/File 5, Charles Madge Papers (C.M.P.), University of Sussex Library.

8. Madge (ed), *Pilot Guide to the General Election*, London, The Pilot Press, 1945, p7.

gradually becoming disillusioned to the point where he turned to extolling drop outs. The fact that he subsequently became profoundly distressed at the 1968 events and ended up reaching a complete state of mental and physical crisis in the mid 1970s, by which time he had become completely disillusioned with sociology, Marxism and any form of leftism, and was reduced to questioning the point of all his past activities,[9] seems like the final twist in a certain kind of trajectory that we are already all too sadly familiar with from numerous other cases. However, this kind of account is inevitably preconditioned by exactly that approach of trying to fit biographical details against a social history background: a certain conformity is unanswerably imposed in retrospect and another name is safely filed away in the footnotes to an unchallengeable historicism. Therefore, I intend to look at Madge's life first, and from the choices and positions he adopted, see what observations can perhaps be made about the post-war settlement. For, of course, Madge was not just a technocrat who became disillusioned: he was first a 1930s Communist poet.

Madge's experience of reporting on the abdication crisis in 1936 for the *Daily Mirror* had led to his disillusion with the press's falsification of public opinion and his founding of Mass-Observation (M-O). His initial letter to the *New Statesman* invoked anthropology and psychoanalysis as the scientific tools required to pick out the clues to the repressed elements of consciousness surfacing in the public upheaval of the crisis - those very elements which were being obscured by the media. This letter was subtitled 'Anthropology at Home'[10] - a phrase that was to stick. However, it might equally have been labelled 'Poetry at Home'. Indeed, Madge's notebooks suggest that 'Popular Poetry' was his working title for M-O. Early ideas included the establishment of 'Coincidence Clubs: groups in colleges, factories and localities', as well as lectures and textbooks. Other scribbled phrases such as 'materialism' and 'class consciousness' suggest Marxist ambitions: 'English people must learn to *like* their surroundings before they can change them'.[11]

These ideas are clearly present in Madge and Humphrey Jennings' article, 'Poetic Description and Mass-Observation', which appeared in *New Verse* in the Spring of 1936, advocating a newspaper that could be read like poetry as shared experience, where everyone is a mass-observer observing both everyone else and their own subjectivity: 'They produce a poetry which is not, as at present, restricted to a handful of esoteric performers. The immediate effect of Mass-Observation is to devalue considerably the status of the "poet". It makes the term "poet" apply not to his performance, but to his profession, like "footballer"'.[12] Jennings and Madge had foreseen that their literary and surrealistic activities were becoming increasingly inseparable from a cultural racket - and M-O was their attempt to move beyond that.[13]

Madge explains his motivation for M-O as a mass science in more explicitly Marxist terms in an article, 'Magic and Materialism', published

9. Madge, 'Autobiography', 2/1, C.M.P., p259.

10. Madge, Letter, *New Statesman and Nation*, 2 January 1937, p12.

11. Madge, notebook, started 9 December 1934, unnumbered pages, 10/-, C.M.P. These notes would presumably date from around December 1936.

12. *New Verse*, 24, (February-March 1937), 2.

13. See Humphrey Jennings, Review of Herbert Read (ed), *Surrealism*, *Contemporary Poetry and Prose*, 8, (December 1936), 168.

in *Left Review* (for which he was a regular contributor and reviewer): 'the clear light of materialism, fearlessly applied to the elucidation of physical phenomena, is withheld longest of all from the study of the human animal himself, because bourgeois society demands that in that sphere the old darkness of magic and religion should continue to reign'.[14] The link of this 'mass science' to 'popular poetry' is made explicit in his argument concerning the threat of residual magic. The remnants of magic (the power of words over things; all forms of idealism) in society are one of the prevailing sources of inequality and although magic remains in Art, poetry is free from this superstition because it 'deals not with the inexplicable, but with what has not yet been explained'.[15] Effectively, Madge is rejecting the ritual, performance and illusion of magic. Poetry, for him, is not performative; it is an act of observation. It is the pure form of empiricism - a poetic empiricism rather than a narrower performative empiricism - that rational science has to aim for. The poet is to be judged on professional criteria, by what has been done.

14. Madge, 'Magic and Materialism', *Left Review*, 3, 1, (February 1937), 31.

15. Ibid., 32.

The initial thrust of M-O culminated in the publication of *May the Twelfth*, the panoramic montage of Coronation Day. This book was famously unsuccessful and widely thought to suffer for having no theoretical framework. But, in fact, it does have a framework, devised by Madge, that of the 3 Social Areas. Where Area 1 is the informal everyday world of family and friends, Area 2 is the public sphere governed by social conventions and Area 3 is the world of celebrity, media and myth: 'M-O is studying the shifting relations between the individual and these three areas, thus seeking to give a more concrete meaning to the abstract word, "society"'.[16] This is an early attempt to map out social eidos. *May the Twelfth* presents the Area 1 experience of the crowds at the Coronation in a way that contradicts the official collective Area 3 account. That is to say, rather than show the crowds lining the Coronation procession route as an adulating mass of subjects, it shows them enjoying themselves much as they pleased by treating the occasion as a public holiday in an almost carnivalesque manner.

16. M-O, 'A Thousand Mass-Observers', c. July 1937, FR A4, Mass-Observation Archive (M-O A), University of Sussex Library.

Whether the book succeeds is debatable (conceivably, Coronations might *only* be able to function in this carnivalesque manner) but the 3 Social Areas provide a usable conceptual framework. As such, they governed Madge's attempts to analyse opinion formation over the remainder of that year. This involved a number of detailed questionnaires concerning smoking, reading habits and advertising. Looking back on that period from January 1940, Madge considered this empirical investigation into opinion formation had been totally unproductive because they had never managed to work out how the broad influences - press, radio, friends - actually interacted with individual consciousness to produce opinion.[17] This point was crucial to the development of M-O, and Madge himself, because it led him to alter his conceptual framework in a way that is highly visible. We can see it in the change from a draft of the first chapter of *First Year's Work* to the published version in March 1938. The draft notes that 'man has a natural

17. Madge, memo to Harrisson, 21/01/40, p3, M-O Hist 1/ 'CM-TH Correspondence', M-O A.

18. Draft of *First Year's Work*, M-O Hist 1/ 'Early Original Papers', M-O A.

19. M-O, *First Year's Work*, London, Lindsey Drummond, 1938, pp9, 1, 11.

20. Ibid., p23.

tendency to conform' and 'that in every [...] case of conformity, there is a question of a relationship in terms of Area 3'.[18] In the published version it is only 'advertisers and political propagandists' who think man is a natural conformist: 'conformity is an intervention from Area 3' which includes 'branded goods such as Sunlight Soap [and] Player's Cigarettes'.[19] This is a major shift in thinking. It involves moving from seeing Area 3 as a part of the material relations of human consciousness, to seeing it as something external to consciousness. A concern with mapping human consciousness including a collective unconscious, becomes a concern about the effects of advertising and propaganda which are invisible but 'investigation brings them out'.[20] It is difficult to see this as other than a return to an acceptance of magic - in the sense that Madge had defined it previously - as the power of words over things. The claim being made for M-O is now narrowly empirical and completely self-reinforcing: it was the very scope of mass-observing in the widest sense that brought to attention the factors Madge selected for more detailed enquiry, but the very act of selection and specific focus shut off the possibility of picking out otherwise repressed elements.

There were at least two reasons for this failure of the investigation into opinion formation that led to M-O's change of conceptual approach. The first concerns the problematic relationship between M-O as popular poetry and M-O as functionalist anthropology, in the context of a rapid running out of patience. While M-O, like poetry in Madge's conception, sought to deal with 'what has not yet been explained', that did not mean that the work it produced would be explicable, any more than poetry is explicable. Clearly the required approach was interpretative rather than explanatory. However, this was of little value to the cause of showing how society functioned there and then and left M-O open to the criticisms of anthropologists. Furthermore, economic pressures on M-O, intensified by the commercial failure of *May the Twelfth*, demanded an instantaneous clarity that could never be forthcoming. Hence, the poetic and related conceptual frameworks had to be abandoned.

The second reason derives more fundamentally from the nature and practice of M-O: it is that their focus on mass and individual subjectivity creates a binary opposition that ignores other forms of intersubjectivity. The theory of the 3 Social Areas, although not maintained for long enough to rectify this deficiency, allows us to see it clearly. The simple fact being that Area 2, the area of social encounters with people who are not close friends or family and, therefore, encompassing what we would now call the public sphere, does not really feature in M-O analysis. Area 3 just acts directly on Area 1: which sometimes is the site for a resistant everyday plenitude as is apparently the case with the Coronation; and sometimes is the site of a banal everydayness which puts up no resistance whatsoever to the blandishments before it, whether they be those of Sunlight Soap or Neville Chamberlain. Clearly, there must be some further forms of social association which act to facilitate the resistance or the lack of the resistance.

If M-O had actually looked for these, they might have been able to make progress on the subject of opinion formation. As it was, it seems likely that this blindness to the possibility of social association suggests unconscious class bias on behalf of M-O. To Madge, the people - apparently incapable of organising themselves beyond the domestic sphere of home, family and friends - appeared defenceless against advertising, the press and the new entertainment industries such as the football pools. The answer, as he came to see it, was to give them, through strong leadership, the social association that they could not provide for themselves.

When M-O returned to longer studies, they retained their distinctive montage documentary style but this was now bounded within a narrow functionalist approach, designed to yield quick results and ward off criticism. This is clear in the Munich chapter of the 1939 Penguin Special, *Britain by Mass-Observation*, edited by Madge and Tom Harrisson. The problem of Press falsification of public opinion is represented as simply a consequence of the gulf between the leaders and the led; and, therefore, something hindering the effective functioning of society. M-O clearly see themselves as resolving the problem by providing a scientific account of what people really think. But this creates a problem for M-O, in that their own documentary techniques - including the subjective experience of the masses, i.e. montages of direct quotes - inevitably throw up examples of everyday social resistance which contradict their newly stated aims by showing that the gap between leaders and led is not simply one of faulty communication, but of deep structural fissure and hostility. It is this contradiction which fuelled M-O's contemporary critics, paraphrased by Calder: 'it is never wholly clear ... whether the primary aim was observation *of* the masses or *by* the masses'.[21] M-O's response is to combine their problem with the problem they are investigating. That is to say, they conclude that the reason there is a gulf between the leaders and the led is because there are distinct private and public spheres, regardless of the fact that it is their own choice of analytical approach which sorts all their material into these two categories:

> Until the last week in September, 1938, the great mass of working people were never observably affected in any marked degree by any crisis within the eighteen months during which we have been making observations, and it was only when the international situation threatened to enter their own homes, as gas, that a real mass response was apparent. In this world of rearmament and fortifications, an Englishman's home is still his castle, although well under half are their own landlords.[22]

This separation of home and real world crisis could still permit more than one interpretation. However, the observation has become predominantly *of* the masses - or, at least, it has become unambiguously presented in that way in this passage - and so the problem appears to be the insulation of the home; rather than the reactionary forces in World politics, which people

21. Angus Calder, 'Introduction to Cresset Library Edition', in M-O, *Britain by Mass-Observation*, London, The Cresset Library, 1986, pxiii.

22. M-O, *Britain*, p217.

could have been considered as consciously seeking to evade as best they could. From such a perspective (of seeing the isolated domestic sphere as a problem), the observations which M-O collected that were *by* the masses, became merely evidence of a set of attitudes which had to be overcome.

This was the overwhelming thrust of their next book, *War Begins at Home*, written during, and about, the Phoney War. Here, a long burst of irritation at the way people are not complying with the war spirit - not going into air-raid shelters at the siren, not carrying their gas masks - leads to the claim that the people can only be made into efficient protagonists of the war, if the war is taken into their homes by compulsion. Although some of the more flamboyant statements to this effect are clearly Harrisson's, the actual structure of the book, which was mainly drafted by Madge, is geared to this viewpoint. The key section is that on the blackout which, being both compulsory, and universally adhered to, is the model they want to propose for the whole conduct of the war. However, in contradiction to their purpose, Madge is obliged to truthfully report that 'it is by a long way the biggest grievance and source of grumbles amongst the imposed war conditions for M-O's national panel respondents and in M-O recorded "overheard" conversations'.[23] Particularly interesting is the effect of the blackout on the home - with total dark outside, and following the closure by decree of just about every form of public entertainment at the outbreak of the war - 'staying in' became a major leisure occupation, even after the cinemas and theatres were allowed to reopen in November. Despite M-O's earlier criticism of home-based attitudes, they welcomed this development: 'Home life has gained a new importance. People are being forced to amuse themselves more, rather than sit and passively watch others do something. So far no government and very few private interests seem to realise the huge new home potentialities which can now be exploited'.[24]

Viewed from today, one is inclined to suspect that the Government emergency measures were probably much more consciously intended to have this effect than M-O allow. Nonetheless, the M-O logic was that fantasy and wishful thinking had only taken hold in the masses because everyday life was resistant to science and rationality, thus offering the masses up to the new leadership forms of football pools and jazz (potentially associated with fascism). With these diversions in abeyance, and war now centred on the Home Front, here was the opportunity for home-dwellers to become the civilian army, unified and responsive to instructions - particularly via the radio - thus bridging the gap between the leaders and the led.

The gap between their conclusions and their documentary methodology was creating large tensions between Madge and Harrisson, which exploded into exchanges of (dictated) thirty page memos in January 1940. Between the rhetoric and personal abuse (fairly generous quantities of both), it is possible to discern the real differences of opinion. Thus, while Madge agrees with Harrisson that there is a need for active leadership for 'bewildered

23. M-O, *War Begins At Home*, London, Chatto and Windus, 1940, p190.

24. Ibid., p194.

masses', he insists that this cannot be M-O's dominant theme: ' … You base your own drive on a leadership idea which affects the whole organisation of M-O and seems foreign to its first character'.[25]

It should be pointed out that the demand for active leadership was in some ways a radical position at the time - an attack on the Chamberlain Government apart from anything else - and the book was reviewed as being radical by Orwell.[26] The difference between Madge and Harrisson was not over the need for this leadership but over the balance between home life and politics. Both were happy that the home was freed from any exterior influences other than the war; but, while Madge's position was that this situation was satisfactory in itself, Harrisson was not content with seeing the private sphere merely in tune with the war effort. He wanted to make everything public in his ongoing commitment to the principle of making everything the people thought known, so that leadership became - to use a phrase - a matter of delivery. In a way this was the classic 'People's War' formula that was also subscribed to, amongst others, by Orwell and J.B. Priestley. This was why Harrisson was so keen to, and later that spring actually did, link up with his friend, Mary Adams, the Director of Home Intelligence at the Ministry of Information (MoI). Both Adams and Harrisson intended for their reports on public morale to feed directly into Government policy. They both became intensely frustrated as it became increasingly clear that their research was only being used to determine issues of propaganda formulation and presentation. Harrisson did in the end manage to change policy on air-raid shelters by publishing an article in the *New Statesman* which came to Churchill's attention causing him to bring the matter up in War Cabinet.[27]

Madge's opinion was that the private sphere of the people could not be entirely overridden in the interests of active leadership, even though the latter was something he believed in. But this left him in the position of always having to publish material that undermined his own conclusions - a fact he recognised as keenly as Harrisson. He said much later, that he was at that time frustrated with M-O because 'one couldn't get solid quantitative results from it'.[28] Obviously the attraction of quantitative results is that the problem of inbuilt contradiction is excluded in theory: your conclusions have to coincide with your results in order for you to publish. Madge had briefly started this kind of work in 1939 investigating the economics of Bolton - M-O's 'Worktown' - in terms, for example, of the patterns of spending. At the time, he corresponded with Keynes who displayed a genuine interest in the project.[29] Then in March 1940, with Harrisson close to securing a deal with the MoI, and Madge's own project of the short-lived M-O newsletter, 'Us', rapidly sinking into a financial black hole, he sent a memo to Keynes suggesting a programme of research geared to providing support for Keynes' ideas put forward in the pamphlet, 'How to pay for the War'.[30] They met, Keynes advanced him fifty pounds, and arranged for Madge to conduct his own survey team under the auspices of

25. Madge, memo to Harrisson, 21/01/40, p3.

26. George Orwell, *The Complete Works*, Vol.12, Peter Davison (ed), London, Secker & Warburg, 1998, pp17-8.

27. See 'Crux' [Richard Crossman], 'London Diary', *New Statesman*, 5 February 1971, p176; and Tom Harrisson, 'War Adjustment', *New Statesman and Nation*, 28 September 1940, pp300-1.

28. Madge, Interview with Calder, March 1979, p.18, M-O Correspondence 3/ 'Madge', M-O A.

29. John M. Keynes, *The Collected Writings of John Maynard Keynes (CW)*, Vol.XXI: *Activities 1931-39*, Donald Moggridge (ed), London, Macmillan, 1982, pp519-22.

30. Keynes, *CW*, Vol.XII: *Economic Articles and Correspondence*, 1983, pp810-5.

the National Institute of Economic and Social Research. It must be emphasised that this was, in the first instance, an M-O project - and seen as such by Keynes - using M-O techniques (all Madge's economic studies are rather distinctively characterised by blocks of direct speech from the public amongst the statistical tables). The attachment to the National Institute was originally a means of bypassing funding criteria. With an irony that did not pass unnoticed by Harrisson and Adams, Madge gained his exemption from military service before any of the mass-observers working for the MoI.[31] By the end of the year, he had publicly left M-O and was taking his survey team around the country, while Keynes was having his reports duplicated as they came in and circulating them round the Treasury.[32]

31. Mary Adams, 'M-O Exemption', memo to Mr Charles, 7 August 1940, 1/A, Mary Adams Papers, M-O A.

The big issue at stake was how to fund the war effort, for which the financial orthodoxy of balanced budgets was clearly unsuitable. Churchill was blocking tax increase and Bevin was blocking a wages freeze.[33] In Keynes' view, this left two alternatives for raising the necessary £500 million: a deferred payment scheme where money was docked from wages as compulsory savings, or an extension of income tax down into the industrial working class. There were two key questions: would deferred pay be more psychologically palatable? And would it reduce existing savings more than income tax? Keynes made these points to Madge in a letter of 1 November 1940 and it is clear that he was relying on Madge's research to find the answer. Earlier in the letter he admits: 'There are a good many points on which we are quite in the dark apart from your figures, which I only hope are right!'.[34]

32. Keynes, CW, Vol.XII, pp821-2; Keynes, CW, XXII: Activities 1939-1945: Internal War Finance, 1978, pp215, 254-5, 274-6, 333-7.

33. Calder, The People's War, p238.

34. Keynes, CW, vol.XII, p822.

What Madge showed in Coventry was that increased wages had not become increased savings. What he showed from Blackburn was that the working class of the North West saved proportionately more than their peers in the more affluent Midlands and South. Madge concluded that the propensity to save was related to a culture of saving and he delineated such a North West culture partly from his extensive M-O knowledge of Bolton. The region was the cradle of the Co-operatives, the Friendly Societies, the Holiday Clubs and Mail-Order and featured important differences in family structure: a much higher proportion of married working class women worked; husbands and working children at home gave their earnings to the wife.[35] Hence less was spent on luxuries and more saved against hardship to come. Madge realised that this family structure was under threat. The Government knew from earnings statistics that the average worker was getting something like 30 per cent more in wages than before the war, so taking great care to exclude families where the main wage earner had been called up, they deduced that the remaining average working class family must be much better off. Madge's research showed otherwise: the average family was worse off because of the loss of income from unmarried sons now in the forces.[36]

35. Madge, 'The Propensity to Save in Blackburn and Bristol', The Economic Journal, L, (December 1940), 429, 430, 435, 437, 447.

36. See Madge, 'A Reply to Dr. Singer's Criticisms', The Manchester School, 13, 2, (1944), 85, 87.

In 1941, Madge published his own opinions in *The Economic Journal*.

He argues that it is necessary to take a broad view of working-class aspirations: 'To be specific, I don't think that money is the sole driving force of working class activity [...] Prestige and social status are sought, even at the expense of economic needs'.[37] But by status he does not mean emulation of the middle classes, he means that the working class need to feel accepted as a valid part of society, not regarded as inferior or uneducated. However the budget was to function (and Madge accepted Keynes' argument that working class consumption had to be reduced), this must not push anyone below the poverty line and it must demonstrate that no inequality ('social rather than economic') can be accepted in society. Furthermore, if it was to be deferred-pay, then the bottom two thirds of the working class should be exempt and left to their exemplary voluntary practice.[38] Of course, with the partial exception of income tax credits, it was not deferred pay - partly because Madge's figures, while showing it to be a popular option, also demonstrated that it would reduce existing savings in all those above the poorer working class. The result was an income tax that met the wartime state's financial needs, while redistributing income *within* the industrial working class: towards the North West and the North in general, at the expense of the South and the Midlands.

What this research had forced Madge to take note of were exactly the Area 2 social associations that M-O had always glossed over. Thus, while in some ways the 1941 budget might appear as unjustly punitive towards the working class as a whole, and as the originating moment of the rigid economic class stratification that predominated in the post-war era, it is also clear that Madge's figures made it the moment when northern working-class culture was saved for the best part of the next forty years until it was to meet its eventual nemesis under the Thatcher Government. It might be that Madge, the wartime economics researcher, was a more radical figure than Madge, the 1930s poet, Communist and Mass-Observer. Or more to the point, it might suggest that the 1940s were not so much of a break with the radical pattern of the 1930s, as a continuation by other means. To this end, there can be no doubt that this work resolved his M-O problems of finding a working-class plenitude he admired getting in the way of the conclusions he wanted to make.

This confidence informs Madge's subsequent war work and particularly his editing and writing of the various Pilot Press publications. His 1943 *Industry After the War* projects the case for a planned mixed economy prepared to continually experiment in finding the best proportion of public to private control - although he does not suggest that this would be the final solution.[39] At the same time he selects the industrial regions of Lancashire and the West Riding, the Clyde and the Tyne as areas where the Government must plan and intervene to ensure that depression never returns.[40] The Trade Unions are encouraged to develop from their concentration on wages and conditions in order to promote collective and co-operative forms of production and consumption. As for ordinary people,

37. Madge, 'Public Opinion and Paying for the War', *The Economic Journal*, LI, (April 1941), 37.

38. Ibid., p46.

39. Madge, *Target for Tomorrow* No.1: *Industry After the War: Who is Going to Run It?*, London, The Pilot Press, 1943, pp56-64.

40. Ibid., p60.

41. Ibid., p63.

'their place in the plan has got to be brought home to them'.[41]

While this sounds the same as the former M-O position, it is really that position consciously extended, because Madge can now conceive of the home as not just the site of isolation, but also the basis for social association and different local common cultures: 'The Englishman's home is his castle *and* he likes to be one of a crowd'.[42] When he wrote this sentence, he was trying to come to terms with the paradoxical nature of the Communist backed Squatter's movement of 1946, where people were organising themselves politically and socially in the attempt to get permanent housing, but the type of housing that most of them desired to live in was a prefab, which in practice encouraged very little communal activity even with next door neighbours. Madge was confident that with 'a little encouragement', a natural balance could be restored. This was what he hoped to achieve as Social Development Officer at Stevenage, stating unequivocally, 'New Towns must be planned as carefully and scientifically as, shall we say, the invasion of Normandy'.[43] Madge envisaged a utilisation of space that would overcome the problem of the isolated Area 1 experience of the home being completely passive before Area 3 media; instead he planned a private sphere restored again to a surrounding rebuilt public sphere:

42. Madge, 'Editor's Commentary', *Pilot Papers*, 1, 4, (November 1946), 6.

43. Madge, 'Reflections from Aston Park', *Architectural Review*, 104, (1948), 110.

> My own personal view is that the whole geography of the housing estate needs turning back to front. Instead of the front-doors and the living-room windows opening on to the asphalt street, with a parallel row of houses returning stare for stare, I envisage a living-room looking on to what is now the back-garden. This would no longer be just a cabbage patch and yard for what are called utilities. It should be a private space, pleasant to walk out into, and leading to further spaces of diminishing privacy, opening out on to trees and grass, tennis courts, children's playgrounds and swings and paddling pools, all of which would be part of what we call the garden common.[44]

44. Madge, 'The Social Pattern of a New Town', *Listener*, 17 February 1949, p268.

Of course, the overwhelming majority of post-war housing was not like this and the New Towns, themselves, never fulfilled their promise. The financial constraints of the late 1940s prompted the rejection of social development as an integral part of the process - one of the factors that contributed to Madge losing his job - and also drove rents up to a point beyond many working class incomes.[45] For the rest of the 1950s, Madge turned his attention to development and education issues in south east Asia.

45. See Madge, 'Tour of the New Towns', *New Statesman and Nation*, 8 September 1951, pp246-7.

In retrospect, given the virtual collapse of the post-war state in the 1970s and the resultant rise of the political right, it might be possible to fault Madge for seeking to preserve the working class in aspic without allowing it the opportunity to develop freely a new consciousness and practices which might have led to a different political outcome of that period. Such a view would see the post-war period as having become mired in state planning and bureaucracy, with the left particularly responsible for a misguided policy of social engineering. There are several points for discussion here.

Firstly, Madge was committed to the promotion of the family due to the widely held fears of the time concerning the perceived decline in Britain's birth rate. At the best, this resulted in an uncritical acceptance of traditional gender roles in the family; but a worst case interpretation would see the wholesale promotion of homelife in the immediate post-war period as part of a more deliberately ideological drive to counter the wartime emancipation of women. As we have seen, Madge was clearly trying to combat domestic isolation; but, viewed from a certain historical perspective, and given the ultimate ineffectiveness of his efforts, the general direction of his work appears unwittingly complicit with these reactionary forces. But, at the same time, Madge's efforts were only ineffective because of a curtailment of planning due to financial considerations. If more post-war planning had followed Madge's ideas - and he made efforts to publicise them - then families would not have been so isolated, which would have gone some way to mitigate the ideological consequences of their post-war promotion.

Secondly, in favouring and promoting a distinctive Northern working-class culture in national policy (contemporary critics did attack the universal applicability of his work by suggesting definite bias, as one critic noted of 1942 research in Leeds: 'the figures establish a suspicion that the sample is overloaded with unskilled workers'[46]), Madge rejected the experience of Coventry, the idea of a new culture of affluent workers that forms the basis of Orwell's hopes for the future in *The Lion and the Unicorn*. The consequence of this was post-war class conflict, particularly in planned and expanded housing estates, between the interwar new middle classes and the post-war working-class 'urban overspill'.[47] Whether such cultures could have flourished together is a difficult question. Arguably, an unbounded new middle-class culture eventually emerged to horrifying effect in the 1980s. While economic libertarianism was the driving force behind the wholesale changes to society in that period, other forms of individual, cultural and sexual libertarianism had grown sufficiently powerful by this time to resist the establishment of a wholly conservative society. From this view point, Madge was an active participant in the political and cultural activity, usually associated with the new left, which prevented the ideological closure of a conformist 'English settlement' in the post-war period, and thus created the necessary space for articulate resistance to develop.[48] His work in the 1960s, which I was considering at the beginning, can now be seen as part of a continuous development with his earlier work of the 1930s and 1940s, in which each setback is met with a change of tactics, geared towards the same overarching strategic aim of the transformation of society.

In this light, it is tempting to relate Madge's pre-war abandonment of magic in favour of materialism to Graham Greene's *The End of the Affair*. The point of that novel was that magic and materialism are linked and that if you reject magic you are left with statistics, dull hate and emptiness,

46. Hans Singer, 'How Widespread are National Savings? A Critique of the Madge Inquiry', *The Manchester School*, 13, 2, (1944), 75.

47. See Vicky Lebeau, 'The Worst of all Possible Worlds?', in R. Silverstone (ed), *Visions of Suburbia*, London, Routledge, 1997, p287.

48. See Tom Steele, *The Emergence of Cultural Studies 1945-65: Cultural Politics, Adult Education and the English Question*, London, Lawrence & Wishart, 1997, p69.

49. Graham Greene, *The End of the Affair*, Harmondsworth, Penguin, 1975, see e.g: pp111-2.

50. Madge, *Society in the Mind*, p152.

51. Ibid., pp29, 135, 138-40.

52. Madge and Barbara Weinberger, *Art Students Observed*, London, Faber and Faber, 1973, p209.

which I take to be Greene's evaluation of the post-war state in 1951.[49] It is clear that following the end of his job at Stevenage, and given the way that the New Town project was starting to unravel, Madge was also disillusioned at that time. After the austerity programmes, arms expenditure and onset of the cold war, the idea of a new society was becoming an illusion. However, Madge's eventual call for an un-social eidos in *Society in the Mind* was not simply the product of a Greene-like pessimism and despair. The point of the aesthetic utopia, as proposed by him in 1964, is that 'Art is in touch with a sphere of mental reality in which illusions are true'.[50]

He could state this because he had rediscovered the link between magic and materialism; and sited it as existing in the first (prehistorical) stage of social eidos - linked to Marx's early concepts of species-being and alienation - where the primitive was also a poet.[51] From this position, we can rewrite Madge's pre-war argument: while ritual, performance and illusion are components of magic that remain sources of reaction when judged in themselves, the endpoint of magic is material. That is to say precisely, a thing that cannot be rendered subject to the power of words and the discourse of language; and which can only be poetically experienced. In stage magic, the end-point is termed the prestige (e.g. the rabbit which appears from out of the hat). Madge, in the same way as he had wanted to take poetry beyond performance, wanted the working class to gain prestige. In the early 1960s, it was still possible to be optimistic about confronting instrumental rationality with a developing aesthetic impulse, within the parameters of post-war planning.

In the event, Madge dispassionately and empirically documented what turned out to be the failure of the national attempt to redirect social eidos towards an aesthetic teleology in *Art Students Observed*. Even as he wrote the study up, many of the country's art colleges were being merged into polytechnics. The key element of this work is his discussion of the 'Art and Language' debate: 'a militant expression of the need to discuss, to defend, to validate and, above all, to *define* activities - those of the artist - which do not fit readily into the frame of reference of modern industrial societies'.[52] This was the defining moment of the 1960s, when Madge's un-social eidos had the opportunity to establish itself - to gain prestige - within a society that could only conceive of it as anti-social; but, the very nature of this effort, its reliance on verbalisation and language, pushed it into the realm of linguistic analysis. Once art is conceived of as an analytic proposition, a tautology, as nothing more than a self-definition, then it can only ever function ritually or performatively.

The extent of Madge's disillusion at the collapse of the post-war project in the 1970s suggests that his aims had been higher than merely creating spaces for resistance and that he had maintained a belief in the planned transformation of society, including - as an integral component - the poetic and aesthetic development of the individual, for more than forty years. In this sense, the post 1973 present we now inhabit is no more magical or material than the post-war state which preceded it, and the inter-war past which preceded that: a series of different illusions maintained by different suspensions of disbelief. Even as the persistence of poetry - the promise of the future in search of its own political becoming - maintains its challenge to this state of affairs, so, despite all else, does the persistence of home:

> I like my prefab. Very much, in spite of minor defects in the design. No one can tell me who designed it - but I should very much like to know (for it is relevant to the issues discussed in this essay) whether the shape of the pretty little aluminium chimney stack was dictated entirely by practical considerations. For me it has real magic - especially when it glitters in the level rays of a westering sun, with an aluminium-coloured moon appearing overhead.[53]

53. Madge, 'Reflections from Aston Park', op. cit., p110.

Mass-Observation, Surrealism, Social Anthropology: A Present-Day Assessment

Jeremy MacClancy

Today, Mass-Observation (M-O) is unjustly remembered in mainly negative terms by the majority of social anthropologists in Britain. In this paper I wish to examine the reasons for these disparaging attitudes and to re-assess M-O, especially in its most experimental, innovative early period, in terms of a more modern, and seemingly more open-minded social anthropology. I will start with the assessments made by two key, contemporary anthropologists on the organisation and its first major work, *May the Twelfth*, a compilation of mass-observations made on the day of the coronation of George VI.

The general reaction of the educated classes to the new organisation was widespread, and mixed. Contributors to a variety of newspapers and magazines regarded its work positively, as a potentially informative approach to further understanding of British life. Several commentators, however, seeking easy copy for light-hearted articles, portrayed M-O as a new sort of entertainment, or parlour game; after all, as Madge and Harrisson had declared, it was something *anyone* could do. Some were less amused, and viewed the movement with alarm, as an infringement on their right to privacy. These critics vilified observers as snoopers, nosey parkers, peeping toms, or worse. In the thundering words of one Labour MP, 'If I catch anyone Mass-Observing me, there's going to be trouble'.

One correspondent thought M-O was generally regarded as 'a silly stunt', another said it seemed 'unbeatable as a sport' while a third found 'it hard to imagine anything dottier'.[1] Evelyn Waugh approved of its founders' 'agreeable touch of levity' and delighted in the 'funny footnotes' of their books.[2] Auden branded them spies and MacNeice summarily dismissed Mass-Observers as 'Madge's lab boys'.[3] Cecil Day Lewis, writing under his detective writer pseudonym Nicholas Blake, lampooned them in *Malice in Wonderland* (1940) and Graham Greene also brought them into the plot of *The Confidential Agent* (1939).

More considered commentators worried about the vaunted 'scientific' basis of M-O's work, the representativeness of its observers, and the supposed 'objectivity' of their observations.[4] The reviewers of *May the Twelfth* for the *Times Literary Supplement* (2 October 1937) and for the *Spectator* (19 November 1937) both thought that the patently left-wing leanings of many observers had led them to revel in reporting the seamier side of the crowds' behaviour. Not *everyone* was drunk, the reviewers claimed. As well as having to suffer these intellectual criticisms, Harrisson was personally crabbed for

1. David Garnett, 'Books in General', *New Statesman and Nation*, 3 July 1937, p17; G.W. Stonier, 'A Thousand Mass-Observers', *New Statesman and Nation*, 9 October 1937, pp532-4; Anthony West, Review of *Anthropology* by A. Goldenweiser, *New Statesman and Nation*, 14 August 1937, p258.

2. Evelyn Waugh, 'The Habits of the English', *Spectator*, 15 April 1938, p663-4.

3. Louis MacNeice, *I crossed the Minch*, London, Faber and Faber, 1939.

4. Geoffrey Gorer, 'Notes on the Way', *Time and Tide*, 24 July 1937, pp1003-5; E.C. Large, 'The Coronation Mass-Observed', *The New English Weekly*, 30 December 1937, pp231-2; T.H. Marshall, 'Is Mass-observation moonshine?', *The Highway*, December 1937, pp48-50.

his 'petulant self-advertisement' and 'unsupported generalisations', Madge for his 'vague eclecticism' and 'chaotic intelligence', and both of them for their condescending air of middle-class intellectuals indulging in a bit of slumming.[5] The publicity-seeking Harrisson was partly to blame for these adverse reactions since he was, for instance, prepared to pose for an article on M-O dressed as a private detective peering through a keyhole.[6]

The response of academic anthropologists was more considered. Bronislaw Malinowski, Professor of Anthropology at the London School of Economics and one of the distinguished intellectuals on M-O's Advisory Panel, gave a qualified welcome to the new organisation. As someone who had repeatedly spoken of the need for, and the political value of, anthropology at home, he was ready to hail the creation of a body such as M-O. For by informing citizens about the nature of their own society, it held the promise of countering the increasing threat of totalitarianism, which seemed to thrive on ignorance. In a long essay which concludes *First Year's Work*, he commended Madge and Harrisson for their initiative, enthusiasm, and accomplishment, and he argued against those academics who were prejudicially opposed to M-O precisely because of the popular sensationalism it had generated. To Malinowski, it was wiser and more profitable to co-operate than to ridicule, for if it were allowed to peter out, it would have to be restarted, 'most likely under less favourable conditions and with a less competent personnel'.[7]

But Malinowski was not happy with much of M-O's methodology. He thought if Madge and Harrisson's approach was to become a useful instrument of social scientific research, they needed to be much more theoretically informed - in a conventional anthropological manner - and much more rigorous. There was little point in telling observers, for instance, to collect conversations taking place in Bolton's public lavatories at precisely 5.30 pm unless the choice of hour could be justified within a broader frame.[8] For the same sorts of reasons, Madge and Harrisson also needed to be more selective. The varieties of response that they had shown occurred during a Coronation or the Two Minutes Silence on Armistice Day were valuable and informative, but sociologists could not be concerned with the almost infinite diversity of feelings at such moments. They could only be interested in those ideas or passions that were felt by sufficiently large groups of people to be symptoms of a tendency towards collective expression.[9] Sociologists and anthropologists were, after all, *social* scientists, not individual psychologists.

Commenting on M-O's more mathematical work, Malinowski felt that once its leaders had worked out a sound theoretical argument for their studies, then the further paraphernalia of scientific work that they occasionally employed - figures and graphs, statistics and charts - could be sited in their appropriate intellectual place. Until that time, this sort of analysis was but a 'pseudo-scientific rig-out' masking lack of forethought.[10]

Malinowski also argued that the potential contribution of M-O to our

5. Gorer, 'Letter', *Time and Tide*, 14 August 1937, p1092-3; Christopher Hobhouse, 'Review of *May the Twelfth*', *Spectator*, 19 November 1937, pp18-20; George Dudman and Patrick Terry, *Challenge to Tom Harrisson*, Oxford, privately printed, 1938; Julian Symons, 'The Case of Mr Madge', *Kingdom Come*, II, 3 (Spring 1941), 73-4.

6. 'Public Busybody No.1', *Daily Mirror*, 6 December 1938.

7. Bronislaw Malinowski, 'A nation-wide intelligence service' in C. Madge and T. Harrisson (eds), *First Year's Work*, London, Lindsay Drummond, 1938, p85.

8. Julian Trevelyan, *Indigo Days*, London, MacGibbon and Kee, 1957, p84.

9. Malinowski, op. cit., p118.

10. Ibid., p89.

knowledge of social processes would only be fully realised when it linked up its particular methods with the results of the already established social sciences. For instance economists, who usually relied on statistically collected data, needed some kind of mass-observation in order to assess the human and social side of production, consumption, and marketing. *Homo economicus* was an academic fiction, which could only be fleshed out by employing the findings of hundreds of observers' reports. Thus in Malinowski's opinion, if the leaders of M-O heeded his suggestions, their organisation would move 'inevitably towards the fully scientific position', as a professionally recognised body working hand-in-hand with its academic brethren.[11]

11. Ibid., pp116-7.

The response of Raymond Firth was far less optimistic. While he acknowledged that M-O was tackling an important series of problems, he questioned its claims to be ethnographically original. M-O could not claim to be pioneers in the use of direct observational techniques because there had been a series of such studies of British working-class life over the previous seventy years. Some of them, moreover, had included long accounts of overheard conversations, reported verbatim, and of memory records dictated by an informant. In this sense all that was distinctive about M-O was the richness of its records and the wide range of its observers.[12] Firth, however, did note that M-O, to its credit, documented institutions and types of behaviour till then uninvestigated (such as extra-family kinship, religion, and politics) and, by enabling comparison between its material and that of the earlier surveys, enabled the making of generalisations about the degree of social change.[13]

12. Raymond Firth, 'An anthropologist's view of Mass-Observation', *Sociological Review*, XXXI, 2 (April 1939), pp170-6.

13. Ibid., p176.

Firth also criticised M-O for failing to integrate the great mass of facts that it presented and for not linking them up with the problems that it stated to be the particular subject of its investigation. For instance, the text of *May the Twelfth*, which was meant to describe Coronation activities, was constantly interrupted with comments on the weather, accounts of people's babies, and arguments about female cyclists. These 'disconnected items' could have been the 'raw material' for other problems, but since their implications were not worked out they were so much lumber weighing down the book.[14]

14. Ibid., p178.

In answer to those journalists who had queried the status of Mass-Observers, Malinowski said that they had to be viewed in the same way as fieldworkers regarded their 'informants': in other words, as members of the studied community, who comment on happenings and take part in them, who supply ethnographers with relevant information and are able to analyse the motives and feelings which account for their fellows' behaviour.[15] Firth might have accepted this formulation but he found it very difficult to discern in the published examples of observers' reports exactly when they were acting as informants on themselves, and when as informants about others.[16] He thought that this duplication of roles would not have caused confusion, if the editors had got full-time observers to corroborate independently the summary statements of their part-time

15. Malinowski, op. cit., p118.

16. Firth, op. cit., p182.

colleagues. But they had not and thus it was occasionally difficult to assess the basis on which the editors made their own generalisations.

Summing M-O up, Firth said he could not share with its leaders their faith in the validity of their methods or results so far. He thought they claimed too much, tried to do too much, and did not give themselves enough time to do even part of that in sufficient thoroughness.[17] He concluded on a note of dismissive condescension: ' ... even though the movement may not consider that it requires to set its house in order, and may make no contribution that will revolutionise modern social science, it has still a value in providing a recreative outlet for its thousand or so Observers, and enabling them to learn something about the behaviour of others than themselves'.[18]

Madge left the organisation in 1940, partly because of a deepening rift between him and Harrisson over the way it should develop. After some years in various kinds of research work, he became in 1950 the first Professor of Sociology at Birmingham University. Harrisson himself joined the war effort and afterwards was appointed director of the national museum of Brunei. In their absence, M-O struggled on for a few more years but eventually evolved into a limited company for market research. Despite its brief life, M-O had a number of significant effects, including the acquainting of a broad swathe of the British public with the aims and methods of anthropology. Yet its innovatory work has neither been mentioned nor discussed in any historical studies of twentieth-century anthropology. The question is, why this neglect?

One part of the answer would be the independent-minded attitudes of Madge and Harrisson. When in 1978 Madge was asked about his reactions and those of Harrisson to the comments made about M-O, he replied, 'Contemporary academic criticism? It didn't bother us'.[19] Since Madge and Harrisson had set their own, extra-mural aims, and were not out to please the professors but to inform the British people about their own behaviour, they could afford to disregard many of the comments made by those they regarded as cloistered anthropologists. For instance, what Firth viewed as needless detail (such as arguments about female cyclists on Coronation Day), they could see as informative sidelights on people's interests and attitudes. As Harrisson argued, it was precisely this kind of detail, the seeming trivia of the present day, which could well be significant tomorrow. Up until now, 'History' had been 'crippled by the absence of information as to what was happening that was not climax, new, "historical"'.[20] M-O aimed to rectify that omission.

Malinowski and Firth both thought *May the Twelfth* an unbalanced account, since Madge and Jennings had paid no attention to the internal structure and symbolism of the central ceremony within Westminster Abbey, to the historical evolution of the royal ritual, or to the way it had been stage-managed by the various organising bodies.[21] But since these topics were within the traditional ken of established anthropology, M-O's free

17. Ibid., pp191-2.

18. Ibid., p193.

19. Charles Madge, Interview by Nicholas Stanley, 1978, transcript in Mass-Observation Archive, University of Sussex.

20. Tom Harrisson, 'Mass-Observation and the Workers' Educational Association', *The Highway*, December 1937, pp46-8.

21. Malinowski, op. cit., pp111-5; Firth, op. cit., p179.

spirits could leave the study of them to more hidebound ethnographers, prepared to toe the disciplinary line.

Firth argued that Madge and Jennings's 'non-selective attitude' meant that, in *May the Twelfth*, 'far from the facts speaking for themselves they speak for the state of mind of those who published them in this form'.[22] However, its editors had provided several ways of reading the book by supplying a highly imaginative variety of indexes. Thus they had not intended that the 'facts' presented be given a definitive sense of unity by the format they had selected. In this sense, the book is deliberately unfinished; its contents could only be unified, and thus made to 'speak', by the work of the reader, who was able to choose how to tread his or her own way through the text.

On the question of the status of their reports, Madge and Harrisson argued that it was a pervasive problem in any kind of observational activity, since even laboratory-bound scientists found it impossible to rule out their own subjective biases.[23] The best way for M-O to accommodate their work to this problem was for observers to provide as much information about themselves as possible and for the observers to have this information corroborated by others. In this way, the subjectivity of an observer could be transformed into objective fact. It was not ignored but turned into a component of the analysis. As Harrisson later came to claim, the distinctiveness of Mass-Observation lay in this qualitative dimension of its work; other studies of British life, which tended to rely on statistics, neglected 'why' for the sake of 'what'. Harrisson and Madge's decision to use a mass of observers also enabled them to claim that they could crosscheck results and, bearing in mind the biases of different observers, could assess critically conflicting reports. As they delighted in pointing out, conventional anthropology could not boast of such advantages: ethnographers went into the field alone, their observations were not checked by others, and no account was taken of their personal biases.

If the leaders of Mass-Observation could pretend to ignore the advice of Malinowski and Firth, they were privately forced to admit the power of some of their arguments. As one member of the original Blackheath group later confessed, though M-O presented interesting possibilities, in practice it posed many problems. The sheaves they were sent by observers proliferated 'like maggots in a cheese';[24] by the end of their first year they had received over 1,700 reports, containing more than 2,300,000 words. As a perceptive journalist noted, this ever-increasing mass of material represented 'infinite regress ... If we could read all the papers and all the books, we could know what we are all thinking. But there never will be time'.[25] In Bolton, Harrisson was stockpiling more information than he knew what to do with; he had promised his publisher the speedy production of three manuscripts dealing with religion, politics and pubs; but unsure how to arrange his material, he constantly had to delay their submission. Madge later admitted that 'the trouble with [the studies on] religion and

22. Firth, op. cit., p178.

23. Madge and Harrisson, *Mass-Observation*, London, Frederick Muller, 1937, pp31-2.

24. Unsigned review, *Listener*, 17 November 1937.

25. *Reynolds News*, 1 May 1938, quoted in Angus Calder, 'Mass-Observation 1937-1949', in M. Bulmer (ed), *Essays on the History of British Sociological Research*, Cambridge, Cambridge University Press, 1985, p129.

politics was that there was too much material. It was very difficult to digest'.[26]

As far as I can judge, Firth's general attitude - if not his tone of condescension - was shared by most of his peers. They were interested in the venture, approved its aims, and appreciated the ingenuity of some of its fieldwork methods. But, unlike Malinowski who was prepared to promote the popularisation of the discipline, they maintained grave doubts about the status of Mass-Observers' reports, and about M-O's 'impressionist' approach to ethnography. Also, while the history of British anthropology demonstrates that the possession of a difficult personality is no necessary bar to success within the discipline, it has to be stated that Harrisson's character endeared neither him, nor the ideas of M-O, to academic anthropologists. Many found him a prickly character to deal with (Firth thought him 'stimulating but a bit of a brigand'[27]) and were irritated by his constant jibes at social scientists for their lethargy and supposed lack of awareness of vital problems. Harrisson, impatient and impetuous, did not like to debate in a dispassionate, painstaking manner, and could simply brush aside others' criticisms when it suited him. He tended to think it more important to state his opinion and to get on with the job *now* than to spend time arguing at length over philosophical points about M-O's methods. He said he wanted 'to cut the cackle and go ahead in an attempt to establish a sensible, normal socio-psycho - whatever else you like oh - anthropology of ourselves'.[28] Priding himself on this no-nonsense approach, he would declaim, 'Fieldwork, not fine words, I say'.[29] A response not likely to go down well with those regarding themselves as responsible professionals trying to uphold the name of the discipline. To them, Harrisson was an unschooled novice more concerned with putting his own name forward, and they judged his best-selling account of Malekula in the New Hebrides (now Vanuatu), *Savage Civilization*, a superior kind of travelogue posing as historical anthropology.[30]

Firth remembers that Malinowski, whose seminars Madge and Harrisson attended for a brief period, told them that if they wanted to do their work properly, they needed to drill themselves in social anthropology and to keep coming to the seminar.[31] Madge claimed he was willing, but was too taken up with the day-to-day running of the National Panel while Harrisson, ever the rebel, refused to submit to discipline. Madge remembers that Harrisson and Malinowski angered one another greatly and that each described the other as a 'crook'.[32] One might consider this clash to be that of, at one level, all-too similar personalities: both were excellent self-promoters, with Harrisson most likely the more effective of the two at that particular skill. For instance, Malinowski liked to boast of the need to do fieldwork, to 'live with the natives'; to Malinowski's anger, Harrisson proclaimed that this should include loving them.

The poet Gavin Ewart remembered the point when he appealed to Madge to 'Cage Me a Harrisson':

26. Madge, Interview, op. cit.

27. Personal communication with the author.

28. Harrisson, op. cit., p46.

29. Harrisson, 'Geoffrey Gorer and Mass-Observation', *Time and Tide*, XVIII, 36, 4 (September 1937), 1167.

30. On doubts about the veracity of some of Harrisson's Vanuatu material, see E.H. Corlette, 'Tom Harrisson's Exploits in the New Hebrides Sharply Challenged by Malekula Resident', *Pacific Islands Monthly*, 21 June 1937, pp17-8 and 'The Claims of T.H. Harrisson. New Hebrides Planter Returns To The Attack', *Pacific Islands Monthly*, 21 February 1938, pp37-8. I thank Judith Heiman for these references. While I was doing fieldwork in Vanuatu in the late 1970s, Nakomaha, the old man with whose family I lived in Sulfa Bay, Tanna, and who had been a Native Policeman in the 1930s, told me that Harrisson, under whom he had worked during the brief period Harrisson was an Acting British District Agent, was a 'wild man' with long hair and a straggly beard.

31. Personal communication with the author.

32. Madge, Interview, op. cit.

O you must learn through loss of love or money:
Harrisson's only useful when he's *funny*.
It's hard to find oneself in the same boat
With people who consistently misquote—
And think of Science with a capital S,
How Harrisson occasions their distress
By baiting poets with his subtle gibes
And 'loving the women' of those savage tribes.
O Madge, my Madge, if you have the power to feel
The supplication of my poor appeal,
Think, you and Science have a world to win,
But Harrisson is the Dog Beneath the Skin—
O put the kennel up and forge the chain,
Let Mass-Observation be itself again![33]

33. Gavin Ewart, 'Cage Me a Harrisson', *Twentieth-Century Verse*, 11 (July 1938), 65-6.

34. Jeremy MacClancy, 'Unconventional Character and Disciplinary Convention. John Layard, Jungian and Anthropologist', in G.W.Stocking (ed), *Malinowski, Rivers, Benedict and Others. Essays in Culture and Personality*, History of Anthropology 4, Wisconsin, University of Wisconsin Press, 1986, pp50-71.

If the 1930s can be seen as a period when British social anthropologists tried to legitimate the academic status of their subject by establishing a common set of disciplinary conventions,[34] it is perhaps understandable that they were reluctant to include Madge, Harrisson, and their outfit within their number. For the broader consequences of M-O were implicitly subversive of university-based anthropologists' attempts to establish the professional nature of their endeavours. The style of intrepid, individualistic fieldwork being established by Malinowski in the 1930s was clearly at odds with M-O's emphasis on research as an essentially collective endeavour. None of M-O's books was presented as having been written by a single person and the majority was simply attributed to M-O collectively. No single full-time Mass-Observer was able to claim exclusive knowledge of a particular society. For part-time contributors, moreover, obeying a Directive or filling in a monthly diary was hardly intrepid.

Furthermore, the democratising endeavours of the organisation menaced the privileged intellectual status of academic anthropologists. By urging people to become their own ethnographers both for their own sake and for that of others, Madge and Harrisson were enabling them to invade (and so partly to redefine) the intellectual territory academic anthropologists were wishing to demarcate as their very own. It is not important here that the types of societies studied by academics and Observers were apparently so different. At that time anthropology might still have been largely defined by its subject matter ('the primitive'), but for the bourgeois intellectuals who ran M-O and for those members of the middle class who read their reports, the lives of the working class, especially the northern working classes who lived in industrialised towns such as Bolton, were just as exotic and as unknown as the Trobriand Islanders. The important consequence of encouraging people to analyse their own social lives was that if, as Madge and Harrisson came close to claiming, anyone could be an anthropologist, what exactly then was so special about the funded work done by academics?

And, just as importantly, if almost anyone could be an anthropologist, why then should people accept academics' particular definition of the subject?

A further reason for the subsequent neglect of the work of M-O was that, quite simply, the organisation lacked an institutional base within academic anthropology, and its founders (like their anthropological contemporaries, Hocart, Layard, and Bateson) left no heirs or successors in a position to install their ancestors in a teaching canon. Their work was effectively forgotten and, to later generations of anthropologists, virtually unknown.[35]

FROM M-O TO POMO

When Jennings left Mass-Observation, the surrealist promise of its original manifesto remained unfulfilled. Examining exactly why this occurred may illuminate the current debate, initiated by postmodernists and continued by them and others on the relations between ethnography and surrealism. Firstly, Jennings and Madge had found it all but impossible to reconstitute the 'collective image'.[36] The root of this problem, particularly important given the central role of the concept in their interpretation of surrealism, lay in their shift of surrealist focus from the individual to the social. For André Breton, the *objet trouvé* had significance primarily for the individual who came upon it, and whose previously felt inner desires it concretised. If others thought the object interesting, that was valuable but not essential; the chanced-upon item had surrealist worth, above all, *because* of the meaning it embodied for its discoverer. But Jennings and Madge, by shifting attention to the social dimension of an object, had created for themselves the problem of identification. In other words, who was 'discovering' what? For, other than their concept of nation-wide 'coincidences', they had no satisfactory criteria for identifying exactly which images had collective significance. And since they claimed to be empiricist they could not rely on their own general knowledge of British culture, otherwise they would lay themselves open to the criticism of being members of a particular social group (bourgeois intellectuals) whose choices were guided by their sub-cultural upbringing. The problem is manifest in Jennings' poems and his wartime documentaries. In these productions, he repeatedly uses, among other images, that of St Paul's Cathedral. For him it was not just that the building signified the heights of British architecture but that its dome brought to mind the forehead of great British thinkers such as Darwin. But how many blitzed Londoners would have been aware of, or even if aware agreed with, this highly intellectual association?

Secondly, Jennings and Madge's notion of a public 'coincidence' - such as Coronation Day - might at first seem specifically surrealist but, shorn of its Breton-based terminology, the idea that a key ritual highlighted the central concerns of its performers was by then already a commonplace among anthropologists. Thirdly, their application of Freudian theory to

35. The only clear exception to this generalisation is David Pocock, Professor of Anthropology and the founding Director of the Mass-Observation Archive at the University of Sussex. The influence of the ideas of the organisation might be discerned in his notion of a 'personal anthropology'. See Pocock, *Understanding Social Anthropology*, Teach Yourself Books, London, Hodder and Stoughton, 1975. See also Dorothy Sheridan, Brian Street and David Bloome, *Writing Ourselves: Mass-Observation and Literacy Practices*, Cresskill, New Jersey, Hampton, 2001, pp95-102.

36. Paul C. Ray, *The Surrealist Movement in England*, Ithaca, Cornell University Press, 1971, p178.

37. See George W. Stocking, 'Anthropology and the Science of the Irrational: Malinowski's Encounter with Freudian Psycho-analysis' in Stocking (ed), *Malinowski, Rivers, Benedict and Others. Essays in Culture and Personality*, History of Anthropology 4, Wisconsin, University of Wisconsin Press, 1986, pp13-49.

38. Dai Vaughan, *Portrait of an Invisible Man. The working life of Stewart McAllister, film editor*, London, British Film Institute, 1983, p68.

39. Cecil Beaton, 'Libyan Diary', *Horizon*, VII, No.37, January 1943, pp38-9.

40. See Jean Jamin, 'L'ethnographie mode d'inemploi', in J. Hainard and R. Kaehr (eds), *Le Mal et la Douleur*, Neuchatel, Musee d'ethnographie, 1986, pp45-79 and 'Anxious Science: Ethnography as a Devil's Dictionary', *Visual Anthropology Review*, 7 (1991), 84-91.

ethnography was not particularly innovative for it, or something very similar, had already been attempted, though not very successfully, by Malinowski and several of his colleagues.[37]

Given these difficulties, it seems that the ultimate importance of surrealism for M-O lay not so much in its general philosophy as in the ethnographic direction in which it led its Blackheath founders. They may have been unable to employ successfully their notion of the collective image but their desire to discern 'the unconscious fears and wishes of the mass' and to draw out its poetic dimension in a scientific manner did lead to that unjustly neglected text *May the Twelfth*. What is so disappointing is that, after the departure of Jennings, Harrisson ensured that the format and aims of that book were not replicated in the later works of M-O. The promise of an ethnographic surreality was given up for the sake of a more mundane reality.

In Britain, generally, the practice of surrealism, made redundant by the effects of the war, steadily declined. For in a bombed hospital, it was far from inconceivable that Lautreamont's famous definition of beauty - 'the chance encounter on a dissecting table of a sewing machine and an umbrella' - might come to be realized.[38] As Cecil Beaton stated, on surveying a Libyan battlefield littered with hundreds of half-buried, half-folded shirts (the remains of a clothing store) and the carcasses of burnt-out tanks, 'The surrealists have anticipated this battle-ground'.[39]

In the Paris of the 1920s, surrealists and ethnologists were, by turns, mistrustful of and attracted towards each others' work. A constructive dialogue rarely occurred between them. They were, above all, but co-participants within the avant-garde of their time. Both may have wished to examine 'the primitive' and to reassess our notions of humankind, but their relationship was in fact less one of mutual influence than of contiguity. Though they moved across a similar terrain, each plotted it according to their own fashion. Surrealists saw their work as a poetics, and ethnologists saw theirs as a science.[40] The evidence of this essay draws out the provisional nature of these self-definitions. For in the London of the late 1930s, surrealists were able to conceive of their endeavours as scientific (however vaguely they defined, and however rhetorically they deployed, that term) while at the same time exposing the irreducible degree of artistry involved in writing ethnography. Unlike, for example, André Breton and Marcel Mauss who thought they were working to different ends, Madge and Malinowski were able to imagine that they were both, at least theoretically, interested in a common goal: the ethnography of their own people.

Today, literary postmodernists like to proclaim the novelty and necessity of their programme: for example, the creation of a plural text, the questioning of ethnographic authority, the recognition of the need for reflexivity, the realisation of the subversive potential of anthropology, the irreducibly literary nature of ethnography, the study of Western industrialised societies, and the recognition of the essentially contested nature of the codes and representations which compose culture.[41] According to this interpretation, the boundary between art and science is blurred, ethnography is an interdisciplinary phenomenon, and the production of ethnographic texts a problematic enterprise.

What is so surprising about the work of these literary postmodernists is that, given their concern with the historicisation of ethnographic production, they have paid so little attention to their intellectual predecessors.[42] For, as the evidence of this paper demonstrates, though their charter for action might be radical, it is not new, but merely replicates many of the original aims and insights of M-O. What is new is the change in the anthropological climate and its institutional structure, from a tightly defined scholastic community predominantly concerned with achieving a methodological consensus to a much more heterogeneous discipline relatively open to experiment. Thus the question to close on must be, if M-O had been created only ten years ago would its ideas and approach still have been neglected so badly?

Sections of this essay come from my article on Mass-Observation and anthropology in Journal of the Royal Anthropological Institute (n.s.) 1, 3 *(September 1995), and reappear here with permission.*

41. For example, James Clifford, 'Introduction: Partial Truths', in J. Clifford and G.E. Marcus (eds), *Writing Culture: The Poetics and Politics of Ethnography*, Berkeley, University of California Press, 1986, pp1-26; George Marcus and Michael Fischer, *Anthropology as Cultural Critique: An Experimental Moment in the Human Sciences*, Chicago, University of Chicago Press, 1986.

42. The only reference that I am aware of by literary postmodernists to the work of Mass-Observation is part of a footnote in an article by Clifford, 'On Ethnographic Surrealism', *Comparative Studies in Society and History*, 23 (1981), 539-64, n14.

GIVING VOICE TO THE ORDINARY: MASS-OBSERVATION AND THE DOCUMENTARY FILM

Elizabeth Cowie

The project of giving voice to the ordinary has been associated with the work of Mass-Observation in the 1930s and, in relation to film, with Humphrey Jennings who co-founded Mass-Observation with Charles Madge and Tom Harrisson. Madge used the phrase 'They speak for themselves' in an article in 1937;[1] but the voices of Mass-Observation are writings - often in the form of diaries. In this paper I will be examining some ways in which the 1930s documentary film was engaged in voicing the ordinary in sounds and images and its relation to the work of Mass-Observation. In particular, I will be considering the role of Ruby Grierson in her collaborations with Edgar Anstey and Arthur Elton on *Housing Problems*, and with John Taylor and Ralph Bond on *Today and Tomorrow* (1937) and *Today We Live* (1937). Ruby Grierson became involved in documentary film through her older brother, John Grierson, the founder of the British documentary film movement, but she worked primarily for Realist and Strand, which were independent associations of film-makers.[2] Rachel Lowe, in her 1979 book *Documentary and Education Films of the 1930's*, writes of Ruby Grierson's 'unusual gift for capturing the natural behaviour of ordinary people'.[3] I want to consider our desire for and pleasure in the 'ordinary' which Rachel Lowe refers to, and to explore the problem of verisimilitude which arises in seeing and hearing the ordinary, that is, ways in which we recognise the 'ordinary' as properly 'real'. A number of interrelated issues arise here, namely, what is being sought in the voicing of the ordinary, and, in so far as this is a desire for testimony as the truth of experience of the 'ordinary' person, the issue of our access to the 'real' of people's lives. The question also arises of, as a corollary, the representability of this 'ordinary' through recorded language, sounds and images, for this voicing is always a discursive construct. This is most immediately evident in terms of film as an audio-visual process involving recording as such and its selectivity, as well as the selections and choices in editing, and the contextualisations provided by, amongst other things, voice-overs and titles. There is in addition and importantly the moment of the historical conjuncture of the speech and its recording, and the discursive construction of the moments of its hearing, its reception, both in terms of different audiences (social, national, racial, gendered, generational) and in terms of different historical times of audiences - the 1930s, the 1970s, or the twenty-first

1. Charles Madge, *Life and Letters Today*, 9 (1937).

2. Biographical information about Ruby Grierson is limited. She died in 1940 at the age of 36, lost at sea when the SS City of Benares was torpedoed and sunk en route to Canada. It is difficult to be certain of her contribution, but the works she was involved in all share certain characteristics, which I want to identify as a strand in 1930s documentary which attempted to include the voice of ordinary people as well as the images and stories of the everyday. Here, then, I am proposing what may be called a revisionist view of the role of documentary film.

3. Rachel Lowe, *The History of the British Film 1928-1939: Documentary and Education Films of the 1930's*, London, Allen & Unwin, 1979.

century. What notions of real and unreal, of verisimilitude and the non-verisimilitudinous, arise for audiences as a result?

RECORDING REALITY AND THE DOCUMENTARY PROJECT

Modernity and its industrial processes of production have transformed the conditions of both work and the look, expanding enormously the scope and scale of productivity through labour as well as the imaging of the world through photography, cinematography, television and now digital video. At the turn of the nineteenth and twentieth centuries the mechanical ears and eyes of the gramophone and cinema's cameras evoked a fantasy of an all-perceiving and all-hearing subject-spectator for whom sight and sound were equivalent to knowledge. It was a desire realised with the electrical recording apparatus of radio and sound films, yet these modern technologies became the proponents of an audio-visual realism that was ever less real.[4] In Brecht's famous words 'As a result, the situation is becoming so complex that less than ever does a simple reproduction of reality tell us anything about reality. A photograph of Krupps or the AEG yields hardly anything about those industries. True reality has taken refuge in the functional'.[5] Film, as simple record of reality, does not of itself produce a knowledge, that is, an understanding, of reality. Hans Richter has summed up the dilemma of film and realist representation for film-makers in the 1930s:

> If the forces that determine men's destinies today have become anonymous, so too has their appearance. Hence today we are obliged to look behind the façade - if facts are to be revealed.

> The cinema is perfectly capable in principle of revealing the *functional* meaning of things and events, for it has *time* at its disposal, it can contract it and thus show the development, the evolution of things. It does not need to take a picture of a 'beautiful' tree, it can also show us a growing one, a falling one, or one swaying in the wind - nature not just as a view, but also as an element, the village not as an idyll, but as a social entity.[6]

What is raised by both Brecht and Richter is the issue of the phenomenal appearance of reality versus the forces - of ownership of property and the means of production - which structure that reality. The documentary film emerged in the work of film-makers in Europe and North America in the 1920s as an aesthetic project of recorded reality represented; not the art of the everyday, but the art constituted by the everyday re-presented by the seeing anew which film made possible. The documentary film was an extraction from and an organisation of reality - in fact, a fabrication, but a fabrication which thereby brought forward a new reality.[7] These films therefore constitute not only a record of reality

4. The history of cinema has been characterised by on the one hand the magician-film-maker Méliès, and on the other hand the scientist-inventors, the Lumière brothers. See John Grierson, the founder of the British documentary film movement, who describes two different possible cinemas, Forsyth Hardy (ed), *Grierson on Documentary*, London, Faber & Faber, 1966, pp69-70.

5. Bertolt Brecht, 'Der Dreigroschenprozess, ein soziologisches Experiment', in *Gesammelte Werke in 20 Bänden*, Band 18, Frankfurt-am-Main, Suhrkamp Verlag, 1967, p161. Quoted by Hans Richter in, *The Struggle for the Film*, B. Brewster (trans), Aldershot, Scolar Press, [1976] 1986, p47.

6. Richter, op. cit.

7. John Grierson first used the term 'document' to describe a film in his review of Flaherty's *Moana* in 1926. On the history of documentary film, see Brian Winston, *Claiming the Real: the documentary revisited*, London, British Film Institute, 1995; and Richard M. Barsam, *Non-Fiction Film, a Critical History*, Bloomington, Indiana University Press, 1992.

but also a discourse of reality.

THE DOCUMENTING OF MASS-OBSERVATION

Mass-Observation was the project for 'Anthropology at Home' launched by Tom Harrisson, Humphrey Jennings and Charles Madge in 1937, in which 'observation' would be the means to get at the facts. However Mass-Observation, they declared,

8. Tom Harrisson, Humphrey Jennings, Charles Madge, letter to the *New Statesman*, 30 January 1937. This followed a letter by Jennings and Madge, who was at the time a journalist with the *Mirror*, responding to Mr Geoffrey Pyke who had written asking for 'that anthropological study of our own civilisation of which we stand in such desperate need', in which they announced that a group had been formed for precisely this purpose. Tom Harrisson, an anthropologist, saw the correspondence and joined forces with Jennings and Madge.

9. Humphrey Jennings and Charles Madge (eds), *May The Twelfth: Mass-Observation Day-Surveys 1937*, London, Faber and Faber, [1937] 1987.

10. See Nick Hubble's very interesting account of Madge's work for Maynard Keynes in this issue.

11. Charles Madge and Tom Harrisson (eds), *First Year's Work*, London, Penguin, 1938, p66.

does not set out in quest of truth or facts for their own sake, or for the sake of an intellectual minority, but aims at exposing them in simple terms to all observers, so that their environment may be understood, and thus constantly transformed. Whatever the political methods called upon to effect the transformation, the knowledge of what has to be transformed is indispensable. The foisting on the mass of ideals or ideas developed by men apart from it, irrespective of its capacities, causes mass misery, intellectual despair and are international shambles.[8]

In their Preface to *May The Twelfth: Mass-Observation Day-Surveys* (1937), Jennings and Madge write that 'The fifty Observers were the vanguard of a developing movement, aiming to apply the methods of science to the complexity of a modern culture'.[9] These Observers were ordinary people drawn from a wide range of social and working backgrounds, of whom Jennings and Madge note that 'A large proportion of them have already shown themselves able to write really useful reports. Professor Julian Huxley has written of some of these that they "would put many orthodox scientists to shame in their simplicity, clearness and objectivity"'. Nevertheless, while Observers were asked to note, for instance, details of dress, which might be related to class, job, family and so on, there is an aspect of Mass-Observation that doesn't deliver only 'objective facts', but also the facts of subjectivity: for example, the facts about how families save also must tell a story about how families desire - or fear - together in relation to the future which their saving looks forward to.[10] Indeed Madge and Harrisson later asserted that 'Mass-Observation has always assumed that its untrained Observers would be *subjective* cameras, each with his or her own distortion. They tell us not what society is like but what it looks like to them'.[11]

A romantic concept of 'the untrained observer' undercuts here the strident empiricism promoted by Huxley's comment, introducing a profound epistemological questioning of modernity's knowledge structures. It is this subjectivism which makes the Mass-Observation material so rich in anthropological terms, while it also limits its role as 'proper' - that is, objective - social history. It is as if, not heeding the division that Jonathan Crary has argued arose between the disciplined observer and the subjective gaze, the camera is no longer the prosthesis enabling true or truer observation, but - in the image of the camera's distorting lens - a metaphor through which the vision of subjectivity is articulated. I want to suggest here, however, that the opposition Crary has posed is challenged by the subjectivism, and the correlative objectivity, being called into play in both Mass-Observation and some of the films of the documentary movement. New aspirations and thereby new definitions of agency are being invoked in relation to subjects as citizens susceptible to the subjectivity of aesthetic, emotional, response.

The subjectivity of 'speaking the ordinary' emerges in relation to the social project arising in the 1930s which sought to enable a wider enfranchisement of views in constituting the 'voice of Britain'. How should this be viewed? Andrew Higson has argued that the Griersonian documentary project 'tried to hold together profoundly contradictory tendencies'.[12] As he notes,

> For Grierson and Rotha, the task of documentary - 'the public service which it is the duty of cinema to perform' - is the 'teaching of citizenship', and the transformation of the spectator into 'a thinking, reasoning and questioning member of the community'.[13]

Nevertheless, Higson says, the form of the documentary film can 'by situating the discussion in the text itself', once more place the spectator citizen 'outside the public sphere', passive - albeit enlightened.[14] Moreover Grierson's many claims for the documentary film, and the state or quasi-state funding he secured, tend to imply that a single 'public interest' can be served, masking the extent to which the public sphere is a contestatory space in which, Higson observes, not all social interests have an equal voice and 'consensus must be negotiated or acquiescence imposed'.[15] Higson concludes by characterising the Griersonian project in Foucauldian terms, as an 'effort to produce and regulate an official public sphere, an attempt to discipline public life'.

> In Grierson's words, 'it was, from the beginning, an adventure in public observation', involving, as Rotha put it, 'presenting one half of the populace to the other'. The public must be educated, they must comprehend the values of citizenship, but they must also be observed, surveyed, analysed, categorised - that is, they must be policed.[16]

The documentary film movement was, however, part of a debate around and struggle for political consensus against state repression in the decade after the General Strike. The incorporation into the public sphere of the working classes - and of course of women following the enfranchisement acts after the First World War - is a social democratic project which opposed the traditional class and gender structures and the vested interests of owners in maintaining an excluded class. No doubt this project and its impetus was partial and incomplete. Certainly it was in large measure subordinate to the

12. Andrew Higson, *Waving the Flag: Constructing a National Cinema in Britain*, Oxford, Oxford University Press, 1995, p186.

13. Ibid., p184.

14. Ibid.

15. Ibid., p185.

16. Ibid.

17. These two films are discussed further in my essay, 'Working images: the representations of documentary film', in Valerie Mainz and Griselda Pollock (eds), *Work and the Image II - Work in Modern Times: Visual Mediations and Social Processes*, Aldershot, Ashgate, 2000.

18. This redefinition was not unilateral or singular, but part of an intense debate on the extent of the role of the new citizen and of state intervention and a progressive civil bureaucracy. Nevertheless the documentary movement, including Grierson, was clearly identified with this centre-left position, As Ian Aitken points out, however, the new move of what I am calling a 'consensual politics' was not confined to the centre-left. For example the later Prime Minister, Harold Macmillan, attempted to establish a new Centre Party with the aim, as described in his book *The Middle Way* (1938), of obtaining a fusion of all that is best in left and right. Ian Aitken, *Film and Reform: John Grierson and the Documentary Film Movement*, London, Routledge, 1990, p171.

19. Higson, op. cit., p197.

continuing elitism and hierarchy of the dominant business interests in Britain in the 1930s, so well summarised and satirised in *Peace and Plenty* (Ivor Montagu and B. Megarry, 1939) and *Hell Unlimited* (Norman Maclaren and Helen Biggar, 1936). Moreover, the movement was, of course, a project of inclusivity rather than class revolution. Yet this itself was revolutionary and needs to be discerned. The 1930s was a period of contestation around the boundaries and modes of widened public participation, of the redefinition of the citizen as more than the male bourgeois, as well as a redefinition of the ownership and hence role of knowledge. In *Coalface* (Alberto Cavalcanti, 1935), for example, the film functions to include the coalminer in the image of British industry and Empire and to extend to this group of workers the idealisation of physical labour and manual exertion, as well as the ethic of work, which were part of, for example, the sports and fitness movements from the turn of the century. Here the coal industry is no longer simply a matter of mines and owners, but also of the men and their families who live, and die, by coal, and the miner is thus re-defined as a key image in the representation of the role of coal for Britain and her empire. Of course this was also the image in the 1910 actuality, *A Day in the Life of a Coalminer*, but there the miner was represented in his and her particularity, whereas in *Coalface* the miner and his sacrifices are a universal, and a component of the success of the British empire.[17] The notion of a state of responsible and informed citizens now includes the worker, producing a redefinition of the 'national interest' as more than the interests of the economic elite and thereby redefining the position of the owners as employers, mitigating their 'absolute' power implicitly and, as seen with hindsight, laying the basis for the wartime national collective interest and the post-war nationalisation of the coal industry.[18]

Andrew Higson indeed notes that,

> There is no denying that such films do extend the boundaries of permissible discourse, the boundaries of the representable, and that in this extension, working-class figures are indeed often placed at the centre of the diegesis - though rarely as active subjects. The system of looking constructed for this cinema, however, suggests a very different reading, since in many ways it situates the spectator as a bourgeois outsider, looking in on this other class as spectacle. From this perspective, the working class are effectively captured - held in place, tamed - as the objects of a benignly authoritative gaze.[19]

The project of inclusivity does not simply 'tame', however, rather it rewrites the 'dangerous, unknown other' as *heimlich*, enacting a process of recognition of the other(s) as part of 'one Britain'. In *Enough to Eat* (1936) science, scientists and the state are charged with a duty to enable good nutrition, but this is not - yet - state, that is national government policy, while the spectator is not only a citizen addressed in terms of her duty to eat better (or to encourage others to do so), but also as an agent who can act to bring this about through knowledge. The working-class poor are victims of poverty but not ignorance in the film, for it carefully demonstrates by interviews and statistical graphs that housewives do know what foods are important for their families, thus showing its own ideological concern to portray them as subjects of knowledge. (This claim clearly contradicting the claims also made by the film for scientific knowledge). Observation and testimony as evidence are central to this film, but the public school youths as well as the urban working-class kids are objects of scrutiny. In contrast to the nineteenth-century informants of Mayhew, the women interviewed are participants in the modernist project of understanding and achieving good nutrition rather than recipients of philanthropy's voyeuristic concern. Action is undertaken not solely through charitable 'hand outs', but also through taxation - local property rates in this case.

In so far as documentary as a mode in the 1930s is exemplary of and a player within the discursive struggles and redefinitions that were arising with the emergence of a new modernity in Britain, the spectator is addressed as an agent as well as a subject of these meanings, that is, she is addressed as a social agent, a subject within a specific historical conjuncture.[20] Films such as *Enough to Eat* do not simply 'know' for and on behalf of the spectator, they also demand a spectator who comes to know. The modernist role assigned to science and knowledge here is homologous to action whereby scientific knowledge itself is an imperative for change and human progress and to be informed about matters of science implies an active relation. Moreover, there is an assumption on the part of film-makers of widely different views in the 1930s that to see is to be impelled to act and that film can function as visual evidence.[21] These views are not simply naive and misguided, as too often we - as later theorists - assume. Rather they attest to the power of the moving images and sounds of film, and to an ideological context of film-making and viewing. The context, the historical - that is, ideological - conjuncture of production and consumption, is also determining of film spectatorship and this is perhaps most true for documentary film.

THE VISION AND VOICE OF THE ORDINARY

In recording actuality, photography and cinematography address two distinct and apparently contradictory desires. On the one hand there is a desire for reality held and reviewable for analysis as a world of materiality available to scientific and rational knowledge, a world of evidence confirmed through observation and logical interpretation. It is a desire for a symbolic or social reality ordered and produced as signification, whereby the observed can be immediately integrated, via a discourse of recognition and classification, into a densely constituted field of knowledge, power and techniques.[22] The camera-eye functions here as a mastering, all-seeing,

20. By 'new modernity' I am assuming that modernity is located at least as early as the industrial revolution in the eighteenth century in Britain, and in the Enlightenment project. The early twentieth century sees new modes of modernity, and modernism.

21. *Spanish Earth* (Joris Ivens, 1937) is an example of such assumptions - it is both a propaganda film for the Spanish Government in its struggle against the Fascists in the civil war, and it seeks to provide visual evidence - of the worthwhile nature of the Republican Government's cause, and of the pernicious involvement of foreign governments demonstrated by the burnt-out German plane and the dead Italian soldiers.

22. This is not the same as desiring to know the true functioning of social reality for if, as Slavoj Zizek argues, 'we come to "know too much", to pierce the true functioning of social reality, this reality would dissolve itself. This is probably the fundamental dimension of "ideology": ideology is not simply "false consciousness", an illusory representation of reality, it is rather this reality itself which is already to be conceived of as "ideological"'. *The Sublime Object of Ideology*, London, Verso, 1989, pp 21-22.

23. With the chemical recording of the camera obscura's images the human observer is displaced by a mechanical seer. Jean-Louis Comolli notes: 'At the very same time that it is thus fascinated and gratified by the multiplicity of scopic instruments which lay a thousand views beneath its gaze, the human eye loses its immemorial privilege; the mechanical eye of the photographic machine now sees *in its place*, and in certain aspects with more sureness. The photograph stands as at once the triumph and the grave of the eye', Jean-Louis Comolli, 'Machines of the Visible', in Stephen Heath and Teresa de Lauretis (eds), *The Cinematic Apparatus,* New York, St Martin's Press, 1980, p123.

24. Jean Baudrillard, *The Evil Demon of Images,* Paul Patton and Paul Foss (trans), Sydney, The Power Institute of Fine Arts, University of Sydney, 1987, p28. Evil, and immorality, are invoked not in relation to morality versus sinfulness, but in a Manichean opposition of rational and irrational.

25. According to Paul Rotha, it was Ruby Grierson's ability to win people's confidence that gave 'a spontaneity and an honesty to the "interviews" that contrasted sharply with the previous,

view, as well as a prosthesis, an aid and supplement to vision whereby we are shown a reality which our own human perceptual apparatus cannot perceive.[23] On the other hand there is a desire for the real not as knowledge but as image, as spectacle. Jean Baudrillard argues that:

> There is a kind of primal pleasure, of anthropological joy in images, a kind of brute fascination unencumbered by aesthetic, moral, social or political judgements. It is because of this that I suggest they are immoral, and that their fundamental power lies in this immorality.[24]

Giving voice and image to the ordinary - the anthropology of our own culture - is clearly not straightforward, but both Mass-Observation and film-makers like Ruby Grierson were concerned to authorise the ordinary. Observation necessarily involves distance, a controlling vision of the observer over the observed, and hence a status of other being assigned to the observed. Documentary films, however, are a specific and particular *performance* of the specular through film as discourse and they cannot be simply aligned with or made equivalent to the surveillance and control of the scopic regimes of the prison, or medicine, to take two of Foucault's studies. The documentary film, for example, does not simply and wholly control the terms for its own reading, and this is shown nowhere more clearly than in the problem of verisimilitude, that is, how far the documentary film succeeds in producing in its spectators a sense of the realness of what it displays, and hence the strangeness or familiarity of what we see. The question, then, is one of how we recognise the ordinary as really real.

Housing Problems (Arthur Elton and Edgar Anstey, 1935), a film widely discussed in terms of its ideological and aesthetic role in 1930s documentary and its importance for social history, notably poses issues of verisimilitude and of the role of the ordinary men and women who voice their stories of slum housing. In this film, encouraged by Ruby Grierson,[25] those living in the slums tell the story of the slums themselves. Are these people only the objects of our eyes and ears, that is, figures to be observed? What is the role of the *mise en scène* of their speech? What is the role of their words and the character of their speech, their enunciation and phrasing? Their speech and statements are framed by the authoritative words of the anonymous voice-over and Councillor Lauder, Chairman of the Stepney Housing Committee, so that far from having their own say, they seem to serve simply to confirm the truth of the problem of slum housing articulated by the voice-over. The formal framing of the informants, it has been said, distances us, preventing identification.[26] Yet while the film's concern is primarily the 'bigger picture' of housing regeneration, the inclusion of 'ordinary people's views' is not fully assimilated. Rather, I suggest, a certain strangeness is produced by these testimonies in relation to the film overall, notwithstanding the familiarity the film evoked in audiences from the community around Stepney. A problem of verisimilitude arises for many modern viewers of the film in relation to the very formal address of some of the informants, and the awkwardness of their poses: Mr Norwood, for example, who stands very straight but behind whom we can see his mantelshelf arrayed with decorative objects. As John Corner observes, however,

> But to be cued by sympathetic embarrassment of this kind into an interpretation of the speaking as somehow inauthentic, perhaps even the result of directorial management (thereby illegitimately 'set up'), is to be oneself a victim of the ideology of spontaneity, of modern television naturalism. Indeed the very awkwardness of non-professional performance in *Housing Problems* can be seen as a guarantee of communicative honesty.[27]

The 'strangeness' here may read as either indicating inauthenticity or on the contrary the truly authentic. The undecidability here poses back to us our demand for the authentically real and its impossibility as anything other than the verisimilar. Mr Norbert had chosen as his *mise en scène* his hearth as home and his ambitions as figured by his mantelshelf, rather than a - more modernist - concern to adduce visual evidence. His words appear as the formality of someone unused to public speaking and this contrasts starkly with his story not only of physical inconvenience but of illness and death, and of infant mortality statistics immortalised in his children's lives cut short.

Mrs Hill, however, is seen on her staircase, describing the damp, the single toilet facility shared by many families, and the vermin in the walls. What is striking is not, or not only, the visual evidence but her mode of speech which circles round to repeat, most noticeably as she reiterates the awful structural condition of the building, 'The whole house is on the crook'. It is a rhetorical device giving emphasis to her words which suggests the insufficiency of the seen and heard as such, and introduces the individual as social subject of speech - the style is part of a community's form of storytelling - and as a psychological subject of speech - figured in the way the particular offence of the crookedness of everything in the house overruns all the other horrors of her housing. The testimonies of *Housing Problems* exceed their proper role as 'realistic' and introduce an imagined space of other stories. For example, Mrs Atribe in voice-over relates how nice her new home is with its cooker and portable copper for washing clothes. The commentary anticipates her next words as: 'All the same, Mrs Atribe will never forget the rats in the house she had before'. We hear her story of the drama one day of a large rat in her room and her husband's efforts to capture and kill it: a drama of event and action and not of the horror of rats and the disease and danger they represent, which remains only implicit. What emerges, I suggest, is a social reality not fully contained

romantic, method of handling people'. (In *Documentary Film*, London, Faber, 1st edition 1986).

26. Higson, op. cit., p200.

27. John Corner, *The Art of Record*, Manchester, Manchester University Press, 1996, p68.

by the film's documentary discourse, a voicing of the ordinary which exceeds the bounds of the structures of cause and explanation, problem and solution which the documentary enacts.

Each of the films Ruby Grierson was involved with are concerned with giving voice to the people they show. *Today We Live* (1937), for example, is about three communities who are seeking funding to build local centres. While scenes are clearly staged, anticipating her war-time propaganda film, *They Also Serve* (1940), the film is also inclusive of dissenting views - such as the unemployed miner in South Wales who consistently objects to the project of building a community centre, arguing that it won't provide them with a job, and that's what they really want. In *Give the Kids a Break* (1937), on which she worked as assistant director to Donald Taylor, the opening sequence of the teacher in a class is clearly acted and scripted for the camera. The scene differs, however, from the usual enactments in 1930s documentaries, such as in *Night Mail* (Harry Watt, Basil Wright, 1936), or *BBC: The Voice of Britain* (Stuart Legg, 1935), organised as it is around diverse and diverting shots of the children at their desks - a girl knitting, some boys playing a game - and focussed through a joke about the spelling of a particularly unpronounceable location. The schoolteacher has set the children the task of writing about what they would like to do on a holiday, and the film shows the accounts they produced. These evoke the imagined spaces desired and anticipated by each child, desires which are realised in the organised and less organised scenes of play of children on holiday that follow. The Glasgow charity which organises these summer vacations for the city's children is represented not by a singular figure, but through a group meeting where the planning and arrangements for the trips is discussed. The film is a record of this holidaymaking as well as an advertisement for the work and an appeal for support. Organised for boys or girls, with camps for Jews and Catholics and Protestants, the images of the tents and the boys lined up outside, as well as the scenes of breakfast and preparing meals, recall scenes from Leni Reifenstahl's *Triumph of the Will* (1936). Here, however, the low-angle shots, and close-in framing which cuts up the scene, present boisterous anarchy rather than organised athleticism. The tone is one of play and playfulness rather than discipline: for example in the series of long-held shots of a teacher with some boys walking down to a beach - some straggling behind, others striding on arm in arm, and one child who bends down to pull up his sock over and over again. Exuberance and freedom are suggested in these scenes. The film certainly offers a spectacle, but of children experiencing pleasure and fun, rather than as objects of controlling observation. The children do perform, however - not only through organised games and activities but also in three set pieces of filming. In one a small boy entertains a group sat around him in a tent, singing and performing, music-hall style, 'Roamin in the Gloamin'. Later a girl regales a group of friends with a comic story, acting all the parts; her broad accent being both familiar and estranging so that it is the non-Glaswegian spectator who is 'strange' or other to this scene as she tries to follow the account of naughty children and animals. Finally, following a collective song, a young boy steps up to sing alone, in a voice rich, melodic and more powerful than his slight and slender frame would lead us to expect, 'Misty Islands of the Highlands'. Though he acts as an experienced performer, arm on his hip as he leans back to project his voice, a different image emerges as his hand drops periodically to tug his short trousers back up around his waist.

Give the Kids Break continues to have the power to delight and move us. Something is documented here, as in *Housing Problems*, which is more than the propaganda of a small Glasgow charity, or an argument for slum clearance. The films not only record and observe, but also enable a sense of the social actors, allowing them not only to have their say, but to speak to us through the gestures and intonations of speech and action. It is, of course, something poetic.

HISTORICAL ENTRIES: MASS-OBSERVATION DIARISTS 1937-2001

Margaretta Jolly

Diary writing was only one part of the original design of Mass-Observation (M-O) and in some ways, its less flashy component. Yet the large group of volunteers who agreed between 1937 and 1945 to write about their everyday lives and environments for the public good was an inspired and perhaps even more original aspect of M-O than Tom Harrisson's team of radical amateur anthropologists. From the perspective of 1981 onwards, when the Mass-Observation project was revived, the interdisciplinarity and democratising of the academy this entailed seem extraordinarily prescient. In this essay I will explore what these unpaid volunteers' relationship was to the challenge of providing an 'anthropology of ourselves' and material for a study of the 'collective unconscious'. How did they interpret their role? And what kind of writing did it produce? In the rich spectrum from private to public time, voice and mood that we will see emerging from the diaries, I will argue that one of the roles of Mass-Observation was to provide an opportunity to write, and in doing so, it produced its own special 'genre' of writing.

It seems odd that the nature of the writing done by the early panel has received little sustained attention from the literary point of view, odd because the single most enduring complaint about Mass-Observation has been its 'unrepresentativity', its 'subjectivity' and 'individuality'. Charles Madge, the driving force behind the establishment of diary-writing as an M-O method, had defended its qualitative interest in 'the world as it is perceived', and it could be argued that it is primarily his early vision that has survived in the current project.[1] Yet both he and the current managers have had to make repeated and extraordinarily similar defences against quantitative critique - and, as Dorothy Sheridan argues in this issue, in many ways Madge increasingly lost conviction in the literary as a means to social knowledge. The following reading of the diaries, then, crystallises around the various disciplinary skirmishes that have defined M-O. However, far from detracting from the project's social aims and uses, I will suggest that it can offer further material for a social history of the 'ordinary' at the meta-level of the relationships between diary writing and gender, age, class and national identity. A reading of the genesis and development of diary writing in M-O thus leads to the thesis that a cultural sociology of writing is part of the logic of M-O itself, perhaps even Harrisson's hope for a 'new synthesis' of social thought. In the final section, I will consider the work of the current Archive's Director and associates in developing such a sociology.

1. Charles Madge and Tom Harrisson, *First Year's Work*, London, Lindsay Drummond, 1938, p66.

2. It was figured as the 'main' motive for only 8 per cent of the slightly more than 200 who replied. Ibid., p67.

3. Mass-Observation Archive reference, (DS382).

4. Ibid., (DS445).

5. Ibid., (DS8).

6. Dorothy Sheridan (ed), *Wartime Women: A Mass-Observation Anthology, 1937-45*, London, Phoenix, 2000, p4. A comprehensive survey and analysis of the panellists has yet to be done. Material from the time includes *First Year's Work*, which contains a section on the 'personnel of Mass-Observation Archive', and two unpublished book

THE DIARISTS AND THEIR DESIGNS

In response to the Directive question 'why did you join Mass-Observation?' sent to the panel in 1937, members repeatedly wrote of their desire to contribute to science, to improve social conditions, to train their powers of observation. This was the aspect Madge and Harrisson focused on in their 1938 résumé of M-O, *First Year's Work*, citing the low score for 'literary or aesthetic' interest as panellists' main motivation.[2] But respondents' descriptions of wanting to 'do good' are constantly interwoven with admissions of pleasure in writing. One spoke of 'an opportunity to express myself' and hoped he would gain 'the ability to write and put together an intelligent essay',[3] another spoke of 'an urge to write or report',[4] while one frankly confessed that 'I like writing but have not a creative enough mind to find satisfactory themes of my own and this seemed to provide me with plenty of material'.[5] It would seem self-evident that enjoying writing was crucial to the production of the diaries, especially when M-O ceased to prompt with requests for day surveys or regular Directive responses. Writing for M-O could also satisfy other psychological and social functions associated with personal diary-keeping. Diary writing allowed not only the development of a writing style and persona but the construction of a confidante out of the projected directors, a therapeutic outlet, a way of managing relationships, identity and time.

It would be impossible to introduce all the diarists here - the 592 people recruited by the end of 1937 rose to at least 3,000 by 1945, and of these about 300 had kept full personal diaries throughout the war.[6] I will therefore focus my discussion on the three diaries that have been published in book length form. These three, unsurprisingly, do not represent a cross-section of the British population then or now - although they do, to an extent, represent the spectra of gender, class and profession within M-O. By and large Panel members were students, librarians, clerical workers, teachers and journalists, and a small number of working-class people involved in politics or adult education. Nearly three-quarters were unmarried, and most were from the South-East.[7] The problems of representativity posed by the make-up of the Panel dogged the founders' largely positivist paradigm, not to mention their quest for the working class voice. But M-O's evident appeal to the lower middle class amateur writer can be valued as charting an under-appreciated radicalism in a group traditionally dismissed as consumerist conservatives.[8] It also provided women with a means of public self-expression in keeping with their traditional skills and inclinations.[9] Thus, precisely because the three diarists, Naomi Mitchison, Nella Last and Edward Stebbing showed exceptional commitment to and enjoyment of writing, by virtue of their length or literary competence, they can be seen to fulfil the brief of the social diary as viewed by Madge. Naomi Mitchison was already an established novelist before she joined M-O, and indeed, was a personal friend of Harrisson. For her, M-O was his

drafts, Celia Fremlin's 'The Crisis: War in Diaries' (File Report 2181), and Yetta Lane's 'Drafts for a Proposed Book on War Diaries' (File Report 621). Nick Stanley provides an analysis of the panel's social makeup in his doctoral thesis 'The Extra Dimension: A Study and Assessment of the Methods Employed by Mass-Observation in its First Period 1937-40', Birmingham Polytechnic, 1981. Margaret Kertesz has analysed those who kept long diaries as part of her thesis 'The Enemy: British Images of the German People during the Second World War', University of Sussex, 1992. The Archive holds copies of both of these. See also the *Guide for Researchers, The Mass-Observation Diaries: An Introduction*, and a file of miscellaneous researchers' notes on diarists, both at the Archive. The website allows for searches for information about the diarists.

7. Angus Calder and Dorothy Sheridan (eds), *Speak for Yourself: A Mass-Observation Anthology 1937-49*, London, Jonathan Cape, 1984, p74.

8. Tom Jeffery, 'Mass-Observation: A Short History', University of Sussex Library, Mass-Observation Archive, 1990.

9. Calder and Sheridan, op. cit., p151.

10. For an amusing snapshot of Harrisson, including her account of painting his toenails red for him before he went on an expedition to the Pacific Islands, see Mitchison's *You May Well Ask: A Memoir 1920-1940*, London, Gollancz, 1979, pp201-2. Mitchison's brother, the scientist J.B.S. Haldane, also joined M-O.

11. Her own response to the Directive on why join M-O begins 'Because Tom Harrisson is one of the few persons of genius whom I have come across and something is likely to come of anything he is interested in'. Interestingly, she omits any reference to personal satisfaction or gain, explaining the point of M-O as 'To get accurate information, which should be of special value to politicians and sociologists and all who have to deal with what people really want'. Mass-Observation Archive reference, D.S. 123.

12. Richard Broad and Suzie Fleming (eds), *Nella Last's War: A Mother's Diary 1939-45*, Bristol, Falling Wall, 1981, p19.

13. Sheridan, *Wartime Women*, op. cit., pp8-9.

14. Edward Stebbing, *Diary of a Decade 1939-50*, Lewes, Sussex, The Book Guild, 1998, px.

idea.[10] A socialist, feminist, Scottish nationalist and Labour Party campaigner, mother and farmer as well as writer, she was herself a member of the left intelligentsia that produced M-O, and for that reason, although she produced one of its most sparkling texts, the project for her was of relatively minor importance.[11] For Nella Last, by contrast, M-O work was her unique foray into public writing. A middle-aged housewife living in the shipbuilding town of Barrow-in-Furness in Lancashire, married to a joiner and shopfitter and involved in the Women's Voluntary Services during the war, her diary vibrates with its early reflection that: 'Next to being a mother I'd have loved to write books - that is, if I'd brains and time. I love to "create", but turned to my home and cooking and find a lot of pleasure in making cakes etc.'[12] Like Last, Edward Stebbing was not a prominent figure, and his self-publication of the diary in 1998 suggests its special significance for him. He joined M-O aged nineteen, a young idealist then unemployed and still living with his family in Essex, but soon a shop assistant in a men's clothing store and then a laboratory technician, having been trained by the army. He represents the progressive-minded working/lower-middle-class, single (white, Christian) young man from the South-East most typical of the Panel.

Attention to the formal aspects of the diaries illuminates the uses of the genre both for the writer and for the readers that have inherited M-O's material. To start with, let us consider the M-O diarists' sense of audience and their related use of 'voice'. Clearly M-O diarists always intended their writing to be read. Yet the M-O panellists' idea of their readers, whether the rarely seen M-O directors or the vague idea of the 'general public' if their work succeeded in entering the M-O Bulletins, reports or books, shaped the writing in very individual ways. Sheridan comments:

> The London Mass-Observers are imagined as kindly, educated, progressive, tolerant and, above all, interested and therefore validating ... Amy Briggs says in passing that she hopes her first instalment is 'up to standard' but this feels like a gesture. She has already decided how she is going to use her diary and the pattern hardly changes. Muriel Green's diary displays a common pattern. At first she concentrates on the impact of the arrival of evacuees in her village. This is 'objective reporting' and presumably how she first thought an M-O diary should be. How different is her 1945 writing where she ponders her future and the possibility that she may be suffering from 'sex starvation'.[13]

In the introduction to his edited diary Edward Stebbing says that M-O, like *Picture Post* of which he was a great fan, was 'really [an] unusual type of journalism'.[14] His format is accordingly one of short summaries of military and domestic news, obviously shaped by M-O interests such as popular response to the blackout, gasmasks, rationing, air raids, and, centrally, the relationship between the press and public opinion, government propaganda and leadership.[15] Stebbing doggedly assesses the Fougasse posters and the anti-VD campaign, the 'hysterical and sensational' *Daily Mirror*, the BBC's decision that 'sentimental' songs should be curbed, the changing rhetoric of Churchill's speeches. We can also see the stamp of M-O's 'observational' methodology: he records the percentages of those 'against' and those 'pro-Jews' at work; transcribes dialogues (often 'Sister' versus 'Me', in which Sister is emotional and confused, 'Me', sceptical and informed); preserves anonymity; reports 'overheards'. But his interpretation of his role as an 'informant' restricts the expression of personal feeling to political opinion. While we learn that he adores coconut creams, is miserable about the rationing of men's suits with 'turn ups', was delighted to be discharged from the army on grounds of ill health, his is a voice abstracted from relationship to any other person or from the diary itself. This prompted one reader to summarise the diary as a 'superficial résumé of activities'.[16] Nevertheless, apart from testifying to the lower-middle class radicalism Tom Jeffery identifies,[17] Stebbing's style interprets M-O's platform of defending the public against propaganda and an upper class state as a popular uncovering of 'the truth'. While 'truth' for him did not involve discussing the intimate, it certainly meant the assertion of individuality, and increasingly, individualism, in the context of the 'British fascism' that seemed ironically so necessary to win the war. One of the rare passages of self-reflection shows just how the diegetic and choric tones of the watcher on the side-lines, the very practice of writing itself, supported his increasing disaffection:

> The main aim of the nations seems to be to plunge themselves into every possible crime and degradation. It is so tragic, it sometimes seems comic. The prospect for 1942 does not seem brighter, but gloomier if anything. I am reconciled to a long and weary war, but as far as I am concerned the world can carry on in its own sweet way. Any part which I shall play in the war effort will be passive, not active. As an onlooker I am greatly interested in world affairs; as a participator I am apathetic. It is impossible to remain outside this war, but I am not actively going to join it. That is the only way to hold onto sanity.[18]

M-O writing offers the solution to participation where 'world affairs' represent the impossible conundrum of a 'just' war, but it also provided an outlet for the individual who felt increasingly swamped by a 'mass' military society. Stebbing's more than usually heartfelt expression of resentment at army life speaks for many of the male soldiers who kept diaries for M-O. The diary ends just after VE-Day with Stebbing's conviction that 'the so-called problems of economics, sociology, and politics' obfuscate the moral nature of problems: 'we are all individually responsible for our own actions'.[19]

Stebbing's sense of audience opens up only a couple of frames of the

15. It should be noted that Stebbing very lightly edited his original text for publication.

16. See the file 'Notes on the Diarists' in the Archive. Margaret Kertesz wrote this.

17. Op. cit.

18. Op. cit., p124.

19. It would seem that Stebbing disliked his extreme expression of this position in the rather self-dramatising final line of the diary. The very final line - 'I feel ashamed to be a member of the human race', is replaced in the edited version with 'Yes, it was a very satirical cuckoo I heard on VE-Day!' Ibid., p321.

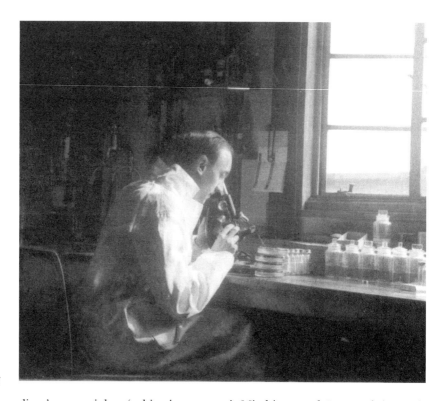

Edward Stebbing

20. In *You May Well Ask*, Mitchison comments that this diary omits the principle occasion for her journey to Vienna, the recovery from a love affair op. cit., p193. She kept other diaries of both travel and state of mind, for example of her trip to the Soviet Union in 1932 which features many portraits of her fellow Fabian Society companions.

21. Op. cit., pp55-56.

diary's potential as 'subjective camera'. Mitchison and Last took it much further. They had the advantage of a zoom lens, providing a more 'mimetic' relationship with events - they are shown, not simply narrated. In Mitchison's case, it is the more unexpected for she was used to public speaking and writing and might have remained within the authoritative tones of her relatively impersonal Directives, or her other public journal, the 1934 *Vienna Diary*, in which she documented the decimation of socialist Vienna.[20] The following account, written after a hiatus from November 1939 during the 'Phoney War', shows that she at least initially conceived of the diary as dependent upon some kind of action recognisable as 'war'. Its use of 'one' or 'we', gives a flavour of her confident authority:

> *Thursday 14 March 1940*   It seems appropriate to re-begin this diary on the day that Finns accepted the Soviet peace terms, and the day that the boats came in after winter fishing. I want to go on with it for a few weeks, anyhow. It seems doubtful whether anything very spectacular will happen within the next few weeks, but one may as well record the moods of this war while they are happening.[21]

Yet it transpires that the diary permits the professional writer to speak off duty, in which recording 'moods' is precisely the point. A year later, she dryly notes 'Of course, one realises that Mass-Obs is a kind of God-Figure - one confesses, one is taken an interest in, encouraged. Will Mass-Obs supersede psychiatry? I always recommend it myself';[22] and June 1943, 'I usually have to listen to people, and I have my human moments of wanting to talk about myself - instead of just putting it into this diary'.[23] Thus alongside chronicling the remote fishing village in Kintyre and the doings of her manor house, the diary plumbs the political and personal ambivalences of an aristocratic socialist, war-anxious mother of endangered children, principled non-monogamist in love with a local fisherman. On returning from a meeting of the local Labour Party she had founded where she and her husband tried not to dominate the working class members, she explicitly aligns writing with lack of dogmatism:

22. Ibid., p154.

23. Ibid., p247.

> [Dick, her husband] is double-minded, which is such a pleasant change from the orthodox Marxists - he knows that this is half true but only half, that there are other ways of looking at the world beside the political, that one never speaks the real truth. That makes him a refreshing companion because I, as a writer, know that too. We both know that you can die for a thing, but all the same that won't make it completely valid, at least for the double-minded, the fully conscious, who are perhaps the ones that matter in any generation. But can you be a good politician if you are like that? I don't know ... [24]

24. Ibid., p51.

But the diary does more than represent 'double-mindedness' or 'ways of looking at the world beside the political' for, as written for M-O, it constantly asserts its faith in a future that will find alternative forms of collective consciousness. In this way, the diary's private-public nature works through Mitchison's political vision, not only because it didn't need to take an immediate stand but also because it suited the intensely personal terms within which she explored the idea of community. The diary documents Mitchison's move towards Scottish nationalism in frustration with the Labour Party, interestingly alongside forthright criticism of both saccharine allied patriotism and fascist nationalism. But her view of 'the right relationship between people and groups of people' was essentially moral and feminist, and she constantly asked herself what the relationship was between the personal and the political.[25] The diary can be seen as a practice as well as representation of this philosophy. Her Foreword, written in 1984 when she was eighty-six and writing for the revived M-O, declares that the diary's significance is its record of the strong hopes for social change during the war: 'I tried to begin the change with personal relations, but Dick, my husband, working with Beveridge and Cole on the political and economic foundations of the welfare state, got much further in the end'.[26] Although she laments the betrayal of those hopes, the diary's very voicing of the private and the sceptical, especially regarding gender relations and children, give it a special place in her own trajectory and the record of the war. As a one-time Observer, Nina Hibbin, reviewed it thus: 'Gradually, as the "dear diary" aspect takes over, something very remarkable happens. You feel you

25. Naomi Mitchison, *The Moral Basis of Politics*, London, Victor Gollancz, 1938, p33. *You May Well Ask* as a retrospective account of this period is entirely structured around the contradictions between her socialist politics and her class and literary practices. See also her 1939 *The Blood of the Martyrs* for the Christian terms in which she had previously explored the kind of experiences necessary for the individual to transcend the limits of self.

26. Op. cit., p13.

*Naomi
Mitchison*

27. Nina Hibbin,
'Writing for Victory',
New Statesman, 19
July 1985.

28. Op. cit., p276.

29. M-O asked for
diarists to send in
their accounts every
three weeks, but Last
sent in a bundle tied
in a cotton, every
week.

30. E.S. Turner in his
review for the *London
Review of Books*
(October 1-14 1981)
chastises Last for her
'heightened' style,
prompted by
consciousness of her
public audience. The
social significance of
Last's literary
ambitions, not to
mention her own
pleasure in them, is
thus missed.

are being drawn into a novel rather than a series of unpremeditated jottings - an epic saga in which the strong-minded, mother-earth heroine struggles to chart her own principled course through conflicting social pressures'.[27]

Diary writing drew out an even more interestingly unique 'voice' for Nella Last. Last's sense of audience quickly became domesticated within the space of the three 'Day Surveys' she wrote in 1938. When we read the diary she began writing in September 1939, we can almost forget she was writing to M-O at all. She mentions filling in the Directive on 'sex' (on 18 June 1941, which characteristically provokes much musing on women's changed roles), and refers to making enquiries for M.O. about 'What will you do on V.E. Day?'.[28] As readers of the diary, however, we would not know that she wrote fifty-six responses to M-O Directives from January 1939 to December 1945 and sent in records of her dreams. We would not even know when she sent instalments in, or what kind of paper she used - striking given her explicitness about other rationed goods.[29] The diary became a fully internalised, self-sufficient process, functioning as a need and a pleasure.[30] Rarely left unwritten for a day, it is the longest in the Archive, covering twenty-nine years and comprising over two million words. As with many more perfunctory diaries, it is where she records the day's achievements, gives recipes and tips on 'making do and mend', forwards opinions on rationing, bombing, domestic policy, evil and violence, what will happen 'after the war'. But the diary also voices her love for the countryside and her pets, her fears for her sons, lively transcriptions of dialogue with family and friends and her resentment at her stuck-in-the-mud husband - he is the only figure never identified by name.

More than with Stebbing or Mitchison, the primary 'event' of Last's diary is her own life story. One of the rare moments when she explicitly refers to the diary gives us a clue to how specific the version of self M-O elicited was:

9 January 1941 After tea, Cliff sat writing for a while before going out to an old boys' dance at the Grammar School. He had put his 'civvies' on, and I was thinking in a hazy kind of way that the war might all be a dream, when he said suddenly and in such a queer way, 'Don't change, dearie - ever - fight *hard* against changing.' I felt startled and wondered what he meant, and he said, 'I've been looking at your Mass Observation diary. Are you really growing different - harder and less tolerant?' I thought carefully for words to express myself, and then said slowly, 'Yes, decidedly - but Arthur and you often told me I'd a weak streak, and should be firmer and refuse to let people put on me'.[31]

'Self observation' was part of the initial remit for the Panel. But as we have seen, many interpreted this to mean observation and recording of their everyday context. However, writing here evidently services the management of identity that psychologists have identified as one of the motivations for keeping a diary. Last merges the public reader with an address by and to her own alter ego - specifically, her 'weak streak', which allowed itself to be tyrannised by her 'petulant', 'little dictator' husband, and, she even admits near the end of the war, by her sons.[32] Last herself identifies her extraordinary conversion as emerging from the effect of taking on war-work in the Women's Voluntary Service (WVS) and Red Cross. With her new public involvement she begins to perceive a contradiction between her emotional and physical independence and skills - her house is 'run like a business', she is after all 'a good manager' - and her economic dependency on her husband.[33] But despite the exhilaration and fury that this simultaneously produces, she remains a Nora thrashing at the door of her 'Doll's House', never seriously able to imagine leaving it, certainly never politicising her situation.[34] Diary-writing and her projected idea of M-O enables and yet also restrains her new insights and desires. Consider the way she describes this particular confrontation with her husband, when he wishes he could see her 'in the glowing silks and velvets I know you always admire in the shops':

Nella Last

31. Op. cit., p100.

32. Op. cit., p296.

33. Op. cit., p255.

34. See Chapter 4 in Roger Bromley, *Lost Narratives: Popular Fictions, Politics and Recent History*, London and New York, Routledge, 1988, for a discussion of how Last's contradictions have proved useful in constructing popular nationalist memories of the war.

> I suppose you would only think I was putting a brave face on if I told you I'd sooner *die* than step into the frame you make for me. Do you know, my dear, that I've never known the content - at times, real happiness - that I've known since the war started? Because you always thought like that and were so afraid of 'doing things', you have at times been very *cruel*. Now my restless spirit is free, and I feel strength and endurance comes stronger with every effort. I'm *not*, as you always fear, wearing myself out - and even so, it's better to wear out than rust out.

35. Op. cit., p255.

'Gosh, but I hope he never comes into money. It would be really terrible to be made to "sit on a cushion and sew a fine seam"'.[35]

The contrast between the angry retort apparently quoted verbatim and the more softened reflection to M-O 'it would be terrible' plays her two voices against each other, the fatalistic wife versus the 'spirited' agent in the act of stepping out of the 'frame' of conventionally objectified woman. Keeping the angry accent in self-quotation mutes the rebellion the diary also records. This kind of 'managing' of a changing sense of self is at its most ironic in her description of a rare row with her husband over their son Cliff's volunteering to be posted overseas. Astonishingly, in a diary so full of fear and longing for the sons taken from her by the military and the state, she defends her son's self-exposure to the risk of death on the grounds that he must not be prevented from living life as she had been:

24 January 1942 When Cliff came in, the storm had blown over. But I said, 'Cliff, will you tell your father exactly how things stand - did you volunteer to go overseas?' Cliff looked calmly down at his father and said, 'Well, not exactly, but I've tried other times to get in a draft, and they knew if an odd one was wanted I was willing.' He went on, 'Anyway, it's what is to be expected.' He was a bit taken aback at his father's face working with emotion, his tear-filled eyes and cry of 'I want you to be SAFE'. I said, 'Safe for what? Till his soul died in his body, and even his body goes back on him, with repeated nervous breakdowns, and bitter inward thoughts turn his blood sour and cripple and torment him?' All he could say was, 'I want you to be *safe*, Cliff.' Cliff was embarrassed - but he is twenty-three and must see things as they are.[36]

36. Op. cit., p191-92.

Last's emerging conviction of the value of 'mother love' supports a vision that mothers would do better at avoiding war altogether. Thus she transforms without fully abandoning the sentiments which she brought to M-O in her early Directive response to the Munich crisis: 'Wish I knew a clever man who would tell me his views. Clever woman would be no use, womens [sic] views limited to welfare of loved men - whether grown up or tiny'.[37]

37. DR 1061, reply to Munich Crisis, September-October 1938.

Last exemplifies the woman for whom M-O provided a form of public engagement from a life otherwise almost totally defined through the private sphere. It is certainly impressive, while ironic, that this amateur form of writing proved so congenial to a woman who displays so lucidly the endless round of unpaid, repetitive and usually unthanked labour involved in housework and mothering. Yet in its early years, alongside her beloved WVS and Red Cross, the diary provided the form through which she seemed able to explore personal boundaries with sometimes very practical results - the move to separate beds from her husband, for example. While Stebbing's inexplicit use of the diary to find himself as a young man in wartime is rich with implications about the nature of individuality, writing and belonging, Last's diary as transitional object is much more dramatic for showing transformation in her fifties by an unrepentantly relational mother. Last shares much with Stebbing as a lower-middle-class and amateur writer finding a place in public record, even if her public politics is never as honed or radical - so absent from Mitchison's rather glamorised record of Scots fisherman, farmers or workers. But Last and Mitchison's use of the diary to advance a maternal perception of the nation, of war, of work, and ultimately of 'history' itself, is arguably the most novel result of the three texts. The diary's relationship to time and the body, upon which this builds, will now be considered as the final aspect of the genre in developing M-O's work.

Self-assertion in and against time is perhaps the supreme psychological function of diary-keeping, naturally augmenting the length and regularity with which a diary is kept. While the present moment predominates, it is stitched between a ceaseless retrospection (of what the diary already holds) and anticipation (of the future reading of the present inscription). Wendy Wiener and George Rosenwald speculate that the diary's function of 'binding time' does not exempt it from the games with memory involved in repression, screening and fantasy, nor does it necessarily reveal the secret or repressed self. Rather, its very proximity to one's personal fantasies of transcendence over time means that it occupies a liminal psychological space very useful to the writer. 'The diary, as an aid to memory', they say, 'secures not only repression but a variety of other advances in adaptation, and it frames these within a mirror for the self ... because it projects the past onto a plane of simultaneity'.[38] This has special relevance for those whose time is limited or controlled by alienated work. Indeed, it can be viewed as a redefinition of time itself against the dominant modes of 'industrial time', in which the clock or calendar measures market forces and the 'process' time that characterises the unpaid, repetitive and interrupted work of domestic and caring labour. For mothers, particularly those on low incomes or with the stresses of a husband like Nella's, writing diaries may be 'playing with time' in the way that Jane Mace has theorised in her study of mothers' literacy (undertaken partly through an M-O directive to the current panel). Mace argues that reading and writing are activities that potentially 'transport' one into a subjective temporality of flow, pleasure and self-loss. Tellingly, she sees this as epitomised in 'diary time', for though a diary is the genre most explicitly defined by the original sin of chronology it is also where an individual measures and redefines the calendar for their own uses.[39]

M-O diaries, conceived of initially within the highly regimented demands of the monthly 'day surveys', then as occasioned by the 'special days' of holidays or public events and finally as records of the war, were not intended to be structured as 'life' records. The initial frame was a collective time, in keeping with the notion of public audience and diegetic or narrative mood. This was overdetermined by the nature of the Second World War as the

38. Wendy J. Wiener and George C. Rosenwald, 'A Moment's Monument: The Psychology of Keeping a Diary', *The Narrative Study of Lives*, 1 (1993), 55.

39. Jane Mace, *Playing with Time: Mothers and the Meaning of Literacy*, London, UCL Press, 1998, p18.

40. A Directive of August 1940 (signed by Harrisson) assures the Panel that 'The stuff that observers have been sending in is quite definitely going to prove of first class importance when the time comes to write a history of this war. In particular, people who are sending in Diaries, and general or special air raid reports have, in the last two months, provided material of first-class interest and importance'.

41. The last account held by the Archive makes no reference to the intention to stop. It may have been that Last died subsequently, or that the papers have been lost.

42. Last's son, Cliff, held M-O itself as partly responsible for this, in having failed to tell its most enthusiastic diarist how talented she was. Cited in Iola Matthews, 'Wartime Creativity and Peaceful Drudgery' *The Age*, 10 (July 1982), 6.

43. Entry dated 5 February 1960.

44. Op. cit., p192.

first 'total' war, in which non-professional writers were often motivated to write as 'witnesses' to history in the making, and indeed encouraged to do so by M-O.[40] Yet the diaries complicate this public chronology. The diary's potential to explore the self in time presents the relationship between private and the public, the individual and collective, as more than 'longitudinal data'. Instead, it can present an insight into the relativity of historical time itself.

Again, Last proves to be much the truest 'diarist'. While all three began explicitly within the remit of the 'war diary', and Mitchison and Stebbing duly ceased writing at the end of the war, she continued until 1967, by which time she was seventy-eight - the longest serving original Panel member. Last's low-key record tells of the dispersal of her women colleagues from the WVS and Red Cross, the moving away of her sons, her husband's nervous decline, the integration of television, domestic technology and convenience food into their lives. But as the diary moves out of the collective time of 'war' and into the individual time of 'life span' in a diary that Last apparently did not intend to end,[41] we are also taken into a game with life and death quite outside the local occasion of war. Last's litany of health complaints, her shrinking round of eating, resting and chatting, can be perceived as the failure of M-O's ideal that diary-keeping would develop the Observer as much as the Observed, or at least shows that 'Observation' may depend upon a situation like the war being sustained.[42] Certainly, the diary shows the limited conditions under which Last was able to identify with the public and feel representative as a mother, a wife and an individual. While her New Year's Day account for 1960 provokes her to assert that she still possesses a 'real liking for pondering over things', and musing over the changed fashions in dress and technology, a month later she writes: 'I wonder at odd times if nowadays with so much and many "history making" events we get to the point when we can not assimilate more "worry" and turn to a trivial "interest"'.[43]

On other hand, Last's dedicated charting of the everyday testifies movingly to the role of diary writing in inhabiting the life span with all the specificity of her social context. A prime example is her distinctive record of what she cooks and how much her cooking is enjoyed by others, a feature that continues long after its response to M-O interest in rationing. The regularity, detail, and sensuous delight involved are one aspect of the diary's investigation into what sustains, measures, and prolongs life, paradoxically through that which is daily and repeated. As the measure of the diary as well as the day's 'rhythm', it is more important even than her descriptions of rising, sleeping and the weather. Thus the diary goes beyond a handbook for 'home economics' in performing itself a kind of temporal economy in its attempt to measure, hoard, spend and save a lifetime. In poignant contrast to her ultimatum during the war that 'it's better to wear out than rust out',[44] as Last enters her sixties and seventies the diary appears to help her endure a numbing routine. It is what Philippe Lejeune has asserted as the diary's attempts to exorcise the vertigo of the end.[45]

Last's invocation of the war as a measure for changes in gender relations is the dramatic plot emphasised by the editors of the published version. But the diary as a whole writes history from a far less glorious aspect.[46] As she declares in a moment of her old exasperation, 'I want people to see me as I *am*, 71, so very tired, rarely feeling well, conscious of "waning". That I'm *not* always able to see the funny side! [sic]'.[47] Yet is this simply a retreat from public to private life and the loss of what was special about an M-O diary? Instead, we can see Last's account as an insight into the conditions under which one's most intimate sense of time is marked by social categories of gender, for example, in the division of the day by cooking and tidying, or caring for a neurasthenic husband. Writing itself as a daily and perhaps liminally-conscious habit both marks that time and allows its escape. In Mace's terms, such a literacy practice testifies to a working woman's exploitation of the temporally 'transporting' potential of personal writing, a way out of the process time of her endless labour as much as a coming to terms with mortality.

Mitchison's diary also represents the relativity of time. The most important example of this is her extraordinary account of giving birth to a baby that died after one day. She was forty-two, and it would have been her seventh child:

> I had better get this over. The induction began to work about 1.30 on the 4th; by 3.15 I had vomited, etc, had a very severe shivering fit, and was beginning to have very adequate first stage pains. I was however very glad it had started [...] I awoke to hear them say I had a lovely little girl; I said that was right, that was what I wanted [...] They said she should not come to me but must stay warm all day; I was rather sad about it, but began reading Agnes Mure MacKenzie's history of Scotland; my throat still a little sore from the chloroform. I was very thirsty. I had got to the chapter on the Bruce when the Nurse came in saying Baby's not so well. It sounded pretty ominous; she and Dr Hunter were in the other room. Rosemary came to me; I asked her to look in; she said She's not responding. I sat up, trying to make up my mind to something which still seemed not quite inevitable. By this time Denny and Val had started for Tarbert to meet Dick. Then Dr Hunter came in and I knew.[48]

The account as a whole exemplifies several temporal modes. Using Katie Holmes' schema for reading women's diaries, we can identify the 'biological time' of labour (from 'first stage pains' on), the 'industrial time' of the 'history of Scotland' and the war, the 'domestic time' of the caring work, here being done for her rather than by her, and finally, the 'individual time' that shapes and is shaped by her diary.[49] Symbolically, she measures the birth by the time it takes her to read 'the history of Scotland'. The relationship between the baby, her deepest involvement in biological time,

45. Philippe Lejeune and Catherine Viollet (eds), *Genèses du Je, manuscrits et autobiographie*, Paris, CNRS Editions, 2000. See also Philippe Lejeune, 'How do Diaries End?', *Biography*, 24, 1 (2001), pp99-112.

46. The diary's editors were Richard Broad, a Thames Television producer who initially intended to make a documentary based on it and Suzie Fleming, a feminist associated with the Wages for Housework Campaign.

47. Entry dated 6 November 1960.

48. Op. cit., pp70-71.

49. Katie Holmes, *Spaces in Her Day: Australian Women's Diaries, 1920s-1930s*, NSW, Australia, Allen & Unwin, 1995.

and national history, twists into further configurations as the account develops. The baby would, on the one hand, have integrated her into the community, taken her through the war. On the other, it would have justified the private self:

> I began to realise how all this small scale life here would have been tolerable with the baby which was to have tied it all together, but now?- I envy Dick having this Ministry of Labour job; I wish I could immediately do something which would employ my mind. I dread going about again and facing people; they will be extremely sympathetic, but damn their sympathy. I feel I shall get landed with agricultural work which would have been tolerable and even delightful with a background of baby - of creation. But intolerable with one's mind empty and groping. To some extent, too, I had used this as an excuse to be out of the war, out of destruction, still on the side of creation; now that's over. I wish I could go to the south and get into an air-raid. But what's the good? The only thing I can do is write. And the only people who can write now are the real successful professionals like Priestley and co, or the equally whole-hearted antis, who can write against. Denny, no doubt, thinks I should do proper *Daily Worker* anti writing, but that's no good for a Liberal anarchist like me. Nor is it really writing.[50]

50. Op. cit., pp71-72.

The diary is demarcated from the professional writing that she reluctantly muses must now be her wartime duty. The next day she miserably records the doctor's advice, that she 'should start writing a book', confessing that 'if only I had my baby I wouldn't need to write a book that probably nobody wants to read'.[51] Personal death in the context of war brings out the diary's engagement with her body in its final years of reproductive capacity and this challenges her own strong belief in historical narrative. The account goes on to germinate a vision of her own alternative history of Scotland, a 'very small-scale history' of Kintyre that would end 'not with vague statements about evictions, but definite family histories'.[52] It is apposite that the novel *The Bull Calves* that came out of this, her only major war writing apart from the diary, pits a narrative of Scots national history against generations of female and specifically maternal resistance. Gill Plain has argued that, stymied by wartime hostility to feminism, Mitchison's most personal politics was displaced into fiction writing.[53] But the diary was equally such a refuge. Writing in it about her child's death, an entry to be 'got over', was not a 'transporting' occasion, through which time felt escapable. The place for even such a painful private death in the war is uncertain in the M-O diary: 'the silly thing is that I realise perfectly that much worse things are happening at this moment to thousands of people (and indeed have done so for a long time), but one cannot generalise as simply as that. I at least cannot change pain into love'.[54] But in mediating the meaning of an individual's place in time, diary-writing's ability to avoid

51. Ibid., p73.

52. Ibid., p73.

53. Gill Plain, *Women's Fiction of the Second World War: Gender, Power and Resistance*, Edinburgh, Edinburgh University Press, 1996.

54. Op. cit., p72.

generalisation, the measuring of pain, did more than provide immediate therapy. It allowed a form of writing that symbolically affirmed reproduction as a higher law than religion or war.

Last and Mitchison's diaristic sense of time, in burrowing through its daily shape to its engagement with questions of mortality, opens up a special relationship between reproductive bodies, ageing and public history. Last makes of this a veritable cause, fantasising about what mothers could do if they were in government. Mitchison, feminist yet also of the managerial class, is far more ambivalent, regularly moaning about how impossible it is to be a professional and a mother. In both cases, though, the M-O diary brings out an alternative shape to the 'public' and conventional notions of war and history. In this light, let me conclude by turning back to Stebbing's diary. What we see is a more confident resting on the category of the war as the alignment of public and private time. This confidence is indicated by his title - the 'diary of a decade' - and his assurance in introducing the sections 'Aftermath I' and 'Aftermath II' that he will not disrupt the public record:

> This is not meant to be an autobiography, nor was the original diary. It is meant as a continuation of the diary - a record of the immediate post-war period as it affected a certain family, written only partly with hindsight. But since it also affected me, inevitably some personal history enters into it. I came from a conventional family background and from a generation whose respectable aims were to marry, settle down, and bring up a family.[55]

55. Op. cit., p337.

Yet, exceeding his aims, this clues us in to the more classically personal uses of the diary as part of his personal rite of passage and individualisation. The subtext of his 'war report' is his leaving home, professional training and a sexual and romantic quest that underlay the many reports of his solitary attendance at dances and concerts. It is not entirely surprising that 'Aftermath I' plunges into the story of a failed courtship with a Dutch woman who had suffered much during the occupation. One of her letters shows that the diary was instrumental in his relationship with her:

> *2 November 1946* 'I read your diary and thought it very nice. Your descriptions are so clear, that your own life is shut out for a moment.' I cannot recall how I sent my diary, since it was quite lengthy - did I send carbon copies? 'Once I took it with me to read in lunchtime'.[56]

56. Op. cit., p330.

As the above demonstrates, the form of dated entries is retained but circled by wistfully nostalgic circumspection, in which poetry and literary comment suddenly appears. 'Aftermath II', recounting his visit with a German Quaker family who had endured even worse than his Dutch amour, steals more time from the public record not only to go beyond the pattern of his work days (clock time), but to engage with others' experience of a terrible public history. But in contrast to Last and Mitchison, this more autobiographical mode is circumscribed by its squeeze into an appendix. Notwithstanding Liz Stanley's warning that readers do not repeat M-O's own essentialising perception of 'sex' as the primary classification of data (such that they file all material by sex rather than age, class, individual), the diaries from this period point to a very different interpretation of 'history' by men and women, even across class and age.[57]

57. Liz Stanley, 'Women Have Servants and Men Never Eat: Issues in Reading Gender, Using the Case Study of Mass-Observation's 1937 Day-Diaries', *Women's History Review*, 4,1 (1995), 85-101.

In this reading of the 'writerly' aspects of the M-O diaries, I am not trying to individualise the record - although there is a possible argument about literary authority that could be made here. It is equally misplaced to blame M-O for merely being a refuge for would-be writers, the suggestion made by Valentine Cunningham in his disappointment that it never did attract 'ordinary' people.[58] While some, such as the more 'proletarian' Bill Naughton, went on to publish novels, this is clearly the wrong question to ask. Rather, it is precisely *as writing*, and specifically, *as diary writing*, that M-O engaged with the seriousness of the evanescent and the nature of the collective, particularly in a time of crisis. If this did not work in any direct way as a revelation of 'the mass', this may not be so much because of the lack of social representativity but because the relationship between the individual, the collective and the written by force, cannot be simple - even, and especially in wartime. Rather it opens up precisely the questions about knowability, communication, shared and non-shared experience that only a holistic kind of data can allow. This is perhaps more than Madge aimed for in the attempt to 'see how, and how far, the individual is linked up with society and its institutions'.[59] It may, however, be the fulfilment of his hope that panellists' writings 'will begin the long task of making Observers conscious of each other's lives, which is after all the main aim of MASS-OBSERVATION'.[60] Such an awareness does not detract from the historical interest of the diaries. Rather we can build upon the evidence that writing itself is part of history and, at some level, pushes against disciplinary limits itself, in providing a 'thick' kind of historiography of the kind argued for by the cultural materialists of recent years. From this point of view, we can begin to build a sociology of public diary writing.

58. Valentine Cunningham, *British Writers of the Thirties*, Oxford, Oxford University Press, 1988, p338.

59. Op. cit., pv.

60. This phrase comes from the very first Directive, probably sent in June 1937 to new Observers, almost certainly drafted by Madge.

A SOCIOLOGY OF THE PUBLIC DIARY: MASS-OBSERVATION TODAY

In this introduction to the diaries, I have argued that the writing process itself can and should be written into the very cultural history that M-O was constructing. Who was likely to keep a diary? What, precisely, did the process and form of diary keeping reveal about the relationship between individual and mass, in war and more generally in a time of a changing contract between state and people? How too did it permit the expression of gender, class, race, sexuality, national or age identity and struggle? I have suggested that in providing answers to such questions the diary's holistic nature does not prevent it from taking its place as historical evidence, and indeed, makes a small claim to change the terms upon which historical narrative is written. The M-O diary as a hybrid of amateur journalism and private diary provides an interestingly particular development of genre, sometimes to great literary effect. It shuttles between collective terms of reference in which no 'sense of an ending' is permitted, and the private interrogation into one's mortality that a private diary involves, a contradiction of particular poignancy in the war diary where questions of survival are both pressing and controlled by nationalist and M-O discourses of a 'greater good'. The individual's shoring up against time is additionally nourished by the belief that writing for M-O is in any case largely for posthumous reading. I have argued that this is most interesting in women's diaries where the historical gulf between public and private identity is widest, and where the content of the diaries in discussing childbearing and rearing seems sometimes to permit an alternative vision of time and survival.

Reading the diaries in this way requires a warmth towards literary analysis and, one might say, an attempt at the philosophical synthesis latent, but never realised, in M-O's initial establishment of the panel. This of course, is not news to the recent practice of cultural historiography nor indeed, to the conception of the current M-O project. The relaunching of a panel of diarists in 1981, under David Pocock and Dorothy Sheridan who were then managing the archiving of M-O's early materials at the University of Sussex, was itself a symptom of the changing paradigms of social science. As Dorothy Sheridan comments:

> We take [the project's rehabilitation] to mean, in the years since the Archive was first established at Sussex in 1970, a renewed, if critical respect, for what Mass-Observation achieved and insights it provided, combined with an interest in the possible replication of some of its methods. It is also a recognition that the fashions in social research, especially in social history, sociology and social anthropology, have shifted since the late 1960s.[61]

Sheridan, who has been Mass-Observation's Director since 1991, has increasingly developed a theoretical framework for the project that responds to such 'shifts in fashion' in suggesting that the project be seen as a precursor to the oral and life history movements of the 1970s on.[62] Rather than seeking to measure or quantify either the writers on the current 400 strong panel or the material in terms of some abstract 'neutral' of class or opinion, she suggests we use the 'case study' approach which 'expands and generalises theories' rather than 'enumerates frequencies'.[63]

It is this perspective that has prompted the latest book to come out of M-O. Sheridan, and the literacy theorists David Street and David Bloome, in *Writing Ourselves: Mass-Observation and Literacy Practices* (2000) have together undertaken the study that most comprehensively 'rehabilitates' the project. Here, they draw upon literacy theory to analyse it as a writing

61. Sheridan cited in Jeffery, op. cit., piii.

62. Dorothy Sheridan, 'Writing to the Archive: Mass-Observation as Autobiography', *Sociology*, 27,1 (1993), 27-40.

63. Dorothy Sheridan, *Damned Anecdotes and Dangerous Confabulations: Mass-Observation as Life History*, University of Sussex, Mass-Observation Archive, 1996.

64. Dorothy Sheridan has also analysed her 'relationship' with Nella Last as a research subject in 'Getting on with Nella Last at the Barrow-in-Furness Red Cross Centre: Romanticism and Ambivalence in Working with Women's Stories', *Women's History Notebooks*, 5,1 (1993), 2-10.

65. Dorothy Sheridan, Brian Street, and David Bloome, *Writing Ourselves: Mass-Observation and Literacy Practices*, Cresskill, New Jersey, Hampton Press, 2000, pp116-17.

66. Ibid., p288.

67. Ken Plummer, *Documents of Life: An Introduction to the Problems and Literature of a Humanistic Method*, London, Unwin Hyman, 1990.

68. For an account of the ongoing attempts to expand the social make-up of the panel, including by using email, see Chapter 2 in Sheridan, Street and Bloome, op. cit. It should be noted that the project has worked with an M-O-style survey of lesbian and gay life in Britain and holds copies of the 'diaries' produced. See National Lesbian and Gay Survey (ed), *What A Lesbian Looks Like: Writings By Lesbians On Their Lives and Lifestyles*

practice that not only involves self-assertion but a relationship, such that traces of letter writing, autobiography, speech making, journalism as well as diary-writing can be found.[64] This fills out the picture I have briefly sketched by considering not only the ethnography of early M-O writing but the writing processes of the current Panel. To do so, they discuss a Directive they designed to lay the foundations for the book in which diarists were asked to keep a log of the 'literacy events' in their day, as well as describe how they perceived their M-O writing and whether for them it was autobiographical or not. The replies are similar to those of the 1930s - an insistence that to write for the public about the public is the primary motor. This is perhaps startling in an intellectual climate that views collective history as having crumbled, and may suggest more public confidence in an idea of nation, community, and certainly, the academy than one might expect. Yet alongside this, the personal meanings of writing in the context of undervalued or marginalised (self)representation and historical experience are constantly evident. I have already offered my own opinion on this - that the presence of mortal impulses more commonly associated (or admitted) in regular diary keeping or autobiography do not ultimately contradict the distinctiveness of its 'public-private' aim. This kind of balancing act is also the conclusion of Sheridan et al, who see it as further evidence for accepting the final logic of M-O diary writing, which is that it can tell us first and foremost *about itself*. Adopting a view that writing must be analysed as a social and ideological rather than merely technical activity, they 'view the exploration of M-O and literacy practices as a "telling case" about the nature of literacy and society'.[65] The central tale they identify is that writing plays a significant role in everyday life outside of educational and professional contexts and in ways that disrupt standard definitions of literacy in its adaptation to multiple 'social, economic, cultural, economic and personal agendas'.[66]

It is important to nuance this shift in the disciplinary debate over M-O. The project today certainly has more in common with Ken Plummer's radical humanist sociology than post-structuralist historiography of the kind practised by Hayden White or Michel Foucault.[67] This is in part because it is still attempting to answer collective questions and is used primarily as a source of social data. (Respondents are also still identified by age, occupation and gender and their writing is classified thematically rather than by individual.) It also, admittedly, perhaps reflects a lack of theoretical backing. It is surely ironic that having come into the right intellectual context to make sense of it, M-O has lost the association with the avant-garde (and the upper class men?) that gave it the edge it had in the 1930s. The quantitative problem therefore won't go away, and few would dispute its ongoing wish - brutally defined by the availability of funding - to expand its panel to include more ethnic minorities, working class, youth, or others underrepresented.[68] Sheridan's direction has made one dramatic change however in putting a feminist perspective at the forefront. This has been expressed in her own analyses and editing of women's writing for M-O and her encouragement of other such archival use. The long connections between women and diary writing particularly benefit from this, as does the record of (lower) middle-class (white) women's experience, now as much as earlier in the century. The revival of the panel rather than the paid observation has also been inspired by the insights of feminist sociology. While feminist thinking across disciplines stresses the situatedness of knowledge, the feminist ideal of sociology as a form of mutual empowerment through dialogue beautifully harmonises with the heightened reflexivity encouraged in the current use of the project by writers, readers and researchers. Sheridan's decision to re-term 'respondents' to the Panel as 'correspondents' was one element to this that also testifies to a related interest in genre.

One of the ironies of the public scepticism about M-O's representativity is that it has invariably been combined with an evident appreciation of precisely what is irreducibly individual about it. The newspaper reviews of the initial project talked of the 'human interest' as much more valuable than scientific value, a back-handed compliment that in fact provides a route into what the diarists were really doing. Press reaction today is similar, regularly going to the Archive for the 'colourful' story or the personalised detail in the seemingly unstoppable stream of documentaries and histories of the war. It can confidently be assumed that fifty years from now, whatever form of media and academy the virtual future holds, its representatives will be coming to Mass-Observation to find out what its panel wrote about Diana's death, the Gulf War, sanitary towel marketing, their experience of the internet ... and what it felt like to be an M-O diarist.

from the Archives of the National Lesbian and Gay Survey, London and New York, Routledge, 1992; and *Proust, Cole Porter, Michelangelo, Marc Almond and Me*, London and New York, Routledge, 1993.

Arresting Cinema: Surveillance And The City-State In The Representation Of Hong Kong

Karen Fang

1. This film is discussed by Esther Yau, 'Border Crossing: Mainland China's Presence in Hong Kong Cinema', in Nick Browne (ed), *New Chinese Cinemas*, Cambridge, Cambridge University Press, 1994, pp180-201. Because of the plethora of recent scholarship on Hong Kong and Hong Kong film, in this essay I cite only the best-known or most useful works.

2. The manifest contradictions of a city-state are (1) that unlike most cities, its central source of power remains state government; and (2) that the imagined community or *de facto* nation is solely constituted by urban culture. Kerrie L. MacPherson, 'The City and the State: Historical Reflections on Hong Kong's Identity in Transition, 1997 and Beyond', *Cities*, 14, 5 (1997), 279-286.

3. The problem with the scholarship on Hong Kong visual culture is that it typically reads the films only narratively. The best work on Hong Kong film and architecture is Ackbar Abbas, *Hong Kong: Culture and the Politics of Disappearance*, Minneapolis, University of Minnesota Press, 1997. See also Stephen Teo, *Hong Kong Cinema: The Extra Dimensions*, London, British Film Institute, 1997; Lisa Odham Stokes and Michael Hoover, *City on Fire*, London, Verso, 1999; David

The critically and commercially successful 1984 film *Long Arm of the Law* offers a canonical introduction to Hong Kong.[1] The movie, about mainland Chinese thieves invading the territory, highlights cinematographically a variety of specific city spaces. A chase sequence early in the film uses travelling shots and fragmented views of the shop windows in the streets of Tsim Sha Tsui, to suggest the city's density, pace, and capitalist economy. The film closes with a shoot-out in a squatters' den in Kowloon Walled City, whose claustrophobic quarters are an appropriate setting to illustrate the hard life and inevitable death of Chinese criminals - as well as of the hapless tenants caught in the crossfire. *Long Arm of the Law* is an action-centred and visually spectacular crime drama, which figures Hong Kong as an imperilled territory resisting violent Chinese invasion. It features a corps of police extras who escalate the mayhem, and conflates cinema with police surveillance by thematically linking criminal arrest with the filmic arrest of freeze-frame. This classic Hong Kong film portrays a city at risk, in which threatened urban spaces are issues of national security, and always in need of additional protection.

Hong Kong is a city-state - a metropolitan entity that is also a nation, and a circumscribed urban territory that remains subject to state sovereignty. The complex polity prompts questions of civic representation and national identity. In Hong Kong for example, citizens enjoy freedoms of speech and a right to public demonstration, but have never attained full democratic representation.[2] *Long Arm of the Law* illuminates these aspects of the city-state polity by two central tropes: the conflation of urban and national spaces, and the thematisation of surveillance as the culture's distinctive characteristic. The peculiarities of city-state status were recently eternalised by the transfer from British colonialism to Chinese communism, conclusively precluding the possibility of self-rule. Significantly, the period from the 1984 Sino-British Joint Declaration negotiating reunification to the 1997 handover also coincided with the great era of Hong Kong cinema - especially the crime-cinema genre - and *Long Arm of the Law* helped to inaugurate this. A profusion of recent scholarship on Hong Kong film has already demonstrated how in Hong Kong national identity is shaped in relation to China, the mainland country and ethnically-similar cultures with which Hong Kong shares both its future and its history.[3] These accounts claim

Hong Kong's commercially-driven cinema as a prime site of civic expression, both because its narratives alluded to popular anxieties, and because the illusory capacity of the medium itself was an apt metaphor for the wealthy but politically-occluded nation. This cinema-centred account of the precarious Hong Kong city-state was affirmed poignantly when the national film industry itself began to fail around 1992, and in the years immediately preceding 1997.[4]

This essay on Hong Kong film, architecture, and police media differs from the existing scholarship on Hong Kong visual culture by emphasising its city-state circumstances as the chief condition for the territory's historical privileging of surveillance and arrest. In contrast to the scholarship that primarily stems from the handover era, my argument uncovers the sites of Hong Kong culture and cinema that show the origin - and the persistence - of surveillance practices, even during reunification. This historical narrative pivots on the 1989 Tiananmen Square massacre in Beijing as a catalytic event whose brutal demonstration of authoritarianism, perhaps surprisingly, only consolidated Hong Kong's surveillance culture. In this dire cultural moment, the culturally-influential Hong Kong film industry began its embrace of the police and video, two social and technological apparatuses of surveillance previously unconsidered as key agents in the preservation of a unique Hong Kong culture. A process of localisation by which the diasporic city nurtured an evolving notion of indigenous sovereignty was an integral phenomenon of the external event.[5] This essay addresses current thinking on democracy and privacy, to locate an apparently paradoxical place where surveillance is constitutive of a free society, and discovers Hong Kong as one of the sites of the spectacular and increasingly commercial forms by which surveillance currently prospers all over the globe.[6] The collusive history of surveillance technology in the territory's real and cinematic geography shows Hong Kong to be the product of a police-entertainment industrial complex.

SURVEILLANCE STATE CINEMA AND CCTV

'Surveillance state cinema' is my term for the films of the handover era, which dramatised city-state circumstances by troping urban attributes as national characteristics, and in which the plot device of surveillance was also exploited for its visual interest. *Long Arm of the Law* is the foundational film of the genre. The movie opens with a scene of Chinese gangsters crossing the border from China to Hong Kong, over which computer data detailing the thieves' criminal records is superimposed. The film thus depicts the physical, geographical, and technological devices by which Hong Kong separates itself from the mainland. The film also politicises the gangsters' criminality. The thieves are revealed to be former members of the Communist military (who prepare for both trespass and heist with a military precision that will be a formidable challenge to the Hong Kong police),

Bordwell, *Planet Hong Kong: Popular Cinema and the Art of Entertainment*, Cambridge, Harvard University Press, 2000; Poshek Fu and David Dresser (eds), *The Cinema of Hong Kong: History, Arts, Identity*, Cambridge, Cambridge University Press, 2000.

4. Once the world's third-largest film industry, the fall of 'Hollywood East' has been dramatic. Over the past decade revenues have fallen by 15-20 per cent per year. By 1992 the historical dominance in Hong Kong of local film was it its end: the top-grossing film of 1993 was an American import.

5. A detailed account of Hong Kong as a 'self-sufficient entity' that emerged 'through shedding its previous national and regional links' is Choi Po-King, 'From dependence to self-sufficiency: rise of the indigenous culture of Hong Kong, 1945-1989', *Asian Culture*, 14 (1990), 161-177.

6. Recent examples include William Bogard, *The Simulation of Surveillance*, Cambridge, Cambridge University Press, 1996; David Lyon, *The Electronic Eye: The Rise of the Surveillance Society*, Minneapolis, University of Minnesota Press, 1994; and Clive Norris and Gary Armstrong, *The Maximum Surveillance Society*, Oxford, Berg, 1999.

and thereby personify the conflation of illegal entry, criminal activity, and Chinese political affiliations, that is central to the surveillance state cinema genre. Both the value of surveillance - and the ability of the film medium to enact it - are dramatised in *Long Arm of the Law* during an episode where undercover cops videotape the Chinese thieves. The surveillance footage is replayed in a briefing that aids the police investigation, and the ability of videotape to pause and project mug shots of the criminals is echoed by the movie's own recurrent use of close-up and freeze-frame. These cinematic moments in *Long Arm of the Law* illustrate the genre's conceit, conflating surveillance technology with the feature film by visualising criminal arrest with a pictorially-transfixing filmic arrest. The movie thus symbolically proffers itself as a means of preventing the assault on metropolitan safety it depicts.

Most of the critical work on Hong Kong film overlooks the fact that this evident anxiety over Chinese intrusion in *Long Arm of the Law* is longstanding, as is the turn to institutional and technological means in order to prevent it. Since its emergence after the Second World War as a newly-industrialised nation, Hong Kong has fostered a vibrant economy whose freedoms and high standard of living exist in stark contrast to the economic deprivations and political restrictions of China. Consequently, the city-state has always deployed surveillance mechanisms to prevent its population from metastasising through an influx of cheap labour in the form of the mainland workers who press to join Hong Kong's Chinese community. *Long Arm of the Law* acknowledges such economic need as the main motivator for illegal entry into Hong Kong. The film includes scenes set in China, where wives and mothers plead for money and modern consumer goods. The film is a particularly legible instance of a venerable fear of Chinese intrusion, because its production was contemporary with reunification negotiations, and it was released in the same year as the Joint Declaration, whose announcement of reunification with China represented the worst-case scenario of this longstanding national nightmare. *Long Arm of the Law* supported the standard critical account of handover-era Hong Kong cinema as being an expression of collective concerns, and - as was the case with many of the films of the surveillance state cinema genre, and certainly all of the films cited in this essay - it was a blockbuster.

The private security camera is the implicit emblem of surveillance state cinema. The likeness between the entertainment medium and the familiar mechanism of property protection is evident in the ways in which the cinematic genre fantasises about protecting a national identity that, under the conditions of the city-state polity, is imaginatively contiguous with its urban landscape. The parallels with surveillance videos are also apparent in the assorted stylised filmic devices the genre harnesses in order to thematise visual acuity. The film evokes surveillance by projecting its narratives of detection and police authority with sophisticated cinematographic embellishments, such as point-of-view shots, telescopic or night vision, timecode or location markers, panning, zoom, close-up, and especially the freeze-frame. This 'surveillance state cinema' genre constituted a major form of cinema production during the reunification years, and played a role in fostering the visually spectacular cinema for which Hong Kong became famed; in this way surveillance aesthetics became embedded in Hong Kong popular culture and national consciousness.[7] Indeed, some of the most memorable characteristics of Hong Kong cinema directly illustrate the genre's self-conscious evocation of surveillance technology. A familiar feature of many Hong Kong films is the conspicuous use of blue-filter, whose monochromaticity replicates the shadowy images of closed-circuit television (CCTV) monitoring. *Long Arm of the Law*, for example, deploys this motif in the film's final image, when the blue-filter which depicts the dead bodies of the thwarted Chinese criminals stands in for the prevailing Hong Kong police.

7. Gangster movies constituted nearly half of local film production in 1989.

Other important surveillance state films include *Project A, Part 2* (1987), a period film pitting municipal police against corrupt British and Chinese officials, and *Heroic Trio* (1994), a superhero movie in which Hong Kong children are abducted by Chinese imperial loyalists. Both films allegorically resolve a national crisis by police intervention, and emphasise Hong Kong as a unique and strictly demarcated society and space. (In *Project A-2*, police jurisdiction is a way of invoking metropolitan autonomy, and in *Heroic Trio* the Chinese subversives occupy a subterranean space which literalises their membership of the criminal underground.) Although *Rouge* (1987) features journalists investigating the betrayal of a fifty-year-old lovers' pact (the 50-year period being an allusion to China's reunification pledge to leave Hong Kong unchanged for half a century), this romance film also qualifies as an

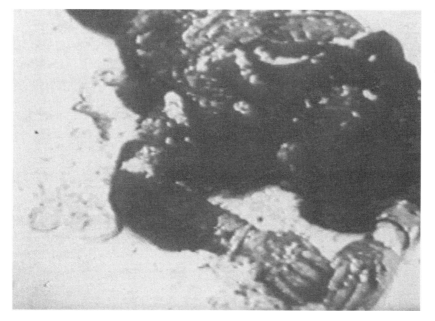

Long Arm of the Law, *courtesy of Johnny Mak Production Co.*

instance of the surveillance state genre because it allegorically deploys the terms of investigative procedure. (The opulent movie also depicts the cityscape with two different types of film, the better to contrast optimistic and cynical perspectives on Hong Kong.) However, by far the most familiar forms of the surveillance state cinema genre are the visually arresting and extremely violent crime films associated with directors such as Tsui Hark, Kirk Wong and John Woo. The apocalyptic trajectories of their films are important because they illustrate the two levels on which surveillance structures such as the security camera function.

A private security camera works both to record illicit acts, thereby enabling criminal capture, and to discourage, by its presence, such acts from being committed. Surveillance state cinema echoed this idea by suggesting that the depiction of violent Chinese intrusion might encourage a defensive national consciousness. But these dual functions of deterrence and apprehension can be contradictory as well as complementary, for in surveillance the commission of a crime also constitutes the system's failure. This apparent paradox of surveillance was epitomised by the relationship between Hong Kong crime cinema and the Tiananmen Square massacre, and was critical to the impact that the Beijing incident had on the Hong Kong film industry.

The high point of surveillance state cinema was the 1989 massacre at Beijing's Tiananmen Square. Although the incident occurred outside of the city-state, the brutal military crackdown was an ominous sign for the future of Hong Kong: it actualised the paranoid narratives of Chinese violence that had already been depicted in Hong Kong film for several years. The historical event's uncanny likeness to Hong Kong's crime cinema tradition was also underscored by the media transmission through which Hong Kong citizens experienced the incident, and was reinforced when Chinese officials shut down broadcasts as the troops moved in. For Hong Kong movie-goers deprived of real images, their screen memories of Chinese violence, retained from surveillance state cinema, provided one way to 'see' the Tiananmen tragedy. But, in keeping with the paradoxes of surveillance technology, if in Hong Kong movie-viewing and film technologies were crucial to people's apprehension of Tiananmen, they were also rendered superfluous by the occurrence of a real event which the cinematic surveillance culture had anticipated. Surveillance state cinema failed as deterrence because it did not stop graphic violence from actually erupting.

In Hong Kong's identification with Tiananmen there was a conflation of the police and the military; and it was the peculiarities of the city-state polity that were responsible for this. In a city-state the police are also the army, and thus in Hong Kong the police were endowed with paramilitary authority. (The territory's colonial history was also a central factor in their status, but is beyond the scope of this essay.) Chinese sovereignty in Hong Kong would be likely to replace the local police with the Chinese People's

Liberation Army (PLA), and this meant that the prospect of reunification, especially after the events of Tiananmen, brought Hong Kong's longstanding anxieties about Chinese incursion into high relief. The threat to the municipal police posed by the Chinese PLA resulted in the costly departures from Hong Kong of major figures in the film industry - departures which paralleled the wider society's trend towards mass emigration, and underscored cinema's status as a microcosm of Hong Kong society.[8] Tiananmen's disastrous legacy for the Hong Kong film industry also included considerable damage to the erstwhile hero of surveillance state cinema - the police figure. The Tiananmen tragedy not only suggested that police might be insufficient protection against the Chinese invasion, but to Hong Kong viewers it also suggested that the police themselves were potential murderers. Thus, in the few successful local films that were made as the industry fell into decline, contemporary concerns about police violence are evident in undercover and rogue cops, or other character types illustrating the likeness of police to criminals; these began to displace the surveillance symbols once vital to Hong Kong cinema.[9]

Hard Boiled (1992) is a noir film that evokes Tiananmen and the subsequent national rise in emigration. The movie opens with two cops considering quitting Hong Kong, and shows the peril of the city when their conversation is interrupted by gunfire; the cop who resisted emigration is killed. Director John Woo conceived the film during Tiananmen, and himself emigrated shortly after the film's completion. His farewell film to Hong Kong cynically interrogates the virtues of surveillance by conflating the misuse of filmic technology with the abuse of police power. During a climactic sequence set in a municipal hospital, the film's villain gains control of the building's video- and audio-monitoring systems; through these he taunts his pursuers, sending his henchmen to mow down victims while the assassins are dressed in fake police uniforms. As an index of the degraded authority accorded to surveillance in this bleak version of urban peril, the film's two police heroes can only retaliate by reclaiming their police identity and deceiving the surveillance technologies. The two cops contrive a false arrest, in which an undercover cop dons a criminal's fake police uniform, bringing the other cop before the security cameras. The violent authoritarianism associated with Tiananmen is suggested not only by the bloodstained police uniforms that circulate throughout the sequence, but also in this ironic moment, when the only way to arrest carnage is to infiltrate the bloodthirsty police. The movie's most Tiananmen-esque moment occurs in the face-off between cop and villain in the final action sequence: the use of a high-angle long shot recalls the famous media image of the protestor confronting a tank during the Tiananmen crackdown. Indeed, Woo astutely extends his frame to depict the media circle monitoring the encounter. The subsequent shot of the cameras rushing in to film the fallen bodies of both cop and villain aptly figures the status of cinematic

8. From 1984-1997 Hong Kong suffered an average emigration of 1 per cent of the population per year.

9. This conflation of police aggression and criminal violence was especially convincing in Hong Kong, because the territory's prohibitions on firearms mean that police and criminals are the only people with guns.

Hard Boiled,
courtesy of
Golden Princess

10. T-L Lui and S.
Chiu, 'Industrial
restructuring and
labour-market
adjustment under
positive non-
interventionism: the
case of Hong Kong',
*Environment and
Planning A*, 25
(1993), 63-79.

11. Videotape
footage captured the
images that were
obstructed from
television
transmission, as well
as transmitted
messages from
student leaders
recounting the
uprising and
denouncing the
Chinese
government.

12. The new video
compact disc (VCD)
technology rampant
in the territory by
the early 1990s only
compounded its
destructive effect.

surveillance after Tiananmen - it is a technology that records tyranny, but cannot prevent it.

Video rather than film is the usual medium of surveillance technology, and its immanence in the genre of surveillance state cinema also accounts for the fall of the Hong Kong film industry. An elision of the difference between film and video was the conceit through which cinema could be read as a surveillance apparatus. In fact, film and video produce disparate visual sensations, and bear notably different cultural connotations. Film is a capital-intensive medium that enables spectacular visual effects, or an illusion of reality, created by artifice. Video is an inexpensive medium whose limited capacity for image enhancement is precisely its virtue. Film was a powerful symbol for Hong Kong, because in financial terms it represented the territory's robust economy, and in visual terms it projected a self-representation which the city-state had hitherto been denied. The value of video, by contrast, as is evident in CCTV-monitoring, and in the pathos of the Tiananmen news footage, is its realism.

The real and symbolic importance of video to Hong Kong cannot be over-emphasised. The manufacture of videotape, its recording/display equipment and associated accessories were crucial to the territory's boom economy during the early 1980s.[10] More relevantly, the portability of video was instrumental in sustaining support in Hong Kong for the Chinese protestors at Tiananmen; it also foreshadowed the abrupt mobility of the disaffected Hong Kong citizens who abandoned Hong Kong after Tiananmen.[11] Video's ability to cross borders exacerbated the decline of the Hong Kong film industry by enabling the rise of a pirate market in videotape technology that cannibalised film industry profits.[12]

After Tiananmen the film industry, once a powerful vehicle for Hong

Kong national identity, suffered a crisis of representation, in both senses of the word. As a visual narrative, in 1989 surveillance state cinema confronted an historical reality that rendered the genre superfluous. As a political symbol, the exhausted genre survived after 1989 only as a poignant reminder of the limitations of this ephemeral and commercial medium. In the subsequent half-life of the Hong Kong film industry, the visual medium which had always been implicit in film superseded film as the pre-eminent cinematic medium of Hong Kong. This changing of the guard from film to video can be seen in other visual elements, such as distortion and truncated frame dimensions, whose presence in Hong Kong cinema imaged the look of video-duplicated film. These cinematographic details also have parallels in the handheld camerawork and grainy images that typified the Tiananmen news footage. However, the superseding of film by video partly coincided with Tiananmen because the technological component had always borne a political element. Many of the pirate operations that undermined the Hong Kong film industry were run by mainland entrepreneurs, who indeed were often the Communist military itself. This interrelation of video and Chinese encroachment even seems to be affirmed by the irony of the acronym for the Chinese state broadcasting station's being 'CCTV'; the appearance of this unfortunately appropriate name on the state's Tiananmen footage underscored its likeness to surveillance video.

'VCDs killed the kung fu star', *The Economist*, 20 March 1999.

MONITORING THE SPACES OF THE CITY-STATE

The imagining of Hong Kong's national territory as a video-monitored urban landscape is linked to the real social and physical antecedents of the contested urban spaces depicted by Hong Kong film. The Hong Kong state centralises and regulates many features of urban life - for example, population density, geographic diversity, and the economy. The territory's geography and built environment dramatise the paradoxes of the city-state: the juxtaposition of infrastructure and services, such as escalators and fast-food counters (which apparently offer free movement and consumer choice at the expedited speed of city life) with the fact that in Hong Kong all land remains state property, and frequently is ordered by compulsory traffic patterns.[13]

The constraints brought to bear on individual agency by the territory's growth are evident in the fortress and carceral architectural styles which characterise both signature buildings and vernacular housing in Hong Kong, and the ubiquitous private security systems. The fact that all persons in the territory are required to carry identification at all times also testifies to the circumscribed experience of urban citizenship in Hong Kong. Ironically, these elements, designed to protect Hong Kong from the vast, authoritarian hinterland it neighbours, only highlight the likeness between the two cultures. Social surveillance is common in urban Chinese societies.[14] Moreover, in Hong Kong, the surveillance system of an affluent and

13. The best work on Hong Kong geography is that of A.R. Cuthbert, e.g, 'The Right to the City: Surveillance, Private Interest and the Public Domain in Hong Kong', *Cities* 14, 5 (1997), 295-311; and 'Under the Volcano: Postmodern Space in Hong Kong', *Postmodern Cities Conference Proceedings, 1993*, Department of Urban and Regional Planning, University of Sydney, pp145-153..

14. On natural surveillance in Chinese culture, see M.C. Cheung, 'Psychopathology Among Chinese People', and D.Y.F. Ho, 'Chinese Patterns of Socialization', both in M.H. Bond, (ed), *The Psychology of the Chinese People*, Hong Kong, Oxford University Press, 1986, pp121-212, 1-37. I thank Roderick Broadhurst of the Departments of Criminology and Sociology of the University of Hong Kong for information regarding natural surveillance in Hong Kong.

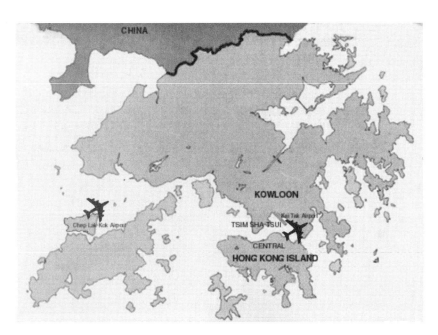

Map, courtesy of author.

exuberantly capitalistic society has become commodified as a means to display wealth.

The controversial film *Cagemen* (1992) deftly depicted the relations between imprisonment, observation and civic expression in Hong Kong. This social realist film portrayed bedspace tenants - the uniquely compact Hong Kong housing form in which individuals occupy barred cubicles no larger than a twin bed - as a socio-architectural synecdoche for the constrained Hong Kong state. The film was censored upon its release in 1992, and this shift in Hong Kong's previously free film culture suggested the complication of surveillance structures after 1989. The film was part of an increasingly politicised understanding of Hong Kong's architecture and geography. The buildings of Tsim Sha Tsui in Kowloon, and the Central district (and, especially, the differences between the two districts), are real sites of urban controversy, giving rise to the contemporary environmental metaphors so provocatively deployed in *Cagemen*.

The Central business district is the political and financial centre of Hong Kong. It is also the geographical originary point of Hong Kong history, and illustrates the polysemic capacity of the city-state to represent simultaneously both municipal and national concerns. In Central, modern corporate skyscrapers like those of the Bank of China and the Hong Kong and Shanghai Bank crowd the colonial buildings of Hong Kong's early years, such as the Legislative Council Building (former site of the Supreme Court), St. John's Cathedral, and the Police Headquarters. These commercial monuments make visible the centrality of capitalism to Hong Kong's existence by obscuring the structures of traditional state authority. The extent to which municipal landmarks might act as metaphors for the politicised contemporary environment of Hong Kong was visible in the rhetorical and architectural debates that occurred over the Central skyline during this period.

The Hong Kong and Shanghai Bank (hereafter HKSB) is a modernist building whose exposed struts and space-age materials assert impregnability. This fortress-architecture effect is enhanced by the building's elevation and restricted access. The first floor of the bank is two storeys above street level, and its single means of entry is an escalator which descends to a panoptic space below the building. The building, designed by British architect Norman Foster, was completed in 1984 (the year of the Joint Declaration); it represented an investment both in the territory's colonial heritage and its future. At that time the bank was the world's single most expensive piece of real estate. Urban mythology figuring the municipal icon as a national symbol embraced its high-tech architecture. Stories described the HKSB building as designed to function for half a century (another allusion to the Chinese fifty year promise), and as capable of being disassembled and reassembled elsewhere (that is, if Chinese sovereignty proved hostile). These narratives highlight the building's mobility and self-sufficiency, figuring the transient image of Hong Kong's culture. Furthermore, the HKSB is the scene of massive weekly gatherings of the city's low-income workers (who primarily stem from the Philippines and other places in Southeast Asia), and thus is an anchor of local immigrant life. Notably, though, both the building's association with recent immigrants and its alleged transportability indicate a lack of any notion of an indigenous Hong Kong identity.

The Bank of China is a postmodern structure of graduated, bevelled towers designed to evoke bamboo, and its pretensions to local and organic qualities forced Hong Kong to attempt to define an urban geography constitutive of its national psyche. The ethnic Chinese architect I. M. Pei aimed to appeal to Hong Kong citizens through the building's rhetorical gestures towards Chinese culture, which also included landscaping and ornamentation suggested by geomancy. But upon its completion in 1989 (the year of Tiananmen), this monument to Chinese ascendancy encountered a hardened anti-China sentiment. Hong Kong citizens accused the bank - then the tallest building in Hong Kong - of destroying urban harmonies and deliberately obscuring local government buildings. These attacks on the Bank of China building - which overlooked similar transgressions by the HKSB and other locally-owned skyscrapers, and arose in spite of the Bank of China's placatory architectural style – were suggestive of a discrete, and immobile, notion of Hong Kong geography that had not previously existed. The defence of local landscape in resistance to the Bank of China building suggested a shift to an anxious assertion of indigenous authority, prompted by reunification and Tiananmen. The 1992 film *Wicked City*, in which the Bank of China building is the place from which a foreign monster launches his hostile take-over of Hong Kong, attests to a notion of local space so cohesive that it can imagine a building in that space as an alien property.

Tsim Sha Tsui is a recreational and shopping district opposite Central on the Kowloon side of the harbour, the region of Hong Kong on the Chinese mainland. As such, concerns over Chinese intrusion have always been acute here. Tsim Sha Tsui in particular is a real or perceived site of crime, due to its warrens of consumption and pleasure, and the illegal immigrants and triad gangs (Hong Kong's form of organised crime, themselves associated with the mainland) who are drawn there.[15] *Long Arm of the Law*, for example, portrays the mainland connections of Kowloon gangs through the sequences set in Kowloon Walled City and Tsim Sha Tsui; and it was often in Kowloon tenements that mainland entrepreneurs carried out their criminal encroachment on the Hong Kong film industry by illegally manufacturing video-duplications.[16] Chungking Mansions, the Kowloon Walled City, and Kai Tak Airport are all spaces of urban surveillance in Kowloon, and, along with the city's subway system, and its connection to the Kowloon-Canton rail station, they are compelled by the city-state's loaded geography to double as symbols of national identity.

Chungking Mansions is a high-rise housing complex located in Tsim Sha Tsui. Its tiny apartments with barred windows exemplify the prison-like architecture of much of Hong Kong housing. However, the Mansions are located in a high-traffic tourist and commercial district, and mostly consist of small businesses and temporary housing. Many of the apartments have been converted into hostel rooms, or offer legal or illegal services, and are visited by travellers, recent immigrants, and other low-income tenants. The Mansions are also believed to be the domain of triads. They thus encapsulate Hong Kong history and national culture in their patterns of settlement and entrepreneurship, and due to their perceived vulnerability to dangerous and illicit tenants, the Mansions also exhibit the surveillance systems characteristic of Hong Kong as a whole. In the Mansions all entry and exit is secured by way of a single closely-monitored passage at the base of each tower. Some proprietors have installed video cameras in stairwells and shop entrances. The surveillance deployed at Chungking Mansions thus internalises the territory's hostile geopolitical environment by conflating alien identity with delinquency, and monitoring a transient or immigrant community as a potentially criminal population.

Kowloon Walled City was a minuscule and hyperpopulated area situated between a thoroughfare and the territorial border. The region was originally a Chinese garrison, overlooked during colonial annexation, and developed as an area free from Hong Kong municipal control. Although the original city walls were soon built over, their facade survived in the massive overdevelopment that lined the area's boundaries. Like Chungking Mansions, the Walled City reproduced Hong Kong history in miniature. Until 1992 the region was inhabited by immigrants and entrepreneurs who

15. The Hong Kong government publishes annual statistics in two reports: the *Crime and Its Victims in Hong Kong* and the *Hong Kong Fight Crime Committee* Reports. In addition to general reportage, in 1992 the most popular Chinese language daily *Ming Pao* published its survey tabulating the population's growing fear index. For the turn in 1988 towards anxieties about illegal immigrants and violence, see John Vegg, 'Illegal Immigration and Cross-Border Crime', in Harold Traver and John Vegg (eds), *Crime and Justice in Hong Kong*, Hong Kong, Oxford University Press 1991, pp83-97.

16. 'China's CD Pirates Find a New Hangout', *BusinessWeek*, 15 December 1997.

tolerated appalling living conditions in exchange for a truly laissez-faire urban environment not on offer in the Hong Kong city-state itself. For the citizens of Hong Kong proper, however, the Walled City's free economy and promise of anonymity was an invidious and embarrassing dystopia, a place which appeared to be a prescient microcosm of a reunified Hong Kong. The Walled City was a haven for criminals and illegal immigrants, who escaped Hong Kong policing by claiming to be Chinese subjects. Inevitably, during the handover era this municipal anomaly full of Chinese criminals and devoid of British law was a prime site of contemporary anti-China agitation. In *Long Arm of the Law*, the extra-jurisdictional shoot-out in the Walled City enacts the contemporary national fantasies of urban surveillance that made the area a major issue in the reunification negotiations in 1984.

But after Tiananmen, reunification preparations aimed at constraining Chinese sovereignty in fact led to repressive measures remarkably similar to the authoritarianism of China. In 1992 all residents of the Walled City were forced to relocate, and it was later razed. What was ostensibly an act of urban improvement was in reality an expression of national political resistance, a municipal issue translated into an act of antagonism against the Chinese state. Ironically, however, the forcible removal by the Hong Kong police of Walled City residents recalled the violence of Tiananmen.

Kai Tak airport was the compact international flight centre in the middle of Kowloon; its location in the urban core symbolised certain aspects of city-state duality, by acknowledging the reliance of this island nation and sea-bound metropolis on international flight, almost as a form of municipal transit. The airport also physically commemorated the modernisation of Hong Kong, formed as it was from the demolished walls of the original

Kowloon Walled City, from Long Arm of the Law, *courtesy of Johnny Mak Production Co.*

Walled City. The airport was imbricated with national consciousness because of its spectacular landings, in which planes descended in harrowing proximity to Kowloon residences, illustrating Hong Kong's voyeuristic as well as transient culture: passengers and residents passed within eyeshot of each other, and planes hovered above street-level as if they were a permanent part of the urban skyline. The experience of landing at Kai Tak is closely associated with cinema, not only because of the frequency with which it appears in Hong Kong film as an establishing shot and a directional metaphor, but also because airlines prepared passengers for the hair-raising experience by screening an instructional in-flight movie. During its tenure it was appropriate that Kai Tak airport occupied the city centre like some sort of capital monument: the entire city of Hong Kong, with its duty-free shopping, transient population, strictly demarcated traffic patterns, and stringent requirements for identity papers, has long seemed like a giant airport.

Reunification intensified the status of the local airport as a symbol of Hong Kong national culture. In 1992 announcements to replace Kai Tak with a new airport were invested with high political significance as British and Chinese officials clashed over construction. Although the passing of Kai Tak was mourned with great nostalgia, Hong Kong citizens also awaited the replacement airport with interest - stimulated by the airport's embodiment of the popular emigration fantasies prompted by the handover. Like the Hong Kong and Shanghai Bank building, the new airport Chep Lap Kok was designed by Norman Foster, and resonated with reunification-era escapist fantasies in its planned location on a larger, less populated, and more distant island, and in its symbolically meaningful opening, scheduled for 1997. More obviously, the new airport recalled the urban flight myths associated with the HKSB municipal symbol, not only as a site of relocation, and as a place that had itself relocated, but also through its very architectural footprint. Chep Lap Kok has the shape of a giant plane.

The Metropolitan Transit Railway (MTR) is Hong Kong's city subway. The MTR spans most of metropolitan Hong Kong, and moves a third of the territory's population every day. Like the Midlevels Escalators, a series of moving stairways that connect Central to a residential district, the MTR epitomises the territory's propensity for traffic control and population monitoring. Both the MTR and the Midlevels Escalators are rife with video- and audio- monitoring. Urban legends abound in which inappropriate behaviour on the Escalators is admonished over loudspeaker. Hong Kong's tendency to incorporate surveillance in urban planning is evident in the subway's history and design. The MTR architecture was partly engineered by local police.[17] Its intestines are characterised by panoptic spaces, strict traffic patterns, and high-technology transfer points that compel user conformity and render delinquency apparent. The MTR directly instantiates the state functions of city infrastructure by effectively policing illegal immigrants. Because

17. Mark S. Gaylord and John F. Galliher, 'Riding the Underground Dragon: Crime Control and Public Order in Hong Kong's Mass Transit Railway', *British Journal of Criminology* 31, 1 (1991), 15-26.

Chep Lak Kok Airport, courtesy of Hong Kong Airport Authority

the MTR connects with the Kowloon-Canton Railway (KCR), the primary means of cross-border travel, it is vulnerable to mainland penetration. (In *Long Arm of the Law* the leader of the Chinese gangsters regularly uses the KCR to trespass into Hong Kong.) But illegal Chinese immigrants are often unfamiliar with urban traffic patterns, and the sophisticated ticket-machine technology of the city subway, and the MTR design exploits this lack of urban sophistication to quickly detain those who blunder in the subway, thereby arresting would-be trespassers.

JOINT-VENTURE CINEMA AND THE POLICE-MEDIA STATE

The Hong Kong Police Force is one of the largest in the world, in absolute and per capita terms. And in addition to their appearances in popular film, the Hong Kong Police themselves operate an extensive media apparatus, which augments their official presence. The Police Public Relations Bureau (PPRB) of the Hong Kong Police commissions recruitment and educational posters which decorate the subways and other city infrastructure, contacts local papers for routine reports on the commendations and civilian awards sponsored by the police, oversees their representation in commercial film, and maintains its own studio and production staff to generate its own releases. Public consumption of police imagery in Hong Kong is enthusiastic.[18] A museum, youth club, and numerous neighbourhood associations run by the police all flourish with regular community interest. The magazine of the Hong Kong Police, *Off Beat*, has a circulation that far exceeds the number of bureau employees,

18. The *Market Survey on Police Recruitment and Advertisements - An Executive Summary*, MDR Technology Limited, 1991, commissioned by the Hong Kong Police, shows a high index of public support for the police.

and an unsolicited history of the Police was a best-selling book. On television the police appear on officially-produced public interest shows that are often the most popular programmes during weekend primetime, and have also been the subject of fictional series (such as *CID*), which have been among the most successful broadcasts in Hong Kong history.[19] With the municipal police thus ubiquitous in urban culture through both official representation and in popular consumption, Hong Kong is a police state that is a media state; paradoxically, the police are also a fourth estate - a highly visible socio-cultural agency in which the police are a site of popular identification.

The Jackie Chan vehicle *Police Story* (1985) illustrates Hong Kong's saturation by police imagery. In the film Chan is a cop selected to represent the force in its next media campaign. Chan is nominated for an award and dispatched by the Police Public Relations Bureau to appear in magazines and television shows (in the movie's sequel Chan also appears on promotional posters adorning station walls). The dialogue of Chan's character repeatedly invokes his police profession, and this is a refrain that recurs in many of Chan's subsequent films, such as the surveillance state cinema film *Project A, Part 2*. The commercially successful movie was an important early film in a screen career that has since become interchangeable with Chan's police identity (even in roles where Chan does not play a policeman, his facility for martial arts, stunts and physical comedy is usually exploited through some sort of investigative or law-enforcement personality). The theme song to *Police Story* is perhaps a unique register of the intimate collaboration between the police and popular media in Hong Kong. The tune, written and performed by Chan, was lent in perpetuity to the Hong Kong Police for use in their own television shows. Chan thus augments his personal publicity by directly associating himself with official police propaganda, and in return promotes the police with his movie-star celebrity, exemplifying the profitable franchise of the police that is possible in Hong Kong consumer culture.

This media-savvy Hong Kong Police was born in the early 1970s, long before reunification, at a time when the legitimacy of the local police was already unstable.[20] As a body of public servants invested with state authority, the police force embodies city-state contradictions. Both its colonial and ethnic Chinese histories further complicate the police symbol in Hong Kong. The British legacy meant that it was perceived as a corrupt and racially privileged body, but, simultaneously, both British and Chinese citizens believed that it was infiltrated by triads. Hence the bureau also suffered from adverse associations with China. Public distrust of the police reached its height in the years between 1969 (when the agency received royal commendation for using force to quell urban demonstrations) and 1974, when the police protested at measures aimed at limiting police authority. This civic unrest was resolved by a swathe of mandates designed to bring the police into line with contemporary culture. These policies increased native employment, and ensured a majority of native representation in the

19. Official police programmes produced by the HKP Police Public Relations Bureau include the Chinese language short programme *Police Call*, the English-language short programme *Police Report*, and the full-length English-language show *Crime Watch*. Radio-Television Hong Kong (RTHK) produces the hosted shows *Police Magazine* and *Deception*, the programme with the Chan song. Kevin Sinclair, *Asia's Finest*, 1983, is the original unsolicited, best-selling book on the HKP.

20. Karen Fang, 'Britain's Finest: The Royal Hong Kong Police' in Antoinette Burton (ed), *After the Imperial Turn*, Duke University Press, forthcoming 2002.

bureau's highest offices. They also combated corruption, and elevated the social standing of the police, by increasing pay and rewarding professional improvement. The police also became accountable to the Independent Commission Against Corruption (ICAC), a powerful external watchdog agency which subjected to surveillance the agents of surveillance. Most importantly, in their efforts to rehabilitate and consolidate police authority the police also tapped into Hong Kong's emerging media culture. It was during this period that the Hong Kong Police founded the Police Public Relations Bureau which, along with the ICAC, devoted considerable resources to media and public relations, including the aforementioned fictional and public interest TV shows. Clearly, it was this era that saw the beginning of the by-now-familiar story, of Hong Kong culture correcting surveillance by intensifying it.

The reunification process of 1984-1997 reprised these longstanding concerns about police identity and power, and they were resolved with the same strategies for restoring political stability that had been employed in the earlier reform era. Reunification-era anxieties about the police focused on the paramilitary authority the police were scheduled to retain until 1997, and on legislation to grant broad increases in police authority.[21] If Hong Kong was to weather reunification the reassertion of police legitimacy was imperative. Thus in 1992, when crime and public cynicism was rampant, the police responded with media strategies first mastered in the earlier reform era. For example, a recurring topic was the unfortunate likeness of the olive-coloured colonial police costumes to Chinese PLA uniforms. The Hong Kong Police astutely recognised that some stabilisation of this embattled national symbol could be effected by preventing this thin green line separating Hong Kong from China from seeming to dissolve into China itself. After considerable deliberation the Police elected to maintain their traditional uniforms as a symbol of local continuity, and deployed a series of press releases to explain this decision.

'Joint-venture' cinema is my term for the film genre that depicts co-operation between the Hong Kong and mainland police. These films exemplify the cultural importance of the Hong Kong police, and, in contrast to films of the surveillance state genre, portray the police succeeding at the maintenance of law and order. The genre also emphasises commerce as a crucial aspect of police work in Hong Kong: the phrase 'joint-venture' is used in many of these films. The romantic comedy series *Her Fatal Ways* (*I-IV;* 1990, 1991, 1992, 1993) illustrates the genre.[22] These movies trace the career of a Chinese cop seduced by the Hong Kong system. In the first film a high-ranking female officer related to Communist Party officials clashes with the Hong Kong cop with whom she is partnered in the territory. But her growing romantic interest in the cop soon precipitates her capitulation to local custom and municipal rule. Her aggressive tactics are shown to be unnecessary, and she abandons her military uniform for flattering urbane clothing.

21. Michael Ng-Quinn, *Bureaucratic Response to Political Change: Theoretical Use of the Atypical Case of the Hong Kong Police*, Hong Kong, Hong Kong Institute of Asia-Pacific Studies, The Chinese University of Hong Kong, 1991. For a review of the internal and handover-related issues confronting the police in the 1984-1997 era, see Raymond Wacks (ed), *Police Powers in Hong Kong: Problems and Prospects*, Hong Kong, Faculty of Law, University of Hong Kong, 1993.

22. This series is discussed in Shu-mei Shih, 'Gender and a New Geopolitics of Desire: The Seduction of Mainland Women in Taiwan and Hong Kong Media', *Signs* 23, 2 (1998), 287-319.

The movie ends with a border scene in which she returns to the mainland. This scene announces a new convention of the joint-venture film by reversing the border-crossings of surveillance state cinema. In the final installment of *Her Fatal Ways*, the mainland policewoman settles in Hong Kong and gets a job in a private security firm. The movie thus portrays commercial culture as both a means of military reform, and the future of the police profession.

Other joint-venture movies include the blockbusters *Police Story III: Supercop* (1992), which follows Jackie Chan to China, and *Rock n' Roll Cop* (1994), in which a Hong Kong cop helps a Chinese policeman attain vengeance on a criminal from Shenzhen. Significantly, such joint-venture films were successful even as surveillance state cinema and the rest of Hong Kong film began to decline. The Jackie Chan vehicles and Kirk Wong films, as well as some others, survived the uncertain handover era by banking on movie careers closely associated with police identities. Like Chan's, the successes in director Kirk Wong's oeuvre are almost entirely of police (or police-type) films. The relationship of the Hong Kong Police with the film industry is a bureaucratic parallel to joint-venture cinema. Indeed, the Hong Kong film industry can be considered as an unofficial component of the police profession. *Long Arm of the Law* was written by Philip Chan, a former police officer turned film director. (Chan is also noted for *The Immigrant Policeman*, 1989, which considers the consequences of officers who leave Hong Kong and forget their roots.) Many Hong Kong film directors grew up with or were trained in the police television shows commissioned by the Hong Kong Police. When John Woo cast

Bodyguard from Beijing, *courtesy of Golden Harvest*

himself as a cop in *Hard Boiled* (as well as in his earlier breakthrough film *A Better Tomorrow*, 1986), the director acknowledged the fluidity between the police and entertainment professions. This real and industry-wide practice of collaboration with the Hong Kong Police also helps account for the universality of surveillance genres, despite their individual artistic visions, among the era's leading film directors.

Bodyguard from Beijing (1994) and *Fist of Legend* (1994) are graphic examples of the yoking of commerce and the police image characteristic of the joint-venture film. These Jet Li vehicles were the joint ventures of a mainland and Hong Kong production company, and were aimed at introducing Li, a mainland star, to the lucrative Hong Kong audience. *Bodyguard from Beijing* is a romance about a PLA officer assigned to protect a Hong Kong woman. She criticises his uniform and cites Hong Kong law to resist the constraints he imposes. At first she destroys the surveillance equipment with which he constantly monitors her. Like other joint-venture films, such as the *Her Fatal Ways* series, the movie romanticises and domesticates the police figure. In the scenes where the cop scans his ward on the CCTV-monitor, surveillance appears as voyeurism and sexual interest. The movie also reproduces another joint-venture convention by concluding with a border scene. However *Bodyguard from Beijing* differs from the usual joint-venture movie by figuring Hong Kong as a lesser place without the Chinese presence. The Hong Kong woman cries as Li's police car departs. The conceit of this quintessential joint-venture film is that the movie itself compensates for the absence of the protective Chinese police. Li's appearance in the cinematic police vehicle (visually figured

Bodyguard from Beijing, courtesy of Golden Harvest

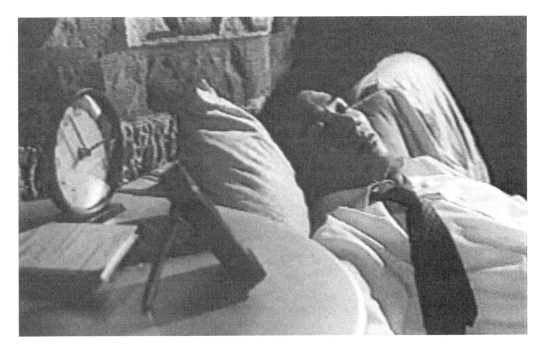

in this scene by the car bedecked with Chinese flags that bears the Chinese cop away) assures his settlement in the Hong Kong market. The suggestion that Hong Kong moviegoers will yearn for Li, just as the film's heroine had come to desire his surveillance, is achieved by an exact correspondence between movie frames and what Li's character views on the surveillance monitor.

Fist of Legend is a remake of the important early Hong Kong film *Fist of Fury* (1972, a.k.a. *The Chinese Connection*), starring Hong Kong screen legend Bruce Lee. The movie is a period film about ethnic Chinese resistance to imperial authorities. Like *Bodyguard from Beijing*, *Fist of Legend* appropriates the conventions of Hong Kong cinema to naturalise the incursion of mainland star Li. The remake revises the ending in *Fist of Fury* to reject the surveillance state cinema conventions that were devised metaphorically to arrest his Chinese presence. The original film concludes with a freeze-frame on the protagonist (Bruce Lee) as he martyrs himself before an imperial firing line. The scene is an arresting cinematic image, but a bleak statement on the viability of nationalism. *Fist of Legend* replaces this filmic arrest with an indeterminate narrative ending where the protagonist (Jet Li) survives to found an underground intelligence network whose mission is to subvert the city's foreign regime, thereby preserving nationalism. The Li film thus exemplifies the appropriation of police cinema to mitigate a potentially politicised commercial endeavour, and illustrates how Hong Kong cinema in the post-Tiananmen era of industrial decline survived by reconsolidating its time-honoured surveillance aesthetics.

These manifold aspects of police media practices, and the actual role police play in the local entertainment industry, as well as the supplementary representation the police gain through their popular imagery, all suggest that in Hong Kong police agency is moving into the realm of the commercial and apolitical. The media agency of the Hong Kong Police realise the spectacular aspects of the surveillance performed by the police and replicated by video technology. Conversely, the cinematic police story genre makes evident the similarity of police to video-monitoring, and the film traditions which emulate it. *Police Story*, for example, concludes with a climactic action sequence that not only uses freeze-frame, but also replays the climax several times. This rupture in cinema's narrative illusion exhibits a video capacity for pausing and replaying that replaces police action with the actor's achievement - in this case, the stunt with which Chan always closes a film. (This idea of police heroism expropriated as cinematic aura is even more obvious in the video-filmed out-takes that play during the film's credits, another Jackie Chan movie trademark.) The conceit illustrates how the moment of criminal arrest in the Hong Kong police film is exchanged for the star's close-up, using film glamour or cinematic celebrity to supplant the police function that originally inspired it.

Official police videos from the reunification era duplicate the stylistic and narrative adaptations that characterise joint-venture cinema of the post-Tiananmen era. During the first reform era the Public Relations Bureau of Hong Kong Police began to make and distribute informational videos designed to promote the weakly-legitimated police. In the reunification era the value of these promotional videos was even greater: not only did they calm public anxieties about reunification; they also helped to ensure Hong Kong's post-handover economic well-being by being mailed to potential outside investors to reassure them of the territory's viability. As in joint-venture cinema, the strategic role of this police representation in maintaining the territory's economic stability was evident in the significant visual and generic change seen in the new police videos. Whereas early police videos had featured fast-paced action-centred narratives showcasing technology and the spectacle of police mobilisation, the videos produced in anticipation of reunification, and especially in the wake of Tiananmen, were replaced by slower-paced, nostalgic narratives set in residential communities, emphasising the contribution of the police to social services.[23] These new police videos paralleled trends in contemporary Hong Kong cinema by featuring a reduced concern for police spectacle in favour of a new emphasis on character development.

The role of the police in combating the video piracy that drove the film industry to near collapse is a less visible, but more commercial, application of Hong Kong's surveillance culture and economy. As piracy escalated, film industry officials who felt that the attenuated duties of the post-reunification police still included border control entreated the Hong Kong police to patrol video production. The police were asked to prevent Chinese pirates from absconding with Hong Kong films, and to combat the illegal video duplications that were then flooding the Hong Kong market.[24] This refiguring of police as customs agents shows their function in local commerce. It also once again assigned a national function to the now solely municipal police agency, and typified the qualified freedoms of the city-state by instituting yet another control on the supposedly free economy of Hong Kong. Thus, as the police were further enmeshed in the local film industry and their place reconsolidated in the national consciousness, they were able to rehabilitate the surveillance they signified, precisely by their strategic relationship to the once-pernicious video technology which was instrumental to the police's reinvention. Although this transition in modes of police agency may have been most evident in the reunification era, it only continued a trend that began decades before. I close with one of the post-Tiananmen reinventions of police cinema, which incorporated the aesthetics of video surveillance to transcend contemporary trends of industrial decline, thereby projecting the post-reunification future of Hong Kong, as well as its consequential film industry.

23. See Hong Kong Police videos such as *A Service of Quality*. During my research in 1998 the Hong Kong Police Public Relations Bureau allowed me to view, but not use, certain videos no longer in use, such as *Policing Hong Kong* (1996). The videos for which I was forbidden use were described as 'misrepresentations' that 'labelled' police activities.

24. See 'Hong Kong fights piracy on the high CDs', *The China Business Review*, November/ December 1999.

Chungking Express (1994) is a romance from the post-Tiananmen era of industrial decline. The movie consists of two police stories set in specific city spaces, whose striking cinematographic details differentiate the film's two parts. The first story, set in Tsim Sha Tsui, features an unconsummated encounter between a detective obsessed with expiry dates and a paranoid smuggler desperate to escape the city. The second story, set in Central, follows the courtship of a beat policeman by a woman who dreams about moving to California. The woman secretly monitors the cop, breaking into his apartment and controlling his life by altering his home and possessions. The colourful, fast-paced, and distinctly cinematic style of the first story contrasts with the over-exposed sequences, shot with a still or hand-held camera, in the second story, whose look is reminiscent of video. Racing through Chungking Mansions, Kai Tak airport, the MTR, the Midlevels Escalators, and the Central Police Headquarters, *Chungking Express* features all of Hong Kong's surveillant urban spaces. Such comprehensive representation of Hong Kong geography, featuring police protagonists and plots of detection, crime, and emigration, suggests *Chungking Express* as a generic variation on surveillance state cinema.

Instead, *Chungking Express* is a homage to the surveillance state genre that is also a deliberate evacuation of the cinema's conceits. The film follows in the later tradition of police joint-venture movies by exchanging the crime story's cynical surveillance for a romantic plot. In the chase sequence with which the film opens, the detective collides with the woman with whom, the voice-over confides, he will soon fall in love. A freeze-frame foregrounds this replacement of surveillance cinema conventions by depicting the woman and not the criminal that the cop had meant to arrest. In the second story the woman's inhabitation of the cop's home testifies to her romantic devotion, and her spying on him while he rides the Midlevels Escalators registers as another sign of affection, thereby reversing and romanticising the actual interpellations that occur in this infrastructure. The movie also follows in the tradition of the joint-venture movie by figuring the police as the agents of commercial investment and inverting the emigration definitive of surveillance state cinema. The woman in the second story departs only to return to Hong Kong, and the cop acquires the fast-food stall where they first met. In the final scene, where the woman draws an aeroplane boarding pass for the cop in order to indicate her desire to renew their relationship, *Chungking Express* re-presents air travel not as a process of departure but instead as one of renewed ties to Hong Kong. The movie's optimism about a discrete Hong Kong identity is also evident in its retraction from the territory's historically- and cinematically-conventionalised criminal geography. In the progression from the film's first to second story, the movie rejects the usual spaces of surveillance state cinema by moving from Tsim Sha Tsui to Central.

Cinematographically, *Chungking Express* differs from surveillance state cinema by recuperating both video and the police symbol, or precisely those things most associated with the genre's decline. The double aesthetics of the movie embraces both film-as-film, and as a medium complemented by video technology. In the first story, lush colour, under-cranking, stop-action, and other sophisticated cinematographic techniques rehabilitate the urban landscape as beautiful. The documentary look of the second story imparts intimacy. The movie also intertextually revises narrative conventions of the surveillance state cinema genre. In the second story, an introductory close-up of actor Tony Leung reproduces a shot from *Hard Boiled*, in which Leung also starred. *Chungking Express*, however, disassociates violence from the police figure by depicting the actor originally associated with that image as a beat policeman (and in fact in the movie the cop seems never to do any police work at all). The movie also replaces with a blue uniform the actual green uniform of this police rank, which was such an inflammatory icon during reunification. It resembles the joint-venture movies of Jet Li by using romance to facilitate a potentially-politicised screen debut. The love interest in the second story is the mainland pop star Faye Wong. The movie's actualisation of joint-venture conceits extends to a reversal of the emigration and capital flight then dominant in the Hong Kong industry. While filming the movie during reunification, the Shanghai-born director Wong Kar-wai, who had trained in the television programmes commissioned by the Hong Kong police, chose, like the cop in his film, to stay in Hong Kong.

The fragmented narratives and cinematographic innovations in *Chungking Express* marked a new aesthetic in Hong Kong film. Spawning numerous imitators, the film was the *Long Arm of the Law* of its time. Of the few Hong Kong movies from this period to achieve significant critical and box office success, many bore the look that *Chungking Express* introduced. The film's importance for Hong Kong was threefold: commercially, the film located a newly profitable vein of representation; visually and generically, the hybrid visual style and domesticated police narrative incorporated video aesthetics and redeemed an exhausted genre; and conceptually, *Chungking Express* projected new ways through which surveillance continued to be constitutive of Hong Kong identity. The film represented urban geography and its agents of surveillance as worthy of investment, not hostile, and committed to a discrete identity and territorial site. The film is a postmodern, post-Tiananmen vision of a post-national polity that continued the conventions of police joint-venture movies by reconsolidating cinematic surveillance as a national symbol. *Chungking Express* was both the end of, and the sequel to, *Long Arm of the Law*.

Films discussed:
A Better Tomorrow	John Woo, 1986
Bodyguard from Beijing	Corey Yuen, 1994

Cagemen	Jacob Cheung, 1992
Chungking Express	Wong Kar-wai, 1994
Fist of Fury (The Chinese Connection)	Lo Wei, 1972
Fist of Legend	Gordon Chan, 1994
Hard Boiled	John Woo, 1992
Her Fatal Ways (1)	Alfred Cheung, 1990
Her Fatal Ways (2)	Alfred Cheung, 1991
Her Fatal Ways (3)	Alfred Cheung, 1992
Her Fatal Ways (4)	Alfred Cheung, 1994
Immigrant Policeman, The	Phillip Chan, 1989
Long Arm of the Law	Johnny Mak, 1984
Police Story	Jackie Chan, 1985
Police Story III: Supercop	Stanley Tong, 1992
Project A, Part II	Jackie Chan, 1987
Rock n' Roll Cop	Kirk Wong, 1994
Rouge	Stanley Kwan, 1987
Wicked City	Tsui Hark, 1997

A Question Of Sport? Butler Contra Laclau Contra Zizek

Jeremy Gilbert

Judith Butler, Ernesto Laclau, Slavoj Zizek, *Contingency, Hegemony, Universality: Contemporary Dialogues on the Left*, Verso, London 2000, 336pp; £15.00 paperback; £45.00 hardback.

Contingency, Hegemony, Universality is a publishing exercise which might either be described as bold, original and refreshing or vain, self-indulgent and infuriating. The book consists of a series of essays by three of the leading theorists currently writing in the English language: Ernesto Laclau, Judith Butler and Slavoj Zizek. A debate - often implicit, occasionally explicit - between these three figures, all of whom claim to occupy the theoretical and political territory of 'radical democracy' first set out by Laclau and Chantal Mouffe in *Hegemony and Socialist Strategy*, has been carried out in the margins and asides of their published works and public appearances for some time now. Essays and books by several of their respective followers, and high-profile essays by Zizek and Butler, have foregrounded their disagreements.

This book seeks to demarcate the differences between its contributors, as well as the points of connection, according to a novel procedure. To begin with each contributor poses a series of eight to ten questions to the others, each expressed in a short paragraph, at the beginning of the book. The questions range across the current theoretical preoccupations of the authors and the historic points of contention between them: the meaning and viability of the Lacanian topology of the subject, in particular the conceptual status of 'the Real'; the nature of political identification; the continued relevance of Laclau and Mouffe's post-structuralist conceptualisation of 'hegemony'; the conceptual and political status of forms of universality; the theory and politics of 'difference' (sexual or otherwise); the political and conceptual status of forms of pluralism and particularism for radical politics today; the relationship between historicism, formalism and transcendentalism in contemporary theory; the relationship between Lacan and other branches of 'post-structuralism'; the philosophical legacies of Hegel and Kant. Each author then replies to these questions in an essay of approximately forty pages. Each then produces a response of similar length to the first three essays, followed by a final response to the preceding discussion. The resulting essays are presented with no index and a rather sketchy guide to contents.

A book largely made up of commentaries on and responses to its own earlier chapters is remarkably difficult to review, spending as it does more than half of its time *reviewing itself.* At its best, the result is a work which combines an uncommon level of rigorous and direct argumentation with something of the thrill of a sports event: one cannot help cheering on each player in turn as they deftly dodge the rhetorical blows of the others, blocking spurious arguments with lightning logic and scoring points with dazzling displays of scholarship and rigour. At its worst, the effect is a frustrating degree of repetition and pedantry, as each author clarifies again and again positions they feel (rightly, in almost all cases) to have been misunderstood by their interlocutors. Readers are likely to find themselves in equal parts annoyed and entertained by the palpable irritation of the contributors with each other as the book draws to a close, having produced few instances of any of them taking the crucial step of answering the others' questions in terms other than their own.

This, perhaps, is the book's greatest weakness, and yet also its greatest strength - and one which this format renders almost inevitable. Ultimately, the authors spend most of the time expounding and clarifying their own positions and the unique theoretical vocabularies within which they are expressed, and upbraiding their interlocutors for failing to comprehend the same issues in the same terms. This is particularly ironic insofar as one of the key points of agreement reached between Butler and Laclau is on the centrality to successful political projects of practices of translation.

It would be quite unfair, however, to charge the authors with equal complicity in this failure to translate. Butler and Laclau at crucial junctures do indeed make the necessary effort to understand the significance of the different valencies each attaches to particular phrases, while the bitterest exchanges in the book occur at the points where the two of them accuse each other of failing to define and properly historicise their *own* terms (a charge which, it might be objected, can always be levelled at any text). Zizek, for his part, is interested only in a one-way translation, redescribing all concepts and phenomena in the language of 'Lacanese' and insisting that that tongue can only ever be understood as a sub-dialect of 'Hegelese'. Like any fundamentalist, the possibility that other languages might ever be desired or even required is simply outside his frame of reference, and the only reason he can entertain for anyone disagreeing with him is that they have not understood; his response to any question is simply to re-state his position in ever more intransigent terms.

The difference between the approach taken by Zizek and his co-contributors is in fact clear from the start. Where the questionnaires produced by Laclau and Butler consist of open-ended questions, every one of Zizek's 'questions' are rhetorical in nature, stridently demanding that the receiver choose between one of two alternatives: a ludicrously simplistic position attributed to Zizek's bogeyman 'postmodernism'/'deconstructionist doxa'/'historicism' and the alternative Hegelian-Lacanian position which Zizek makes no secret of his intention to defend, come what may. For example, when Butler asks, 'Can the ahistorical recourse to the Lacanian bar be reconciled with the strategic question that hegemony poses, or does it stand as a quasi-transcendental limit on all possible subject-formation and, hence, as indifferent to politics?', it may be clear where her sympathies lie (with a position which is sceptical towards the political utility of Lacanian ideas), but she is clearly asking for genuine clarification of the views of her colleagues. When, by contrast, Zizek asks, 'Is the Lacanian Real the ultimate bedrock, the firm referent of the symbolic process, or does it stand for its totally non-substantial inherent limit, point of failure, which maintains the gap between reality and its symbolisation, and thus sets in motion the contingent process of historicisation-symbolisation?', there is no question of there actually being a question. Not only is it clear that Zizek is certain as to what the answer is going to be (the latter); his question is framed according to a distinction which can only produce the Zizekian response, since no one who knows anything about Lacan is going to defend the former position - unless on the grounds that Zizek's alternative is a false one. Every one of Zizek's 'questions' takes this form, a form which demonstrates his apparent inability even to imagine what it would be like to think outside of his Hegelian-Lacanian orthodoxy.

It would be unfair, not to say unsporting, simply to write off Zizek's contribution. The constant re-statement of his basic positions provokes him, by the time of the final instalment, to present an exposition of Lacan-Hegel of unparalleled lucidity, making quite clear that the terms in which he understands the Lacanian schema are not at all vulnerable to the usual criticisms of it, and indeed present a considerable challenge to any theoretical model predicated on such critiques. As little as Zizek seems to understand the positions of anyone else, he unquestionably remains the key expositor of Lacanian cultural theory in the current era, and the first half of his final essay is a unique defence of Lacanian Hegelianism which casts it in terms refreshingly different from the provocatively metaphysical rhetoric for which he has become famous.

And yet, typically for a theoretical player of such verve and brilliance, it is at precisely the moments when Zizek appears to be at the peak of his form that his game collapses, and he crosses the line into absurdity. Zizek's stunning defence of Lacan and Hegel falls apart when he attempts to reverse the flow of argument and go on the offensive against his perceived enemies. Like so many critics of 'multiculturalism', 'postmodernism' and 'cultural studies' (all, we are assured, players on the same team), Zizek fails to cite even one example of these ubiquitous and mercurial foes. Not a single reference to a text or author is offered in the attacks on these supposed enemies with which Zizek closes his last two contributions. Despite Zizek's early assertion that the answer to the question 'class struggle or postmodernism?' is 'yes please' (a joke he evidently thinks original enough to need explaining), he clearly regards the latter as the enemy of the former. Speaking in the name of a Marxism so orthodox it would have embarrassed

Trotsky (never mind Marx), Zizek's closing attempts to marry it with his Lacanian fundamentalism appear by turns merely clumsy and excruciatingly embarrassing. His assertion that 'capitalism is the Real' of contemporary politics, his suggestion that the world class system can be mapped according to the tripartite topology of symbolic (the 'workers': presumably everyone from primary school teachers to millionaire market analysts), imaginary (the conservative 'middle classes' who still believe in 'the wholeness of society', wherever they are) and real (the lumpen masses) is simply a sociological absurdity, especially from any kind of Marxian perspective, and one which it would really have been kinder for some editor to dispense with. Zizek's reliance on analogical and allegorical arguments which see the logic of symbolic/imaginary/real reproduced at every level of experience carries no logical weight at all, as pointed out by both Laclau and Butler.

At the end of the day, Zizek is only convincing when playing on his Lacanian home ground. In particular, his attempts to bolt a crude Marxist account of the determining effects of 'capitalism' as the absolute horizon of the contemporary and the need for history-changing revolutionary 'acts' onto the sophisticated Lacanian framework which made his reputation is simply no match for a wily old Althusserian like Ernesto Laclau. What is most impressive about the latter's contribution is not merely its displays of technical skill in the matter of abstract argumentation, but the weight of scholarship which underpins it. Laclau's arguments against Zizek's logic - and his accusations that Zizek is, in the end, an apolitical thinker incapable of moving beyond the limits of purely psychoanalytic thought - must ultimately be judged according to the taste and discernment of the reader. The moments when he scores most decisively against his opponent are when he deflects some shot from Zizek with a deftly understated gesture, revealing at last his far greater experience of the game. It is easy to forget, given the nature of their recent outputs and the tone of the early parts of this work, and especially given Zizek's appeals to a Marxist tradition he claims to uphold, that of the two it is Laclau who has the greater standing as a scholar of Marxism, while for Zizek Marx is implicitly read as a follower and interpreter of Hegel of rather less importance than Lacan. For me the most devastating blow which Laclau strikes in the whole book is where he quietly points out that Zizek's 'Marxism' simply ignores the entire past century of Marxist thought and debate. Similarly, to Zizek's insistence that capitalism is 'the Real' which contemporary theoretical discourse, in its complicity with neo-liberal hegemony, forecloses, Laclau merely replies that this cannot be the case as 'capitalism' is quite clearly only effective *within* a symbolic order.

It is his authority as a scholar which is also most convincing in Laclau's disagreements with Butler. In this case, the object of disagreement is the proper interpretation and implications of the work of Lacan, which Laclau believes do not lend support to an essentialist account of sexual difference in the manner that Butler fears. However much the reader may be won over by Butler's lucidity and passionate political commitment, always more engaging than Zizek's quixotic bluster or Laclau's dry detachment, one is left with the sense that her criticisms of the Lacanian vocabulary are based on a certain textbook understanding of Lacan which bears little relation to Lacan as read by experts on his work such as Zizek and Laclau.

Even if this is the case, however, it does not excuse Zizek's and Laclau's reluctance to engage properly with the issues raised by the facts which are the source of Butler's anxiety: that there *is* an account of Lacan's ideas which is widely circulated in the Anglophone academy and which is implicitly, if not explicitly, essentialist and homophobic in its implications; that there *really are* Lacanian psychoanalysts running around making explicitly homophobic statements in the French press and elsewhere. What is particularly strange is that none of the contributors tackle the issue of the problematic implications of making 'castration', 'sexual difference' and 'the Real' virtually synonymous terms with as much directness as Zizek does in the appendix to his earlier volume *The Metastases of Enjoyment*. Instead, this issue, like that of the historical status of concepts such as 'hegemony' and indeed 'historicity', gives rise to the most protracted three-way conflict of the book, that accurately described by Butler as its 'comedy of formalisms'. Within this comedy, each of the contributors comes to accuse the others of being excessively formalist or empiricist in the implications of their arguments and to refer this disagreement to a misplaced understanding of the significance of Hegel's critique of Kant and a misunderstanding of the relationship between Hegel and Lacan. Zizek has no doubt either that Lacan is the second-coming of Hegel or that simply to find Laclau guilty of 'Kantianism' is to prove him wrong; Laclau disputes the authority of Hegel, as anyone so imbued with the thought of Althusser and Derrida must, while denying that Lacan's thought is fundamentally Hegelian in nature; Butler defends Hegel but remains sceptical that the implicit anti-essentialism of his thought is in fact compatible with Lacan. What emerges, as Laclau points out, is an intriguing absence of clear lines of demarcation.

At least, that is a fair interpretation as long as each of these issues is regarded as of similar importance. However, what really emerges by the end of the book is on the one hand a set of scholastic, exegetic disputes over the proper understanding of Lacan and Hegel and on the other a real political gulf separating Laclau and Butler on the one side from Zizek on the other. While the former remain committed to the 'left postmodernist' project of radical and plural democracy, resolutely refusing the distinction between 'revolutionary' and 'reformist' politics, Zizek commits himself to the class struggle and revolution against capitalism, condemning those who decline to do likewise as petit-bourgeois lapdogs of neo-liberalism.

In the process it is actually Butler who emerges as the most appealing player, and it is clear why she is the one who has cast the most powerful spell over the English-speaking audience in recent years. It is the simple readability of Butler's contributions, the rate at which they generate concepts and arguments which are readily understood and easy to apply elsewhere, which marks them out. Laclau may be right, for instance, that his concept of 'equivalence' is theoretically preferable to Butler's 'translation' (both of them attempts to describe the logic by which elements are reconfigured within a hegemonic operation), but it is not nearly so suggestive or as amenable to an audience more used to thinking in terms of poetics than formal logic. It is Butler's straightforward indignation at the apparent unconcern with which Lacanian theorists trample over the basic assumptions of queer feminism which is easier to sympathise with than either Zizek's macho posturing or Laclau's intimidating scholarship. Even when she trips and falls, as she appears to when in direct confrontation with Laclau, she has our sympathy, even though it is he who displays that knowledge and skill which finally leaves him in control of the game.

Not that such skill is always required. In particular, Zizek's unqualified, unjustified and unsubstantiated assessments, often framed as rhetorical questions ('Is it not obvious that … ?'), are as easy to refute as they are to make. On the other hand, Zizek's insistent demand that a position be taken on the question of capitalism, its effects, and its possible replacement is a timely provocation to 'post-Marxist' thought. While Laclau and Butler have both made incisive and important remarks on the implications of their work for the theorisation of capitalism and its relationship to culture, politics and the state, what has yet to emerge is an adequate theoretical formulation of the grounds upon which the post-revolutionary left might oppose - or not - various types of capitalist formation. Whatever his weaknesses, Zizek's capacity to ask the questions which must be answered (how like a psychoanalyst!) remains his enduring strength, while the sense that those questions *are* answerable within the frameworks articulated by Laclau and Butler, but have not been (quite), haunts the work from beginning to end. *Contingency, Hegemony, Universality* is at last a satisfying and enlightening - not to mention entertaining, if exhausting - work which comes highly recommended. But we will have to wait for a re-match to see if those answers are really there, or if their promise is merely a manifestation of the *objet petit a*, luring us and our three players onwards towards a goal which is never quite reached.

Zizek Against The Fashionable Intelligence: On Totalitarianism

Lois Wheller

Slavoj Zizek, *Did Somebody Say Totalitarianism? Five Interventions in the (Mis)Use of a Notion*, Verso, London and New York 2001, 280pp; £16 hardback.

Readers of Slavoj Zizek's previous work will be familiar with the ideological mechanisms and totalitarian state systems, in particular Stalinist Communism and Nazi Fascism, explored in *Did Somebody Say Totalitarianism?* This addition to Zizek's oeuvre significantly extends his concerns, investigating both the notion of totalitarianism and the ideological function of the term itself within academic debate. The threat of totalitarianism, discerned by critics in any argument that even brushes with a prescriptive or universalising mode, comes charged not only with overtones of fascism and racism, but with the unspeakability of a specific violent history that these terms evoke. Zizek argues that 'the notion of "totalitarianism", far from being an effective theoretical concept is a kind of *stopgap*' which inhibits not only action but intellectual thought (p3). Often deployed to neutralise rather than critique, the concept of totalitarianism has, perhaps paradoxically, contributed to the fencing in of political philosophy. As the introduction states, *Did Somebody Say Totalitarianism?* does not offer a historical account of totalitarianism or even argue for its redemption or reappropriation. Instead, Zizek adopts a typically broad frame of reference, from Antigone to the films of John Woo, and weaves together five interventions that reverberate with an anxiety over political agency in current Leftist academia.

Rather than forming a single exposition, this collection of essays is united through an attack on those 'conformist liberal scoundrels' that Zizek loves to hate. His writing has been fuelled by the 'burning question of how we are to reformulate a Leftist, anti-capitalist political project in our era of global capitalism and its ideological supplement, liberal-democratic multiculturalism'.[1] In *Did Somebody Say Totalitarianism?* he contends that the new populist Right in the West has usurped the anti-capitalist stance of the Left. Without either its radical position or scope for political engagement, the left is now forced to shuttle between artificially constructed poles of democracy and totalitarianism that ensure a liberal democratic hegemony. Whilst Zizek's caricature of liberal democracy may put some readers on guard, a disjunction between theory and practice, and a surplus of taboos generated by this anxiety - of which the Political Correctness row

1. Slavoj Zizek, *The Ticklish Subject: The Absent Centre of Political Ontology*, Verso, London and New York 1999, p4.

is but a small part - is perceived as a significant cause of unproductive friction in certain academic disciplines. In *Did Somebody Say Totalitarianism?* Zizek deploys his distinctive blend of Lacanian psychoanalysis and Hegelian dialectics to formulate a materialist response to metaphysical notions of totality and political structures of totalitarianism that is as urgent and antagonistic as it is engagingly playful.

The range of material and its fragmented presentation makes this book easy to dip into, but the exploration of mythic narrative structures in the first intervention usefully prefaces a more specific examination of tragedy in relation to twentieth century totalitarianism in the following chapters. In order to ask whether the violence perpetrated under Nazi Fascism and Stalinist Communism can still be interpreted in terms of tragedy, the book's opening chapter, entitled 'The Myth and Its Vicissitudes', examines changes that have occurred in our understanding of tragedy since the classical era. Zizek's concern is to provide a temporal narrative that demonstrates a logical progression from comedy to tragedy, thereby refusing the myth its conventional status as a 'starting point' (p26). Rather than reading Hamlet as a secondary distortion of the Oedipus myth, Zizek argues that the Hamlet narrative in fact preceded its incarnation as myth in the Oedipus story. Likewise, analysis of three successive treatments of Marcel Pagnol's *Jean de Florette* and *Manon des Sources* reveal that the mythical structures of tragedy and Fate are most prominent in Claude Berri's 1987 film version. The main 'lesson' for Zizek's reader is not that contemporary myths are inauthentic, but that '*myth as such is a fake*' (p26). Yet the tripartite classification of the traditional, early modern and contemporary hero which emerges from Zizek's analysis of late Romanticism, Modernism, Postmodernism, somewhat curiously echoes the mythological matrix of three generations that he draws out of the Oedipus family myth. Whilst explicitly distancing himself from the nostalgic yearning for authentic tragedy which he discerns in Lacan's anti-Americanism, Zizek's argument nonetheless positions Greek tragedy proper above contemporary action films, undermining his own impressive movement between the canonical and the popular, that later enables an insightful Levinasian reading of John Woo's *Face Off*.

A grounding exploration of tragedy is, however, important to the bold probing of Nazism and the Holocaust in the second chapter. Zizek is fully aware that he risks repeating 'the anti-Semitic negation of its uniqueness' when he argues that representations of the Holocaust as the 'untouchable exception' contribute to the occlusion of a violent history of Western colonisation and the splintering of current anti-capitalist forces (p67). The near comic speculation into Hitler's psyche used to introduce these concerns supports Zizek's claim that an increase in Holocaust comedies can be correlated with its elevation into 'the unspeakable Evil' (p68). This chapter provides readings of several comic and tragi-comic Holocaust films, setting them against the tragic narrative of *Schindler's List* which is classed as a failure. Interpreting the victim of the extermination camps, the figure of the 'Muslim', as 'beyond tragedy' rather than 'dehumanised', Zizek argues that the Holocaust cannot be represented successfully as a tragedy. Building on his allusion to the totalitarian dynamic of laughter in *The Sublime Object of Ideology*, Zizek resists any simple association of comedy with liberty and unpicks a paradoxical generation of tragedy through cruel humour. In particular, Zizek's analysis of the comic aspect to the automative gestures of the 'Muslim' figure brings his argument right up against the representational difficulties of the subject and opens up challenging correlations of comedy and suffering. The imagery that informs the Bakhtinian carnivalesque and the writing of Sarah Kofman, Robert Antelme, Maurice Blanchot and Julia Kristeva come to this reader's mind. Considering the work of these writers, it is disappointing that this engaging section does not consider the theme of 'the stranger within ourselves' (p57), a 'fashionable thesis' which is rejected outright in the previous chapter.

Through a reading of Vaclav Havel's *The Power of the Powerless*, chapter 3 returns to themes addressed elsewhere in Zizek's work, in particular Stalinist totalitarianism and the miscommunication between the Western Left and dissidents of late socialism in East Europe. This chapter unfolds numerous paradoxes of ethical law that 'harbour a genuine tragic dimension overlooked by standard liberal diatribes against "totalitarianism"' (p101). For example, the old Bolshevik redefinition of "'severe justice'... in terms of excessive forgiveness and generosity" is informed by a *structurally* perverse logic of public confession and unfulfillable economy of duty and is not, therefore, simply a false legitimation of state violence. Any simple notions of belief, betrayal, loyalty or apathy, or any tidy oppositions between ethics and totalitarianism, public action and private belief, are rigorously dispelled. This discussion extends analysis of the Stalinist show trials in *The Ticklish Subject*, where horror defies description and the tragic dimension is absent from the victims' fate ' - that is, they were not tragic heroes, but something more horrible and simultaneously more comical'.[2] The suggestion is that our understanding of tragic and comic structures informs our interpretations of ethical law, problematising distinctions drawn between mental states of innocence and guilt and between acts of collaboration and resistance, but surely also between the terms of conformist and radical politics that motivate this text.

Challenging the conceptual and ethical primacy of melancholy in current criticism, chapter 4, 'Melancholy and the Act', proposes an exit to this theoretical 'stop-gap' through a Lacanian interpretation of *the act*. The echoes of postcolonial criticism, most notably of Aijaz Ahmad's *In Theory* and E San Juan's *Beyond Theory*, in Zizek's anti-theoretical materialism make his provocative statements concerning a cynical and melancholic attachment to the gesture of loss in postcolonial studies and queer theory sound a little glib. Even less satisfactory is the argument that homosexual desire could fade with legislation that accommodates gay couples. The remainder of

2. Ibid., pp320-21.

this chapter could be read as a response to Simon Critchley's political appropriations of Derrida, Levinas and Lacan in *Ethics-Politics-Subjectivity*. Zizek contrasts melancholic attachment to the messianic longing brought out in Critchley's reading of a Derridean 'democracy to come', but states that both melancholic and messianic longing preclude the possibility of the act or the decision, leading instead to passivity or pragmatism. Whereas *The Sublime Object of Ideology* finds in Hegel 'the strongest affirmation yet of difference and contingency',[3] *Did Somebody Say Totalitarianism?* attempts to divorce itself further from the 'deconstructionist political doxa' in which 'any stance that does not endorse the mantra of contingency/displacement/finitude is dismissed as potentially "totalitarian"' (p6). Derrida's democratic deconstruction is interpreted as a total renunciation of actual political measures that contrasts with the dynamic possibilities for change accommodated in a Lacanian conception of the act. In conclusion, Zizek relocates naivety in the assumption that reality is a given rather than in the belief that we can break from reality, but it is not clear where this interesting reversal leaves the numerous, and varied, cynics whom he attacks.

Departing from the philosophical, political and literary emphases of the four previous interventions, Zizek's final chapter, 'Are Cultural Studies Really Totalitarian?', examines the relation of the Freudian Real to the scientific Real and argues for the need to probe the parameters of philosophy and science without reducing either discipline to the other. As Zizek identifies, the critical-theoretical prohibition on both naive empiricism and non-historical metaphysics has opened up an abyss between philosophy and science. His analysis of 'popular science' and the 'Third Culture' suggests that this gap is, and perhaps must be, unbridgeable. Yet Zizek's useful insistence on the reiteration of naive questions, concerning the structure of the universe and the human psyche, does not necessarily lead to a Lacanian privileging of 'hard' science. It is not specified how we are to pursue Zizek's call to untangle real science from its popular ideological counterpart. The scientific discourse addressed here does, however, suggest some major omissions in the field of philosophy and offers a different viewpoint from which to examine the assumptions that inform the stand-off over theoretical and political agency in the social sciences. But perhaps more significantly, and as Zizek notes, it is the scientific specialist who has begun to displace the often less intelligible theorist from the humanities as public spokesperson, a cultural shift which particularly threatens the role, authority and credibility of the Leftist intellectual.

Packed with examples drawn from popular culture and current events, including the *Big Brother* television shows, the Wachowski brothers' *The Matrix*, (the Millennium bug, right wing politics in Austria and the recent Bosnian conflict), the conclusion of *Did Somebody Say Totalitarianism?* is, like the previous chapters, both engagingly nostalgic and up to the minute. Whilst such cultural references may appear to make these interventions acutely political and practical, they also risk a sensationalism which is

3. Slavoj Zizek, *The Sublime Object of Ideology*, Verso, London and New York 1989, p7.

counterproductive to this text's anti-capitalist and demythologising project. In contrast, it is out of 'a concern with sobriety' that Derrida's *Politics of Friendship* 'deliberately refrain[s] from recourse to "illustrations" to "actualize" our analysis or in an attempt to demonstrate their necessity today'.[4] It is perhaps such a tension of *currency* that finds *Did Somebody Say Totalitarianism?* framing its insightful analysis in yet another attack on fashionable permissiveness, postmodern cynicism or elitist theoretical jargon. Zizek distances himself from all academic vogues, criticising the rise in popularity of Hannah Arendt (pp2-3) as well as the recent 'return to ethics' which 'shamefully exploits the horrors of Gulag or Holocaust as the ultimate bogey for blackmailing us into renouncing all serious radical engagement' (p4). Nonetheless, the language of *Did Somebody Say Totalitarianism?* frequently evokes such a critical call for a 'return', whether to art, literature, politics or ethics, each one an instance of what Zygmunt Bauman calls "that seriousness which the socially produced world made all but laughable".[5]

Zizek continues to be an excellent and necessary exponent of Lacanian psychoanalysis at a time where Lacan has fallen from favour in certain academic circles (perhaps even to Zizek's secret delight). Zizek's Lacanian twist on ethics, democracy, tragedy and comedy in *Did Somebody Say Totalitarianism?* is rigorous in its detail and refreshingly unfettered. But at times the tone seems to express antagonism for antagonism's sake. Bemoaning a 'false universal critical capacity to pass judgement on everything, without proper knowledge' (p224), and providing a brief 'test' of his readers' 'implicit racism' (p235), this book risks shielding the academic taboos that it otherwise effectively challenges.

4. Jacques Derrida, *Politics of Friendship*, George Collins (trans), Verso, London and New York 1997, p272.

5. Zygmunt Bauman, *Postmodernity and its Discontents*, Polity Press, Cambridge 1997, p 126.

Vulgarity, He Said: T.J. Clark's Modernism

Herman Rapaport

T.J. Clark, *Farewell to an Idea: Episodes from a History of Modernism*, Yale University Press, London 1999, pp450 plus 252 illustrations; £30.00 hardback.

Ever since the 1980s people have started to ask, 'what exactly *was* modernity?' For a long time we thought we knew. Modernity, the experts said, had to do with a delegitimation of the past that had its sources in Darwin, Marx, Nietzsche, and Freud. Moreover, in anticipation of a full scale cultural revolution, some nineteenth-century artists were intuitively resisting the rational coherence of a bourgeois world picture. One can even hear this in as conservative a composer as Bruckner, whose symphonies are made up of sections that sound like titanic fragments loosely strewn rather than carefully put together. Mahler, Wagner, and Debussy are similar cases, and were followed by an even more radical decentring of harmony by Stravinsky and Schoenberg. The parallels in literature and painting are well known and have often been used to show that an old cultural order was breaking up because, as the Yeatsian cliché had it, the centre wasn't holding. But metaphors and crumbling empires aside, what exactly *had* happened? Had a new age simply come about through a convergence of social-political changes? Had the West somehow passed through a major epistemic break? Had an entire world picture been shattered because the past had been intellectually discredited? Or was the horror of World War One mainly to blame? The answer we've been given is all of the above and then some.

Of course, these questions assume that the modern results from destabilising events of great magnitude. Although T.J. Clark's *Farewell to an Idea: Episodes from a History of Modernism* doesn't invalidate any of these accounts - in some respects, it bolsters them - it actually goes a long way towards downplaying the rhetoric of crisis and upheaval that has been a common theme for historians of the field. Part of this is reflected in the fact that Clark's examples - David, Pissarro, the Suprematists - are not generally included among what modernists have often identified as modernism's spectacular fireworks. The two big exceptions are Clark's accounts of Picasso's cubist paintings of 1908-1912 and his full scale analysis of Jackson Pollock's major phase.

What makes this a landmark study is that it brilliantly downplays the well known contours of modernist history in favour of looking at particulars within that history that do and do not fit the familiar master narratives. And seeing those particulars is the genius of this project. Also welcome is that Clark has let the cat out of the bag concerning what happens when art historians *look* at art. Anyone who reads interpretations of paintings has probably noticed that even straightforward descriptions can be misleading, as in the case of Meyer Schapiro's failure to notice that Van Gogh's pair of painted peasant shoes is not really a pair of shoes at all, since in order to have a pair one would need a left and right shoe. Worse, interpretations of paintings often project fantasies onto the work. Heidegger's much discredited account of the peasant woman who was supposedly the wearer of the shoes Schapiro was talking about is typical of this hermeneutical practice.

In Clark's book, we get the rare admission that the relationship between perception and conception is extremely vexed and that there is a major problem concerning the hermeneutics of looking. For one thing, one needs some prosthetic fantasies in order to get an analysis on the right track. What we learn from Clark is that the process of looking and interpreting requires us to indulge in heuristic fantasies that can't be empirically justified. Moreover, Clark teaches us that we don't have an adequate vocabulary for talking about visual art; that often we depend upon anecdotal contexts; that we're not able to tell for sure which particular visual structure should be privileged in a work; and, ultimately, that we're compromised by the fact that one can never be absolutely sure that one's conception of the work is the right conception. Do we really know what El Lissitzky had in mind when he engaged in 'agitprop'? Is it possible to stabilise a history of revolution in process long enough to construct a context for interpreting art? Did Picasso actually understand the conceptual issues he was facing when he painted his most path breaking cubist works? And can we know let alone evaluate with any certainty just what he was doing when he revised his great cubist canvases?

Clark's answer to such questions is yes and no. Though such negative capability is refreshing, it does have the downside of appearing thin and inconclusive. No matter how sophisticated we are, perhaps we still hanker after some master narratives. Happily Clark does have a central thesis, which goes like this. At around the time of the French Revolution an artist such as Jacques-Louis David had to deal with radical contingencies within the life-world that posed a new problem for art: one can't see exactly what it is that one has to represent, because 'reality' is too much in flux. This is the radical epistemic break that modernists have somehow not made enough of, their attention being drawn to issues like the death of God, the Freudian discovery of psycho-sexuality, and the advent of mass man and consumer culture. Instead of taking such a thematic approach to history, Clark notices instances in which art has to struggle with the unrepresentability of a changing life-world which follows from the fact that this world is never stable enough to be seen as a thing in itself. His opening chapter on David is a brilliant exposition of this thesis, because it is based on the fact that the figure of Marat, whom David painted in the summer of 1793, was being figured or constructed by a number of political revolutionary factions, and that this conflict of interpretations was highly unstable and therefore in flux for some months. David was asked by the Jacobin faction to find a way of depicting Marat that was politically acceptable to revolutionaries but politically useful to the Jacobins. To put this crudely, David was being asked to put a bit of media spin on a figure whose martyrdom was threatening to blossom into a cult so strong that it could render the Jacobins far less powerful than they were. How was David to construct an image that would hegemonically win the day? David *couldn't* know the solution, according to Clark, because he was living at a time when change was too radical and coming too fast. In a sense, he had to paint the picture blind, which is to say, blind to many of the things going on around him. The relation of the work to the political life-world was therefore in suspension until the work was put on display in the fall of 1793, a display that David presumably orchestrated, and that allowed for a retroactive political interpretation. Of course, David was lucky that matters turned out well, for in truth *Death of Marat* is perhaps the best example we have of art as lucky wager at the risky gaming table of revolution.

Later, in a chapter on Suprematism, Clark will investigate an instance in which art is less successful at playing at revolution, given that the politics of the Soviet revolution - its wheel of fortune - will turn against a community of artists dedicated to the cause. There too the question of revolution as radical contingency is raised within a historical context that is far less transparent than the French Revolution, though much closer to us in time. Unlike David, who is trying to spin a hot political issue, painters like Lissitzki and Malevich appear to be pushing the limits of philosophical thinking within a revolutionary context that could conceivably prepare the way for a significant epistemic break in the relation of art and society, that break having to do with destroying the distance between art and ordinary material existence without negating or wiping art out. After all, within bourgeois culture, kitsch or something near to it is often the result when this distance is compromised. In order to hang on to art, the Suprematists insisted on an aggressively intellectual approach to abstractionism so that it couldn't be turned into kitsch or its close cousin, trendy but functional design. This, at least, is what I deduce from Clark's reproduction of Aleksandr Tseitlin's *Ration Card* of 1920 which just about leaves functionality behind, though not quite (its arche-trace is still there). But how were works like this supposed to fit into all the various 'mood swings among those responsible for running the economy' in 1920? That's where the chaos of the Soviet revolution far outstrips the chaos of the French Revolution, or so it seems, given Clark's detailed historical descriptions. Again, as in the case of David, Clark will have to broach the issue of art in relation to terror (recall that David, like the Museum Section of the French Revolution, was in the camp of the terrorists). Perhaps most importantly, whereas the relation of art to revolution can be known retroactively in the case of David, it *cannot* in the case of the Suprematists, because the Soviet life world was so chaotic and, eventually, so authoritarian and crushingly disastrous that one can't learn much by way of retroaction. This, I'm afraid, is where Lacan's insight about the subject coming into being as a meaningful entity in the backwash of the signifier fails us, according to what we read in Clark, because in the case of the Soviet revolution the logic of the signifier has come apart at the seams and isn't entirely readable or reconstructable.

In contrast to these wide screen chapters of armies clashing in the night, there is a muted chapter on Pissarro (no one's favourite impressionist) who was sympathetic to anarchism. But Pissarro (and this may be his tragedy) didn't get to live in the midst of social revolt. Clark examines paintings of peasant life in the country that are motivated politically in terms of content and execution wherein the contingency of everyday life is reflected as a dematerialization of bourgeois reification (or thing-presentation). Although Clark doesn't say so, Pissarro was concerned with transforming the image into an aura that was radically mutable, though modal, in the seventeenth century sense of maintaining a tonality of luminescent sobriety (desentimentalisation). It would have been useful if Clark had talked a bit more about Millet, whose paintings of peasants have always struck me as rather close to the poetry of Trakl, where one senses an enormous pent up violence in the gentle particulars of nature. To put the matter baldly, Millet's peasants conceal a furious wrath in the stillness of their gazes. Is this the consequence of Millet's construction of depth? In the case of Pissarro the viewer experiences disenchantment where wrath might otherwise appear; or, if one thinks of Poussin, where the sublime (that sublimated side of wrath) might otherwise manifest itself. The technical cause seems to be Pissarro's modernist (Greenbergian) flatness.

Of *Two Young Peasant Women* (1892), Clark says that 'the key to the picture's colour organisation is the fact that its two peasants are taking their rest in a translucent foreground shade, with here and there a trace of sunlight coming through the leaves onto their fists or foreheads' (p65). But one isn't necessarily aware of this, since the shade isn't thrown over the colour but emanates out of its very optical interplay, so that its presence is hardly detectable. This makes for tricky viewing, because one isn't sure what one is looking at, exactly. And this, Clark will go on to show, is a deliberate feature of Pissarro's art that turns the experience of looking into an exercise of undecidable perception, with the proviso, and an important one, that the conditions of lighting are precisely right. For this painting requires strong daylight in order not to look merely 'sullen' (Clark's adjective). Under artificial light we will see nothing but a drab painting that is incapable of materialising and dematerialising before our eyes. Apparently, Pissarro didn't think of art as artefact, but as a phenomenon of the outdoors.

Two Young Peasant Women would be incidental to the history of modernism were it not that it represented an attempt to change the history of art. At least, this was Pissarro's intention when he exhibited the work in 1892. This is the time, Clark reminds us, when Van Gogh's paintings start to be shown and catapulted to fame, a time when a new wave of modernism erupts that will obscure Pissarro, though from Pissarro's perspective it represents a step back in the history of painting. After all, his aesthetic of optical dematerialization wagers on the eventfulness of what is contingent within the interplay of natural relations between the work, the light, and the optical capacities of the viewer. The new wave of modernism emerging in 1892, and championed by Cézanne to some extent, betrayed that impulse, because it made a transition from an emphasis upon the work as event (the mobile interplay of light freed from the rigidity of form) to the work as structure (as transgressive formalism).

In a chapter on Cézanne, Clark explores how another painter of disenchantment and anti-sentimentality dissolves concrete reference and mimesis by way of structure rather than atmosphere, representation rather than performance, with emphasis falling on the depiction of psycho-sexual constructions as well as superseding single point perspective. Here is a thread that Clark doesn't widely develop - namely, the correspondence between sexual figures in Cézanne (this is where the disenchantment comes in) and that of other modernist painters. The flippant thing to say, I suppose, is that given the list of painters concerned with the psycho-sexual, one would have to include, well, just about everyone. So we can quickly surmise the reason Clark didn't go far in that direction. Yet, we might nevertheless ask why at the very least we didn't get a corresponding chapter on Willem de Kooning's monsters of sexual and maternal affection, with perhaps some detours into the marriage between Jackson Pollock and Lee Krasner.

My impression is that readers will find the two most significant chapters in Clark's study to be those on Picasso and Pollock, for this is where our hankering for masters and master narratives comes in. As is the case elsewhere, Clark compares photographs of works with the works themselves as we now have them. With regard to Picasso, Clark examines a moment when the history of painting appears to hang in the balance. In other words, to those who insist on modernism as an epistemic break Clark gives what must be the most highly charged moment in the history of modern art, the years 1908-1912. The thesis is a bit complex, but it boils down to the following point: Picasso faked an epistemic break that he was unable to produce and ended up being credited for having made an advance that, if one looks carefully, wasn't really made. Hence Clark downgrades Picasso to master illusionist, someone who has done what painters have always done: fooling the eye. No paradigm busting here, just a lot of showmanship and trickery, a point Clark backs up with meticulous observations about how Picasso manipulated illusionistic techniques that were hardly new to the visual arts. The depressing thought that maybe the arts don't have epistemic veracity (they just pose as if they do) is central to the notion that we need to say farewell to the idea of modern art - that idea being that art *has* epistemic clout. More generally, he's suggesting that whatever the idea of modern art may be, it's more like a utopian horizon or an idea to come that not only never really came about but that is no longer conceivable as a real possibility since its historical moment of advent has now passed. This is the debatable ground of Clark's study, debatable because it's not really clear that modernism *is* dead and gone. Maybe, one could argue, we're just living in a phase of modernity without quite realising it. Anyway, isn't it clear today that postmodernism was a 1980s historical fantasy? That today it's horribly dated as a stylistic vogue in which architectural fashion played such an enormous role? Clark wriggles out of this sort of debate by breaking off his study in the 1950s. But, as we will see, he seems to be of the view that after Pollock American art, at least, went into some sort of major decline. 'Vulgar', he calls it.

Obviously no artist in the twentieth century had the good fortune to find him- or herself at the forefront of art history in the way Picasso did. Jackson Pollock was a close runner up. Still, Clark wants to know whether this was essentially a media stunt or not. Clearly the New York intelligentsia - Greenberg and company - were cheering Pollock on as a major event in the history of modern art. Had some kind of tawdry truth emerged when magazines like *Vogue* used his paintings as designer backdrops for pretty blonde models? The thought that the epistemic break of abstract expressionism was a media stunt is the thesis of a book by Serge Guibaut, who wrote about how New York was the Grinch that stole modern art from France. But, as Clark's chapter on Picasso has taught us, Picasso had already shown everyone how this sort of fakery is done. Hence it is highly misleading to say that New York simply stole the idea of modern art; what it stole was the *illusion* that there is an idea of modern art as epistemic break. In fact, Clark suspects that all art does is stage or fake this event in a way rather similar to the advertisers' cameramen at *Vogue* who posed their models as if they were busting up the bourgeois world picture by giving it one right in the kisser. That is Clark's disenchanted reading of this history and what leads him to suspect that art under capitalism is merely vulgar, 'in your face' stuff.

'He was, need I say it, a petty bourgeois artist of a tragically undiluted type - one of those pure products of America (of Riverside County, California) we like to believe will go crazy strictly on their own class terms.' (p300) Like Picasso, Pollock didn't have the sort of intellectual background that would have enabled him to deal with anything as major as an epistemic rupture in the history of Western art. And yet, he did make an enormous breakthrough that cannot be denied. He alone had gone beyond what Clark calls 'the grid' (for example, the schema laid bare in Mondrian's late works). Whatever one wishes to say of Pollock, he manages to free form from geometry in a way that is extraordinarily convincing. Was it a conjuring trick? This is where Clark starts to have reservations about the fakery thesis, because a close formal examination of the work discredits the kind of cynicism that chalks Pollock up to Madison Avenue hype.

Then there is the contingency and instability factor. Pollock, too, couldn't really see his work completely, because it was in process. 'But what [Pollock] seemed increasingly to want in practice was a situation where the synthesis of aspects - the reading - came about as part of a sequence of movements: it took place but was never arrested.' (p326) Yet as Clark notes, Pollock and his friend Clement Greenberg did manage to look at the paintings in ways that they could be viewed as propositions. This, we recall, was already at work in David. The real question is, what kind of proposition does a painting make?

Clark often underscores the metaphorical ways in which modern art proposes something, as if the modern work of art was what Jean-Francois Lyotard once called 'paralogical.' It simulates a definitive statement about something without possessing the means really to make that statement valid. But what is it that modern art doesn't possess? According to Clark, it is certainty. In the case of Pollock we can't be certain the works are really as discomposed as they appear, or that they are as abstract as they appear, or that they are as unrhetorical as they appear, or that they are as anti-figural as they appear, or anti-painterly as they appear, or anti-perspectival as they appear. Clark takes pains to show us this and in so doing gives us a brilliant lesson in close examination of visual works. There is more to learn from a couple of pages of these speculations than in most of the art books in print, whatever the veracity of Clark's overall thesis. The main sticking point is that there is so much speculation and change of direction that we don't know whether to hate Pollock's work or love it. Even Clark is so unsettled that he gives us three endings, none of them particularly convincing.

This unravelling of focus is a prelude to the last chapter which ends on that sour note of the vulgar. Pollock's work may be redeemable. But when one turns to Hans Hofmann, Adolph Gottlieb, Mark Rothko and Willem de Kooning, the big ugly secret about Pollock's work is hard to miss. Abstract expressionism as a whole is in bad taste. 'A good Hoffmann,' Clark writes, 'has to have a surface somewhere between ice cream, chocolate, stucco and flock wallpaper. Its colours have to *reek* of Nature - of the worst kind of Woolworth forest-glade-with-waterfall-and thunderstorm-brewing. Its title should turn the knife in the wound' (p397). Hoffmann is the symptom of what art has become under the reign of the bourgeoisie; one can imagine Clark making similar comments about Morris Louis (painting as candy for the eye), Helen Frankenthaler (department store abstractionism), and Jules Olitski (kitchen counter-top aesthetic). As if to hold back the big guns, Clark spares us plates of Warhol's famous silk-screens of money, David Salle's sex playmates-cum-graffiti, Cindy Sherman's female grotesques (deformed women again), and Nan Goldin's wasted youths on beds smoking a fag after a bad fuck.

Vulgarity - there you have it. If one thinks about this a bit, one immediately realises it is the obvious next step in a decline from sublimity (Poussin, but also Turner), to disenchantment (Manet, Courbet, Pissarro, the lot), to vulgarity (Robert Mapplethorpe, Jeff Koons, and Lucas Samaras). No doubt, putting the shoe on the American foot is a bit unfair if one considers the vulgarity of painters like Kirschner, Klimt, and Grosz parading their whores onto the painterly stage, Duchamp's urinal and peep show gynaecology, Picasso's spread eagled models lusting for penetration, Dali's kitsch Jesus and kitsch Gala, and Bacon's 'gross-out' scenes of religious desk murderers. You could go even further back in time to the infamous painting *Origin of the World* by Courbet, once owned by Lacan, that now hangs in the Musée D'Orsay. If one looks at it from a certain perspective, one will notice that it brings the sublime, the disenchanted, and the vulgar into relation, something whose traces can be seen in the work of Warhol, Salle, Koons, and many others. It's here that Clark's history lesson falls on deaf ears: mine. I simply don't buy into his decline-of-Western-art scenario.

In the end, though, I'm less interested in taking issue with Clark's unsatisfactory ending, which reminds me a bit of the degenerate art thesis sponsored by fascism in the 1930s, than in holding out the possibility for a more careful examination of the vulgar as a cultural distinction. I'm also not overly concerned with the fact that Clark's thesis about the instability of the life-world in the arts is so general that it becomes blunted as an analytical tool, if not questionable as an epochal characteristic (was the Reformation any more stable?). Rather, I think we should pay attention to the particulars of Clark's painterly analysis which opens the possibility for considerable reflection on the most basic issues of what is at stake when we look at art, the premise being that perhaps this looking may be greatly restricted, given all the things we can't know. Yes, it's the 'blindness and insight' argument all over again; but this time from the perspective of someone who is not simply making clever arguments, and who deals with the particulars of what it is one cannot see or know that constitute the thing one is trying to perceive. Just *what* did Picasso think he was looking at in 1912? And how could *we* ever determine this? Do we know how to look at cubism? If so, how do we know? And *what* was it that Pollock thought he saw when he looked at his drip paintings hanging on the studio wall? According to whose principles did he decide a work was finished or not - his own or Clement Greenberg's? In any case, how is any principle applied to an art as unstable or unresolved as Pollock's in the early 50s? Are we any closer to such answers in the case of Suprematism or David's *Marat*? As I said, all of this is very uncertain. But admitting this is more than half the battle; it's an act of liberation.

THE LIMITATIONS OF 'DUCKOLOGY'

Adam Roberts

Eleanor Byrne and Martin McQuillan, *Deconstructing Disney*, Pluto Press, London and Sterling, Virginia 1999, 216pp; £13.99 paperback.

Deconstructing Disney is a timely, impressively inventive, extremely entertaining and deeply flawed book. It is hard to disagree with the tenets of the book: of course Disney represents a hugely significant body of cultural texts, and not nearly enough properly theorised critical study of that body has been undertaken. Of course the ideological bases out of which these American texts are produced are the same bases as determine American foreign policy (amongst other things), so there are good reasons for reading these films with a view to their historical, cultural and political contexts. Many readers are going to be sympathetic with Byrne and McQuillan's overall perspective; although this does not mean that they're going to be entirely convinced by declarations that, for instance, *The Lion King* is 'about' South African apartheid (pp82-93). Isn't it a little more complex than that? Which is to say: doesn't ideology construct questions of race, political opposition or otherwise, and intertextuality in a rather more complex manner?

On the other hand, given that Byrne and McQuillan's critical idiom is polemic, the fact that it provoked a series of strong disagreements in at least one reader (this one) is certainly a good rather than a bad thing. And there are prodigious strengths in this book; the fact that it has no pretensions beyond wanting to 'open a move in the wider strategy of criticism' (p17) frees it up to make a large number of rhizomatic connections between Disney texts, contexts and theory, many of which are very interesting. Sometimes, by the same token, it comes over as random, even frantic, in its yoking-togethers. The whole is uneven.

Byrne and McQuillan begin by emphasising how soft a target Disney is to left-sympathetic theoretically-informed criticism. Previous critics have arraigned the corporation for 'sexism, racism, conservatism, heterosexism, andro-centrism, imperialism (cultural), imperialism (economic), literary vandalism, jingoism, aberrant sexuality, censorship, propaganda, paranoia, homophobia, exploitation, ecological devastation, anti-union repression, FBI collaboration, corporate raiding, and stereotyping'. 'It would seem,' say the authors, 'only a matter of time before conclusive proof is discovered linking Walt Disney to the assassination of J.F. Kennedy and the production of anti-personnel landmines' (p1). As the reader stifles her chortles, she goes on to read that we must 'not only ask questions about Disney', but also 'ask questions about the questions we have been taught to ask about Disney' (p7); and that 'if we are interested in the political circumstances which oppress us then we can never know too much about Disney' (p18). It is, they claim, using Ariel Dorfman and Armand Mattelart's awkward phrase, 'a study in "Duckology"' (p17).

There is a problem with the authors' use of humour. There is clearly nothing wrong with critics using humour per se, especially if the writing has a polemical aspect. The problem is that Byrne and McQuillan's humour isn't very funny. Like the John F. Kennedy gag quoted above, too many of the jokes here are obvious, or actively wince-inducing, and instead of pointing up the thrust of the thesis, or making the whole thing livelier and sparklier, they come over as flat and tired. 'There is something fishy about the *Little Mermaid*' (p22). 'Serbs sat watching *Aladdin* on video while their country was at war with America ... perhaps this episode is a case of a spoonful of sugar helping the bombs go down' (p176). Or take the following reading of *The Lion King*.

'Yes Simba, let me explain. When we die our bodies become grass and the antelope eat the grass and so we are all connected in the great Circle of Life'. This seems a thin argument even by Disney's philosophical standards; it is Hamlet's advice to Claudius that 'a king may go through the guts of a beggar' ... the lions manage to square the circle even if they do not acknowledge that they are talking shit (pp86-7).

The thinness of the lion's 'circle-of-life' philosophy, which was inflated by the Elton John song that functions as an ideological short-hand for the film as a whole, is a very interesting thing indeed; it mediates capitalist consumption and oppression through mystical obscurity that contains within it the necessary but repressed transformation of Capital into refuse. Its contradiction goes to the heart of the contradictions of contemporary ideological constructions of society. But Byrne and McQuillan's punchline here undersells what could have been a more interesting point.

On a par with this, the authors sometimes use bad jokes in order to set up serious points, which can read as plain pompous. An example is the 'perhaps over-familiar Glasgow pun' they cite in their introduction: 'what's the difference between Bing Crosby and Walt Disney? Bing sings but Walt Disnae' (p17). In itself, this, to my ear, lacks the chuckle-factor; but worse is the way Byrne and McQuillan laboriously explain the joke beforehand ('[in] Glasgwegian dialect ... "disney" is a homonym of "disnae", meaning "does not"'), and go on to make points about negativity and deconstruction ('deconstruction disnae do enough') on the back of it. As with the tiresome punning associated with 1980s deconstruction ('sexual/textual' bah!), you end up just wanting them to stop.

The meat of the book is a series of readings of major Disney films from 1989 to the present (from *The Little Mermaid* onwards); so 'classic' Disney such as *Dumbo* - a 'parable of tactical aerial bombing' it seems (p16) - and *Pinocchio* get only glancing mentions. Let me give an example of the sort of reading the book favours. The section dealing with Disney's *Hercules* (1997) begins with a quotation from Toni Morrison: 'Bill Clinton is the closest thing we have to a black president'. It goes on to specify two public engagements, from the many, that Clinton undertook after the Lewinsky scandal burst, as it were, over the blue dress of the world media: 'attendance at an all-black southern Baptist church and appearing on stage at the end of a performance of the broadway production of Disney's *The Lion King*' (p151). From this constellation of reference, the authors go on to assert that Disney disavows race by 'encod[ing] black experience as white'. This is relevant for *Hercules*, the argument continues, because '*Hercules* is a more or less explicit character reference for the Clinton defence team' and 'it is the only Disney feature-length animation in which African-Americans appear as themselves'. Assuming we don't want to quarrel with this last assertion (although it seems to involve a rather fuzzy sense of 'representation' to argue that animated painted-pots represent African Americans 'as themselves' where, say, animated crows do not) - we then proceed to the reading itself. The authors' eclectic referencing (Star Wars, Fidel Castro, Michael Jordan and so on) embellishes and to some extent tries to veil a straightforward reading of the text as political allegory: Hercules is Clinton; Zeus is Abraham Lincoln ('his statue resembles the monument to Lincoln on Capitol Hill' (p154)), or maybe John F. Kennedy, but either way the mythic authoritarian strong-father figure of the American political establishment; Meg is Monica Lewinski and so on. This fairly banal reading of the text as coding an easily mapped political significance is complicated a little by the cross-vectors of race, and livened up by the verve of intertextual reference deployed, but doesn't escape a certain flatness for all that. One problem is that it seems arbitrary: given the conjunction of race and political icon-status that the authors want to bring to this text (although its not entirely clear why), does the Toni Morrison quotation really authorise the Clinton/Kennedy reading of Hercules/Zeus? Why not, say, Jesse Jackson/Martin Luther King? Why, when texts like *Aladdin* are related directly to the explicit Arabic context ('*Aladdin* is a representation of the Gulf War', p81), and *The Lion King* to the explicit black-African experience, is this Greek text not seen as articulating something more racially Greek, or Mediterranean? There was certainly unhappiness amongst some Greeks at the cavalier fashion in which Disney had appropriated their culture. If this doesn't merit a mention, where the disapproval of 'the General Secretariat of the Arab League' at 'negative portrayals of Arabs' in Disney films does (p7), it may say more about the calcified sense of approved left-wing causes than the actual texture of ideological signification implicit in these texts.

A deeper problem with this reading of *Hercules*, it seems to me, is that its undeclared assumption of a surface/depth model of text is both rather rusty, and also at odds with the deconstructivist and postmodern patina of the book as a whole. Quite apart from anything else, seeing this sort of pattern in the carpet can lead to distortions of the primary text, and a degree of crudity. Can we really buy *Aladdin* as 'the story of an evil Islamic dictator' (p74), even if Byrne and McQuillan qualify the assertion with an 'on a superficial level'? In the case of this movie the code comes over as muddled. Aladdin himself, apparently, is 'a Palestinian "street rat" whose antics in the marketplace and ongoing feud with the palace guards call to mind the teenage revolutionaries who raised *intifada* against Israeli troops' (p76). But somehow, at the same time, authority in this film is not Jewish, but Islamic, 'Jafar ... a cross between the Ayatollah and Saddam Hussein' who 'is encoded with the familiar markers of Western racism, wearing black clerical robes and a "sinister" Islamic moustache and goatee' (p77). What is going on here? How can a goatee, 'sinister' or otherwise, carry the weight of Western orientalist racism? *Aladdin* makes no explicit reference to Islam at all, unless a general visual shorthand for stylised 'Arab-ness' necessarily embodies this. (An equivalent syllogism: Edward Said is an Arab; therefore he is Muslim). But the beauty of this sort of argument is that evidence in the text supports it, and lack of evidence supports it even more potently. Assume we want to read *Aladdin* as being 'about' the Arab-Israeli conflict. What do we do with the fact that there are no Jews in the film? Not a problem: the very absence of Jews is significant, since 'Israel is a ghostly absence from Aladdin as a film which responds to the specific historical conjunction of the Gulf War' (p77). Since we have already decided the film is about 'the specific historical conjunction of the Gulf War' and 'the intifada', its absence of Jews must in fact constitute a sort of haunting presence. Besides, *Aladdin* reminds Byrne and McQuillan (although it didn't me) of *Raiders of the Lost Ark*, and there's a load of Jewish stuff in that film which can be sleight-of-handed over into the Disney text, so that 'the Ark of the Covenant as representative of Israel "yet to come"' filled with ghostly Jews somehow illuminates *Aladdin* as well. Out of this comes the reading: Aladdin as Arab (plucky street-boy fighting the intifada, Aladdin) and Jew (bad authority figure, who is also oddly the anti-Islamic caricature, Jafar) fight for the magical, wise-cracking smart-ass genie who 'is an encoding of American support' (p78) - hence his 'technological prosthesis', the magic carpet which gives him command of the militarily crucial aerial arena.

Byrne and McQuillan conclude by asserting that 'these films open themselves onto the entire history of the West and act as a symptomatic concentration of all the ideological contests which are currently being fought in our world today ... [if] there is no "limit" to deconstruction, we would like to add that there is no "limit" to Disney' (pp168-69). Fair enough; but this is very specifically *not the same thing* as 'I can write down anything that pops into my head about these Disney texts, it's all equally valid'. The very importance of Disney means that more thoroughly thought-through readings are required.

BOOKNOTES

Ulrich Lehmann, *Tigersprung: Fashion in Modernity,* MIT Press, Cambridge, Massachusetts and London 2000, 532pp; £27.50 hardback.

Ulrich Lehmann's *Tigersprung* knits together work from Baudelaire, Mallarmé, Simmel, Benjamin, and various dadaists and surrealists to articulate a 'philosophy of fashion' as it emerges amongst a European cultural avant-garde between 1840 and 1940. For the writers discussed in Tigersprung the connections between *la mode* and *modernité* (or *Mode und Moderne*) are more than just etymological: viewing modern life through the optic of sartorial fashion is both compelling and necessary. If modernity witnesses the contradictory amalgam of rationalism and irrationalism, of the eternal and the ephemeral, of newness and repetition, then such themes are writ large in fashion. *La mode* becomes the 'royal road' (so to speak) for understanding the decidedly undecided qualities of modernity.

The foregrounding of fashion allows Lehmann to rework overly familiar accounts of cultural modernity. At times this includes resurrecting seemingly minor figures and placing them at the centre of a cultural formation; for instance, the enigmatic dandy Jacques Vaché is seen here as the essential *animateur* of French dada and proto-surrealism. At other times it means privileging work that could be seen as relatively incidental to a writer's oeuvre: here, the fashion magazine *La Dernière Mode* becomes Mallarmé's most significant production. More generally, though, it allows for a sense of the everyday lives of these theorists and artists to be registered. One of the arguments continually encountered in *Tigersprung* is that sartorial fashion is an attempt intimately to inhabit modernity (as a second skin), so it is of more than passing interest to find that Georg Simmel, for instance, opted for bespoke English tailoring. A photograph of the dapper sociologist is accompanied by the information that Simmel sports a 'summer suit in cool wool, waistcoat in off-white gabardine, white cotton shirt with detachable collar and cuffs, assorted silk tie. The perfect relaxed outfit for the intellectual-about-town' (p128).

Tigersprung takes its title from Benjamin's assertion that fashion (and by extension all that is modern) is the 'tiger's leap into the past'. Fashion thus registers a modernising impulse that struggles to 'draw its poetry from the future' (as Marx would say) by continually quoting the past. Parisian haute couture, of course, evidences such tiger's leaps, as does the (male) surrealist penchant for monocle and top hat. It would, however, also be worth considering connections between fashion and avant-gardism at moments of more emphatic social revolution: the work-suit designed by the Soviet artist Rodchenko in the early 1920s, for instance.

If *Tigersprung* leaves the reader with a sense of unanswered questions (the uneven rhythms of male and female fashion, although continually discussed, never really come into clear focus), this should be taken as a sign of the continued relevance of investigating *la mode* of modernity.

Ben Highmore

Michèle Barrett and Duncan Barrett, *Star Trek: The Human Frontier*, Polity, Cambridge 2001, 264 pp; £50.00 hardback, £14.99 paperback.

There are only a handful of book length surveys of *Star Trek*, and this mother-and-son collaboration is a welcome contribution to those. It provides a valuable overview of the programme from its original appearance 35 years ago, tracing the ways in which successive series have reproduced and challenged the original 'liberal humanist' ethos of *Star Trek*. The first section of the book is particularly interesting in this respect. Here the Barretts trace the numerous nautical allusions in *Star Trek* to the British and American naval discourses of the late eighteenth and early nineteenth centuries. These in turn are seen both to represent the ideals of modernity - progress, exploration, freedom - and to facilitate its hegemony through acts of colonisation. *Star Trek* emerges from this reading with an ambivalent investment in modernity, celebrating its humanist, rational ideals whilst also attempting to distance itself from colonising tendencies. This section does an excellent job in situating *Star Trek* within the tradition of nautical fiction, as well as providing a specifically British perspective on the second *Star Trek* series, *The Next Generation*, in which the Royal Navy features repeatedly as an idealised reference point. Given that most writing on *Star Trek* comes from the States and situates the series in relation to American culture, this is an unusual and valuable critical position.

My chief criticism is of the book's third section, where the Barretts discuss the two most recent series, *Deep Space Nine* and *Voyager*, which they identify as postmodern, and consequently as rejecting or undermining many of the principles which lie at the essentially modern heart of *Star Trek*. Whilst I fundamentally agree with this point, the negative way in which the Barretts define postmodernity weakens their argument. It is too easily identified as what modernity is not; hence the appearance of religion, insanity and moral ambiguity are focused on as examples of how the modern qualities of reason, humanism and clarity are brought into question. The explanation for why this shift in perspective should happen in the mid-1990s is inadequate, and there is a tendency to collapse the considerable historical and cultural distance between the original series and *The Next Generation* in order that they may both be read as modern. This is particularly problematic given that the latter did not finish until 1994, by which time *Deep Space Nine* had already started, while the original series finished 25 years earlier.

The Barretts' definition of the postmodern also falls short of engaging with the idea of the posthuman. They justify this position by arguing that both the original conception of *Star Trek* and its popular reception are fundamentally humanist; consequently, a 'posthumanist' reading would simply be inappropriate. As such they miss the valuable opportunity of reading *Star Trek* against its own grain and discovering posthuman uncertainties lurking behind its overtly humanist agenda.

Megan Stern

Laura Chrisman and Benita Parry (eds), *Postcolonial Theory and Criticism* (The English Association Essays and Studies series Vol. 52), DS Brewer, Cambridge, 2000; £30.00 cloth, 168pp.

This is a diverse collection of essays whose subjects range from a critique of diaspora and postcolonial theory, questions of subaltern representation and agency, interventions in the way contemporary postcolonial studies shapes up in the US, and more overtly 'literary' readings of works by Rudyard Kipling, Jack London, Robert Louis Stevenson and Hanif Kureshi. These essays are collected together because of their commitment towards a more grounded, localised and materialist approach to cultural and philosophical analysis. For example, Tim Watson's essay on *Kim* explores how the text functions as a fictionalised space which negotiates the problems raised by Indian and Irish nationalism. There is a complex and richly textured treatment of colonialism and disease in South Seas texts, by Lawrence Phillips, and a very suggestive (if all too brief) discussion by Gautam Premnath of how one might try to understand Homi Bhabha's theorisations of hybridity in the context of the political terrain of Thatcherite Britain, or R. Radhakrishnan's diasporic displacement within the 'transformations in the state-civil society relationship in the USA during the epoch of Reagan' (p61).

Alongside these pieces are disciplinary interventions on the shape and future of postcolonial studies in the US context (Vilashini Cooppan), and more theoretical interventions on the nature of subalternity, particularly in the Latin American context (Fernando Coronil). Ato Quayson's essay reminds us of the ethical dimensions of postcolonial studies. While exploring the value and productivity of interdisciplinarity in postcolonial theory, such as we find in Bhabha's deconstructive crossings and Mbembe's 'cultural studies' approach to political subjectivity, Quayson cautions that such interdisciplinarity should not become caught in a theoretical loop but must move towards political effectivity. For all this volume's ostensible commitment to a materialist approach, it will probably be read more for its notable interventions in, refinement of and supplements to the existing canon of high postcolonial theory.

Gail Low

Gary Bridge and Sophie Watson (eds), *A Companion to the City*, Blackwell, Oxford 2000; 640pp; £80 hardback.

If cities demand interdisciplinarity, as the editors of this volume forcefully assert, then anthologies may well be the destiny of the written city. There is after all something 'urban' about 58 contributors crammed in between the covers of a book, all clamouring (very politely, of course) for the reader's attention. And if the urban is an unmanageable totality (a cacophony of competing images, differences, economies, and so on, blaring out descants from hundreds of cities across the globe) then recourse to 'team work' might be considered essential. Yet even a compilation on this scale (600 or so pages long) seems to suggest the impossibility of anything but an amalgam of partial views. As one of the contributors puts it, 'cities do not add up. Rather they accumulate' (p406).

The vast majority of the chapters in *A Companion to the City* were specially commissioned by the editors, whose cast list brings together some less-familiar names with 'old-hands' such as Saskia Sassen, Richard Sennett and Ed Soja. One task that the editors have set themselves has been to redress 'a tendency within urban studies' towards 'analysis and argument based on Western cities and Western assumptions of cultural, social, and economic life, with little attention paid to the profound differences of social, cultural, and economic processes and the local specificity of cities across the world' (pp1-2). Here the success of a more global perspective doesn't rely simply on the addition of non-Western urban centres to the catalogue of cities considered, but on also offering cross-cultural perspectives on Western metropolitan centres (London as articulated in Caribbean novels, for instance). This physical and cultural expansion is accompanied by various speculative considerations of how urban studies might account for less visible (and less textual) aspects of urban experience (smells and tastes, performative experience, and so on). Such suggestive possibilities for future urban studies are sketched alongside more familiar geographical discussions of mapping, planning and policy.

Yet the question that the urban still poses (and that this volume necessarily avoids) is the possibility of a writing practice that can attend to the polyphony of the urban: that can register the accumulation of the city not as a series of discrete views but as a multi-layered weave. From this perspective, anthologies might be seen as stopgaps that try to manage the awkward overabundance of the city, while urban studies awaits the invention of more 'orchestral' forms of attention.

Ben Highmore

Back Issues

1 **Peter Wollen** on fashion and orientalism / **Denise Riley** on 'women' and feminism / **Dick Hebdige**'s sociology of the sublime / **Laura Marcus** on autobiographies / **John Tagg** should art historians know their place? / **Franco Bianchini** on the GLC's cultural policies / **Homi K Bhabha**, **Stephen Feuchtwang** and **Barbara Harlow** on Fanon.

2 **Mary Kelly, Elizabeth Cowie** and **Norman Bryson** on Kelly's Interim / **Greil Marcus** on subversive entertainment / **Georgina Born** on modern music culture / **Geoffrey Nowell-Smith** on popular culture / **Ien Ang** on 'progressive television' / **Alan Sinfield** on modernism and English Studies in the Cold War / **Tony Bennett** on Eagleton.

3 *TRAVELLING THEORY* – **Julia Kristeva** on the melancholic imaginary / **David Edgar** on carnival and drama / **Kobena Mercer** black hair – style politics / **Jacques Ranciere** on journeys into new worlds / **Peter Hulme**'s Caribbean diary / **Bill Schwarz** on travelling stars / **Ginette Vincendeau** on *chanteuses realistes* / **Steve Connor** on Springsteen / **Christopher Norris** on Gasché's Derrida.

4 *CULTURAL TECHNOLOGIES*
Out of print

5 *IDENTITIES*
Out of print

6 *THE BLUES* – **Jacqueline Rose** on Margaret Thatcher and Ruth Ellis / **James Donald** how English is it? / **Benita Parry** on Kipling's imperialism / **John Silver** on Carpentier / **Mitra Tabrizian** and **Andy Golding**'s blues / **Barbara Creed** on *Blue Velvet* / **Joseph Bristow** on masculinity / **Graham Murdock** on Moretti's *Bildungsroman* / **Edmond Wright** on post Humptydumptyism.

7 *MODERNISM/MASOCHISM* – **Victor Burgin**'s Tokyo / **Linda Williams** on feminine masochism and feminist criticism / **John Tagg** on criticism, photography and technological change / **Geoff Bennington** *l'arroseur arrose(e)* / **Emilia Steuerman** on Habermas vs Lyotard / **Paul Crowther** on the Kantian sublime, the avant-garde and the postmodern / **Mark Cousins** on Levi Strauss on Mauss / **Iain Chambers** being 'British' / **Adrian Forty** on lofts and gardens / **Lisa Tickner** on Griselda Pollock.

8 *TECHNO-ECOLOGIES* – **Peter Wollen** cinema: Americanism and the robot / **John Keane** on the liberty of the press / **S.P. Mohanty** on the philosophical basis of political criticism / **David Kazanjian** and **Anahid Kassabian** naming the Armenian genocide / **Paul Théberge** the 'sound' of music / **David Tomas** the technophilic body / **Felix Guattari** the three ecologies / **Margaret Whitford** on Sartre.

9 *ON ENJOYMENT* – **Slavoj Zizek** the undergrowth of enjoyment / **Peter Osborne** aesthetic autonomy and the crisis of theory / **Rachel Bowlby** the judgement of Paris (and the choice of Kristeva) / **Joseph Bristow** being gay: politics, identity, pleasure / **Gail Ching-Liang Low** white skins black masks / **Christine Holmlund** I Love Luce / **Line Grenier** from diversity to indifference / **Mark Cousins** is chastity a perversion? / **Simon Critchley** review of Christopher Norris.

10 *RADICAL DIFFERENCE* – **McKenzie Wark** on the Beijing demonstrations / **Paul Hirst** on relativism / **Cindy Patton** African AIDS / **Anna Marie Smith** Section 28 / **Tracey Moffatt** something more / **Susan Willis** Afro-American culture and commodity culture / **Hazel V. Carby** on C.L.R.James / **David Lloyd** on materialist aesthetics / **Peter Redman** Aids and cultural politics.

Schubert's sexuality / **Barbara Engh** after 'his master's voice' / **Herbert Schnadelbach** the cultural legacy of critical theory / **Sean Homer** the Frankfurt school, the father and the social fantasy / **Deborah Parsons** flaneur or flaneuse? / **Graeme Gilloch** the return of the flaneur / **Esther Leslie** space and west end girls / **Eamonn Carrabine and Brian Longhurst** mosaics of omnivorousness / **Kate Soper** despairing of happiness.

39 COOL MOVES – **Dick Pountain and David Robins** cool rules: anatomy of an attitude / **Rita Felski** the invention of everyday life / **Steven Connor** integuments: the scar, the sheen, the screen / **Mariam Fraser** creative affects / **Guy Hocquenghem** on homosex, or is homosexuality a curable vice? / **Bill Marshall** / commentary: 'on homo sex' / **Fred Botting** the art of smoking in an age of techno-moral consumption / **Anny Brooksbank Jones** Avon's calling: global consumption and microcultural practice in a latin american frame / **Gregory Stephens** 'you can sample anything': *zebrahead*, 'black' music, and multiracial audiences / **Syed Manzurul Islam** forming minoritarian communities: nomadic ethics for the postcolonial world.

40 CULTURE/CHINA – **Stephanie Hemelryk Donald** la chine in culture/ china / **John Cayley** a stranger to yourself / **Wanning Sun** internet, memory and the chinese diaspora / **Audrey Yue and Gay Hawkins** going south / **Souchou Yao** xiao ye: food, alterity and the pleasure of chineseness in malaysia / **Katie Hill** allegorical figures / **Shu-mei Shih** globalisation and minoritisation / **Richard Read** alienation, aesthetic distance and absorption in Tsai Mingliang's *vive l'amour* / **Harriett Evans** fashioning identities, consuming passions / **Tamara Jacka** other china/china's others.

41 THE FUTURE OF DIALOGUE – **Michelle Barrett** the great war and postmodern memory / **Stephen Bygrave** 'and art thou nothing?' / **Denis Flannery** sibling love and queer subjectivity / **John Hood-Williams** and **Wendy Cealey Harrison** gendered melancholy or general melancholy? / **Lucy Hartley** conflict not conversation / **Ken Hirschkop** it's good to talk / **Simon Jarvis** the future of monologue / **Laura Marcus** oedipus express / **Nicky Marsh** 'doing the call and response' / **Peter Middleton** the burden of intersubjectivity /**Saul Newman** universalism /particularism / **Sujala Singh** secularist faith in Salman Rushdie's *midnight's children*

42 THE RUINS OF CHILDHOOD – **Adam Phillips** children again / **Douglas Oliver** mongol in the woods / **Vicky Lebeau** another child of violence / **Bernard O'Donoghue** unknownst to the people / **David Marriott** 'the derived life of fiction' / **Tanya Horeck** 'let me tell you a story' / **Marian Partington** letter to Lucy / **John Wilkinson** *from* proud flesh / **Vincent Quinn** fostering the nation / **Lindsay Smith** 'infantia' / **Christine Clegg** 'no one is seduced here' / **Bernard O'Donoghue** command of english / **Sebastian Mitchell** 'but cast their eyes on these little wretched beings' / **Stephanie Hemelryk Donald** the necessary privations of growing up.

43 MOBILITIES – **Tim Cresswell** mobilities **Tim Cresswell** the production of mobilities / **Ginette Verstraete** technological frontiers / **Don Mitchell** the devil's arm / **Vikki Bell** negotiating and narrating emplacement / **Alan Finlayson** culture, politics and cultural politics in northern ireland / **Eleanor Byrne and Martin McQuillan** walt disney's ape man / **Rebecca Beasley** art as propaganda for literary modernism / **Eluned Summers Bremners** post-traumatic woundings.

Back issues cost £14.99 each
Make cheques payable to *Lawrence & Wishart* and send to:
Lawrence & Wishart, 99a Wallis Road, London E9 5LN

Why not Subscribe?

New Formations is published three times a year. Make sure of your copy by subscribing.

SUBSCRIPTION RATES FOR 2001 (3 ISSUES)

Individual Subscriptions
UK & Rest of World   *£40.00*

Institutional Subscriptions
UK & Rest of World   *£120.00*

Back issues: *£14.99 plus £1 post and packing for individuals*
                   £34.99 plus £1 post and packing for institutions

Please send one year's subscription
starting with Issue Number ―――――――――――――

I enclose payment of ――――――――――――――――――――

Please send me ――――― copies of back issue no. ――――――――

I enclose total payment of ―――――――――――――――――

Name ――――――――――――――――――――――――――――

Address ――――――――――――――――――――――――――――

――――――――――――――――――――――― Postcode ――――――――

Please return this form with cheque or money order (sterling only)
payable to *Lawrence & Wishart* and send to:
Lawrence and Wishart, 99a Wallis Road, London E9 5LN